The Human Factor in Machine Translation

Machine translation has become increasingly popular, especially with the introduction of neural machine translation in major online translation systems. However, despite the rapid advances in machine translation, the role of a human translator remains crucial. As illustrated by the chapters in this book, man-machine interaction is essential in machine translation, localisation, terminology management, and crowdsourcing translation. In fact, the importance of a human translator before, during, and after machine processing, cannot be overemphasised as human intervention is the best way to ensure the translation quality of machine translation. This volume explores the role of a human translator in machine translation from various perspectives, affording a comprehensive look at this topical research area. This book is essential reading for anyone involved in translation studies, machine translation or interested in translation technology.

Chan Sin-wai is Professor in the School of Humanities and Social Science, The Chinese University of Hong Kong, Shenzhen. He was formerly Professor and Chairman of the Department of Translation, The Chinese University of Hong Kong. He was also Director of the Master of Arts in Computer-aided Translation Programme and Director of the Centre for Translation Technology. He is Visiting Professor of Harbin Engineering University, Visiting Professor of Beihang University, Visiting Professor of Dailian Maritime University, and was a member of the Translation Technology Committee of the International Federation of Translators (FIT).

Routledge Studies in Translation Technology

Series Editor: Chan Sin-wai

The Future of Translation Technology
Towards a World without Babel
Chan Sin-wai

The Human Factor in Machine Translation
Edited by Chan Sin-wai

For more information on this series, please visit www.routledge.com/series/RSITT

The Human Factor in Machine Translation

Edited by Chan Sin-wai

LONDON AND NEW YORK

First published 2018
by Routledge
2 Park Square, Milton Park, Abingdon, Oxon OX14 4RN

and by Routledge
711 Third Avenue, New York, NY 10017

Routledge is an imprint of the Taylor & Francis Group, an informa business

© 2018 selection and editorial matter, Chan Sin-wai; individual chapters, the contributors

The right of Chan Sin-wai to be identified as the author of the editorial material, and of the authors for their individual chapters, has been asserted in accordance with sections 77 and 78 of the Copyright, Designs and Patents Act 1988.

All rights reserved. No part of this book may be reprinted or reproduced or utilised in any form or by any electronic, mechanical, or other means, now known or hereafter invented, including photocopying and recording, or in any information storage or retrieval system, without permission in writing from the publishers.

Trademark notice: Product or corporate names may be trademarks or registered trademarks, and are used only for identification and explanation without intent to infringe.

British Library Cataloguing-in-Publication Data
A catalogue record for this book is available from the British Library

Library of Congress Cataloging-in-Publication Data
A catalog record for this book has been requested

ISBN: 978-1-138-55121-3 (hbk)
ISBN: 978-1-315-14753-6 (ebk)

Typeset in Galliard
by Apex CoVantage, LLC

Contents

List of figures	vii
List of tables	ix
List of contributors	xi
Introduction CHAN SIN-WAI	1
1 Localizing websites using machine translation: exploring connections between user eXperience and translatability LYNNE BOWKER AND JAIRO BUITRAGO CIRO	7
2 Norms and controlled language for machine translation SYLVIANE CARDEY	30
3 Caught in the web of translation: reflections on the compilation of three translation encyclopedias CHAN SIN-WAI	51
4 A comparative study of term extraction methods in translation JIANG CHENG AND WANG MIN	64
5 Introducing corpus rhetoric into translation quality assessment: a case study of the white papers on China's national defense QIAN DUOXIU	83
6 Evaluating term extraction tools: system performance vs user perception OLIVIA KWONG OI YEE	100

Contents

7   Terminology resources in support of global communication 118
    KARA WARBURTON

8   Corpora and CAT-based CN-EN translation of
    Chinese culture 137
    XU BIN

9   Issues of language structure in machine translation
    between English and Kiswahili 153
    SARAH NDANU M. NGESU

10 Quality estimation of machine translation for literature 183
    MOZHGAN GHASSEMIAZGHANDI AND
    TENGKU SEPORA TENGKU MAHADI

11 Optimising the use of computer translation systems
    by examining disciplinary differences and characteristics
    of genres as well as various approaches applied in
    computer translation 209
    CECILIA WONG SHUK MAN

12 Crowdsourcing translation in contemporary China:
    theories and practices 236
    CAO YIXIN

    Index 255

Figures

2.1	Chomsky Type Schema with double arcs which if suppressed lead us to Tesnière	32
2.2	Structure covering several Arabic utterances from the simplest to the most complex	33
2.3	Example of our linguistic programming using a spreadsheet table	35
2.4	Trace for the machine translation of *maintenir le train d'atterrissage en position DOWN* (Keep the landing gear on DOWN position) to English	37
2.5	Example of rules for machine translation and sense mining	38
2.6	User interface	40
2.7	Schema of the LiSe Project	45
2.8	Translations Output	47
2.9	System for extracting terms represented by a user-entered definition	49
4.1	Specific words and corresponding colours	67
4.2	Results of Chinese text segmentation and POS tagging	67
4.3	Results of English text segmentation and POS tagging	68
4.4	Results calculated by C-value	76
4.5	Results calculated by TF-IDF	76
4.6	Results calculated by BSCF	77
4.7	Results calculated by hybrid method	77
4.8	Precisions of the four methods at different orders of magnitude	78
4.9	Recall of four methods at different orders of magnitude	78
4.10	F indexes of four methods at different orders of magnitude	79
5.1	Main menu	86
5.2	MTV	87
5.3	STV	88
5.4	DocuScope STV sample analysis	91
5.5	Sample demonstration of DocuScope identification	93
5.6	DocuScope analysis of the White Paper in 2012	96
6.1	Evaluation of term extraction results	108
7.1	A synset for controlled authoring in TermWeb	121

7.2	Terms related to "water", from Eurovoc	127
7.3	A multi-level subject field taxonomy in TermWeb	129
7.4	Relations between "forest" and other concepts in TermWeb	130
7.5	Automatic inverse relation between "cloud forest" and "forest" in TermWeb	130
7.6	Terminological entry with a picture in TermWeb	131
7.7	Setting up an automated workflow in TermWeb	132
7.8	Sample workflows for a large organisation	133
7.9	A concept map in TermWeb	134
8.1	The concordance results of "chengchi"	147
8.2	The concordance results of "shi"	149
10.1	Human evaluation of differed levels of post-editing efforts	185

Tables

1.1	Examples of UX-oriented guidelines and translatability-oriented guidelines	15
1.2	Some elements of overlap and contradiction between UX-oriented guidelines and translatability-oriented guidelines	16
1.3	Examples of differences in the texts when the two different sets of guidelines are applied	17
1.4	Comparison of the preferences of different groups of target language respondents	21
1.5	Comparison of user preferences for raw machine translation and post-edited machine translation	24
1.6	Comparison of user preferences for source text and post-edited machine translation	25
1.7	General comparison of the preferences of the source- and target-language respondents, which demonstrate opposing tendencies	26
3.1	List of contributors (1995 encyclopedia)	53
3.2	List of contributors (2015 encyclopedia)	58
3.3	List of contributors (2018 encyclopedia)	62
4.1	Sample candidate terms extracted by C-value	69
4.2	Sample candidate terms extracted by TF-IDF	70
4.3	Sample candidate terms extracted by BSCF	72
4.4	Sample candidate terms extracted by the hybrid method	73
4.5	Results of terms extracted by BSCF in 12 texts	74
4.6	Results calculated by four methods when order of magnitude is 16	75
4.7	Results calculated by the four methods when order of magnitude is 156	75
4.8	Results calculated by four methods when order of magnitude is 1568	75
5.1	Factor analysis result and the relative strengths of positive and negative factors	89
5.2	Chinese segmented and rhetoric strategies explained (Part 1)	94
5.3	Chinese segmented and rhetoric strategies explained (Part 2)	94

5.4	Number of rhetorical devices in the White Papers (2000–2012)	96
6.1	Data size for automatic term extraction	109
6.2	"Precision" and "Recall" for SDL MultiTerm Extract	110
6.3	Matched terms	110
8.1	Statistics of alignment	141
9.1	Comparison of machine translated text and human translation text	168
9.2	Analysis of responses from informants for questions 1–4	177
9.3	Analysis of frequency of scores (1): Customer satisfaction on machine translation between English and Kiswahili	178
9.4	Analysis of frequency of scores (2)	178
9.5	Average score per question: Responses on customer satisfaction on English to Kiswahili machine translation	178
11.1	Special features of genre and translation principles	216
11.2	Machine translation approaches' suitability match for different genres	221
11.3	Scales for fluency and fidelity (based on LDC 2005)	222
11.4	Evaluation scores comparison	223
11.5	Comparison of the translations of Extract 1 and Extract 2	224
11.6	Comparison of translation segments generated by machine translation systems for Extract 1	232
11.7	Glossary of Extract 1	234
11.8	Comparison of translation segments generated by machine translation systems for Extracts 1 and 2 with Glossary	234

Contributors

Lynne Bowker is Full Professor at the School of Translation and Interpretation at the University of Ottawa, and is also the Vice Dean of the Faculty of Graduate and Postdoctoral Studies.

Cao Yixin is a PhD candidate at the Department of Linguistics and Translation, City University of Hong Kong. She obtained her BA and MA degrees from Sun Yat-Sen University, China.

Sylviane Cardey is Senior Member of the Institut Universitaire de France and Tenured Professor of Linguistics and Natural Language Processing in the University of Franche-Comté, Besançon, France.

Chan Sin-wai, is Professor at the School of Humanities and Social Science, The Chinese University of Hong Kong, Shenzhen. To date, he has published 52 books in 64 volumes.

Jairo Buitrago Ciro is a student on uOttawa's Master of Information Studies programme.

Mozhgan Ghassemiazghandi is a PhD candidate in translation studies at the University Sains Malaysia. She works as a freelance translator for a number of international organizations and private clients.

Jiang Cheng, is Director of the Department of English for EST Translation and Vice Director of the MTI Center of the University of Shanghai for Science and Technology.

Olivia Kwong Oi Yee is Associate Professor at the Department of Translation, The Chinese University of Hong Kong. Her research interests span many bilingual and pan-Chinese language processing issues.

Tengku Sepora Tengku Mahadi is Full Professor and Dean of the School of Languages, Literacies and Translation at the University Sains Malaysia. She lectures in translation theories and practice.

Sarah Ndanu Mwangangl Ngesu is Lecturer at the South Eastern Kenya University. She has taught at the South Eastern Kenya University and the Kenyatta University.

Qian Duoxiu is Associate Professor and Vice Dean of the School of Foreign Languages and Head of the Department of Translation and Interpretation of Beihang University, Beijing, China.

Wang Min obtained her BA degree from Nanjing University of Science and Technology in 2011 and MTI degree from University of Shanghai for Science and Technology in 2015.

Kara Warburton was the lead terminologist for IBM for 15 years and is a recognized expert in terminology management. She has taught terminology management in professional workshops and universities.

Cecilia Wong Shuk Man taught at the City University of Hong Kong, Hong Kong Polytechnic University, and the Department of Translation of The Chinese University of Hong Kong (part-time).

Xu Bin is Associate Professor and Director of the English Department of the School of Foreign Languages at Shandong Normal University. He conducts research on translation studies and computer-aided translation.

Introduction

Chan Sin-wai

Despite the rapid advances of translation technology, the human factor in machine translation is as important as ever. This is very much in evidence when we study all the chapters in this volume.

The first chapter is entitled "Localizing Websites using Machine Translation: Exploring Connections between User eXperience and Translatability" by Lynne Bowker and Jairo Buitrago Ciro, both of the University of Ottawa, Canada. UX – or "User eXperience" – is concerned with the user-centred design of a website: it focuses on the total subjective experience of the user and on whether the site meets the user's needs. Questions include whether the site is easy to use, attractive, and appropriate. Since the web is a multimedia platform, UX often focuses on visual aspects of the site (e.g. font, icons, colours, navigation). Yet, much web content is text-based, and there has been some effort to consider text as part UX. For example, some organizations produce style guides for content creators that suggest the particular tone and voice that should be adopted to appeal to site users. While UX guidelines aim to make web content engaging, other types of guidelines may also come into play. For instance, as organizations increasingly engage in website localization, controlled language guidelines may be applied to ensure that text can be more easily translated, typically by a machine translation system. The question of whether UX and translatability guidelines are compatible or in conflict becomes increasingly relevant, particularly when it comes to balancing time, cost, and quality. This chapter reports on a multilingual recipient evaluation of web content that has been created according to two different sets of guidelines, and then translated using machine translation. The results indicate that there are some areas where the two sets of guidelines are compatible, but other areas where they are in conflict.

Chapter 2, by Sylviane Cardey of the Université de Franche-Comté, is entitled "Norms and Controlled Language for Machine Translation". Sylviane examines the relationship between machine translation and sense mining and notices that in translating, meaning can be paraphrased in different surface representations in the source language as well as in the target language(s), whereas in sense mining, meaning is searched from surface representations in different languages. It is therefore interesting to see how such a relationship can be applied to which domains and languages. A norms-oriented approach has been conducted to make a comparative study on norms between several languages, such as Arabic, Chinese, English, French, Japanese, Russian, and Thai. It is found that the generation and use of controlled language for machine translation for the safety domain results in the avoidance of pitfalls and removal of the need of post-editing.

Chan Sin-wai of The Chinese University of Hong Kong, Shenzhen, puts the human factor in machine translation in an encyclopaedic way by sharing his experience in editing three encyclopedias, all of which are in some ways related to translation technology. This chapter, entitled "Caught in the Web of Translation: Reflections on the Compilation of Three Translation Encyclopedias", reveals the process of encyclopedia compilation and discusses how encyclopedias enlarge the areas of translation and open up new frontiers in translation technology. Reflections and discussions in the chapter are based on the three translation encyclopedias that the author has compiled: *Encyclopedia of Translation* (1995), *The Routledge Encyclopedia of Translation Technology* (2015), and *An Encyclopedia of Practical Translation and Interpreting* (2018). *The Encyclopedia of Translation*, co-edited with David Pollard, was the first in the field and comprised contributions of eighty-nine experts. *The Routledge Encyclopedia of Translation Technology* is the first definitive reference to provide a comprehensive overview of the general, regional, and topical aspects of translation technology, covering forty-nine topics. Finally, the *Encyclopedia of Practical Translation and Interpreting*, scheduled for publication in 2018, will provide a general and authoritative reference for translation teachers, professionals, and practitioners, as well as students working on practical writings, with special reference of the language pair of Chinese and English. It will cover around twenty topics in the areas of practical translation and interpreting, to be written by prominent scholars, researchers, experts, and up-coming specialists in the field and industry.

Jiang Cheng and Wang Min, both from the College of Foreign Languages, University of Shanghai for Science and Technology, contribute a chapter entitled "A Comparative Study of Term Extraction Methods in Translation", which makes a comparative study of term extraction performances of four representative term extraction methods, i.e. C-value algorithm, TF-IDF algorithm, nonstatistical algorithm, and combined algorithm. An experiment was conducted to test the measurable indicators of term extraction performances of each method. By analyzing the data collected from the experiment, they found that while the first three algorithms have their advantages and disadvantages when considering measurable indicators of term extraction performance in terms of precision rate, recall rate, and F index, the combined algorithm performs better than the other three term extraction algorithms in term recognition. Their findings are of theoretical significance as they help to improve term extraction methods and develop term extraction tools for translation, which plays an important role in enhancing the overall efficiency and quality of the translation.

Chapter 5, by Qian Duoxiu of Beihang University in China, is entitled "Introducing Corpus Rhetoric into Translation Quality Assessment: A Case Study of the White Papers on China's National Defense". In translation studies, quality assessment has always been a challenging issue. As a means of inter-cultural and inter-lingual communication, translation and its effect on the target readers have been largely studied from the stylistic perspective, based on a detailed analysis at different linguistic levels. This chapter introduces a corpus-based rhetorical approach to the evaluation of translation to see how faithful it is to the original in calling on the audience for similar actions intended for the original audience. DocuScope, a rhetorical analysis tool, together with Minitab, are used for this specific purpose. The White Papers on China's National Defense (2000–2012) are the texts under study. It is found that the translated text is an accurate transfer of communicative effect. It proves that the effect of translation, particularly the persuasive effect, can be quantitatively measured and evaluated. The study and the method used here can be adopted in the assessment of translation of texts on a larger scale and in other domains.

Chapter 6, by Olivia Kwong Oi Yee of the Department of Translation, The Chinese University of Hong Kong, is about the evaluation of term extraction tools. Term extraction tools for translators may exist in the form of stand-alone applications or a component in a suite of computer-aided translation software. They often take a set of texts provided by the user, run some algorithm over the text and suggest term candidates, and leave the potential terms for the user to verify. The value of automatic term extraction to translators thus heavily depends on whether the time saved from automating the term collection step outweighs the effort to be spent subsequently on cleaning up the suggested term list, given that most translators are already used to keeping and continuously accumulating their own glossaries manually. While studies in natural language processing have often reported encouraging system performance for automatic term extraction, different kinds of comments have been made by term extraction software users. This chapter aims to account for this discrepancy by analyzing term extraction results from existing tools, and discussing how factors such as output quality, software design, user expectation, and work habit, might affect the general perception of these tools.

Kara Warburton of Termologic Terminology Consulting takes up the issue of terminology a step further by putting it in a global context. In Chapter 7, entitled "Terminology Resources in Support of Global Communication", she claims that terminology in electronic database form is becoming a language resource that is leveraged in increasingly new ways to support global communication. To maximize their reuse potential, terminology resources must be structured and managed according to the latest standards and best practices. In this chapter, Warburton presents some of the functions, features, and end-uses of repurposable terminology resources. Beginning with a review of essential standards, methodologies, and principles of terminology management, Warburton then demonstrates how terminology resources in the modern era have evolved from simple spreadsheets containing equivalents in two languages to highly-structured knowledge systems developed with state-of-the-art database technologies. Sophisticated terminology management systems that can store a wide range of information types in an unlimited number of languages are now available.

Warburton demonstrates some of the features that distinguish these systems from their predecessors, such as support for ontological relations, workflows, and multimedia. These systems enable terminology resources, previously developed to support only the translation industry, to be repurposed for innovative extended applications, such as controlled authoring and search engine optimization (SEO). However, computer-assisted translation tools are still the predominant technology used to manage terminology, and their translation-oriented focus is slowing down the pace of change.

Xu Bin, of Shandong Normal University in China, discusses "Corpora and CAT-based CN-EN Translation of Chinese Culture" in Chapter 8. As China takes a more active attitude in promoting Chinese culture in the world since the turn of the century, a lot of research has been done in this field. However, based on a thorough survey of the literature since 2000, the author finds that among the related papers, very few touch upon the topic of the significance of borrowing solutions from former translated works of Chinese culture (or history, philosophy, etc.) in the translating process, let alone realizing the usefulness of terminology mining and computer-aided translation. In terms of translating Chinese works into English, the author holds that a turn in the research is required, i.e., turning from focusing on the studies of translation ethics and strategies in general to exploring more specific strategies such as the application of terminology technologies, computer-aided translation, and the corpus-based approaches in the translation of Chinese culture works into English.

Chapter 9, entitled "Issues of Language Structure in Machine Translation between English and Kiswahili", is written by Sarah Ndanu M. Ngesu, who teaches at the South Eastern Kenya University in Kenya. This chapter examines issues of language in Machine Translation between English and Kiswahili. Structurally, English is an infusional language while Kiswahili is an agglutinating language. Language structure in Machine Translation (MT) and its effect on the accuracy in translation of texts from one language to another has been influenced by modernization and crosscultural dynamism brought about by globalization. There is a need to identify strategic models involving accuracy in automation in translation. This might involve linguistic exploration of aspects of lexicon, syntax, semantics, and pragmatics in machine translated texts. This chapter identifies, categorizes, and discusses issues of language structure between English and Kiswahili in Machine Translation on aspects of lexicon, syntax, and semantics. The primary aim of this chapter is to identify complexities of language structure between English and Kiswahili languages that pose great challenges to machine translation. The study is guided by three questions: Are there causes of mismatches and inaccuracies in machine-translated texts from English into Kiswahili? How effective are the machine-translated texts from English into Kiswahili in relation to consumer satisfaction? Machine Translation is relatively new and its issues are a grey area. This chapter therefore sets out to examine these unique issues in machine translation and give suggestions where possible on how these issues could be handled in machine translation. Data used in this chapter was collected from sampled texts from the internet that was translated by computer and also by a human translator. Common communication phrases were sampled using purposive sampling. Cases of mistranslations were classified into three categories, namely lexicon, syntax, and semantics. A comparison was done between the machine translation and human-translated texts. A questionnaire was formulated and tested on respondents. These translations and the responses from the respondents was analyzed, interpreted, and discussed. The results were statistically analyzed and significant levels interpreted to form the basis for reliable conclusions and recommendations.

In Chapter 10, Mozhgan Ghassemiazghandi and Tengku Sepora Tengku Mahadi, both of the School of Languages, Literacies and Translation of the University Sains Malaysia, believe that machine translation has reached levels of performance that allow for its integration into real-world translation workflows. Despite the high speed and various advantages of this technology, the fact that varying quality of machine translation requires different levels of post-editing effort has raised a need to assess their quality and predict the required post-editing effort. The aim of the current study is to investigate the quality estimation of translation freedom and narrowness of the domain in literary texts. It is a pilot study on machine translation for the literary text with a novel being translated from English to Persian. The training data is created by translating literary texts with machine translation and then post-editing the results, in order to assess the translatability of these texts with machine translation. This study sheds light on the applicability of machine translation to literature, as machine translation and literature might seem incompatible at first glance. From the small number of selected examples in the literature, it can be concluded that there are many mistranslations and near-mistranslations and potentially ambiguous translations. Machine translation in literature is a useful tool restricted only to the aspect of memory and time. The product is not yet a high-quality translation without the intervention of human intelligence.

Chpater 11 is on machine translation by Cecilia Wong Shuk Man, entitled "Optimizing the Use of Computer Translation Systems by Examining Disciplinary Differences and Characteristics of Genres as well as the Various Approaches Applied in Computer Translation". It is generally agreed that "fidelity", "fluency", and "elegance" are the traditional three standards of translation suggested by Yan Fu. Scholars have different views on the third criterion, such as Tung C. (2010), who suggested using "felicity" to substitute for "elegance". No matter which principle we follow, there are different ways to translate. Literal translation, for instance, is done by translating the explicit word meanings of the text, whereas free translation is done by translating messages expressed or intentions of the writers in order to achieve specific effects, such as emotional impact. It is obvious and generally agreed that computer translation is more suitable or specifically, more useful for translating texts that need literal translation with absolute consistency. After decades of development, it is still an unreachable goal to generate fully automatic high quality translation for free translation texts. However, as supported by abundant recent research, computer translation can extensively increase the productivity of translators. This chapter aims at examining the feasibility in enjoying the advantages brought by the computer translation development in doing free translation. The discussion focuses on disciplinary differences of genres, approaches employed in computer translation systems, as well as aids or extra measures being used and suggested to be incorporated in computer translation systems to facilitate better performance.

The last chapter, Chapter 12, is about crowdsourcing translation in China by Cao Yixin of the Department of Linguistics and Translation, the City University of Hong Kong. According to Cao, recent years have seen the augmentation of attention both in crowdsourcing and crowdsourcing translation activities, from either the industry or the academic circle. In terms of translation, several case studies have been done in this area. However, current research lacks a solid theoretical review of the concept and focus more on the individual cases rather than the entire sociocultural backdrop. China is a country that witnesses the prospering crowdsourcing translation activities nowadays; however, the value and the cultural-political significance of such activities have been under-estimated. When did crowdsourcing translation communities come into shape in China? Why have they become popular among the audience? What are their potentials in the future? These questions remain to be explored.

Under such considerations, this chapter contributes to a more comprehensive understanding of the nature of crowdsourcing translation, as well as its practicing contexts. Specifically, it aims at setting a theoretical foundation for the future discussions of crowdsourcing, crowdsourcing translation, and crowdsourcing translation activities in China. To reach such a goal, this chapter firstly focuses on the definition of crowdsourcing and crowdsourcing translation. The theoretical history of crowdsourcing is traced together with an introduction of general crowdsourcing examples. Based on the theoretical discussions, the latter half of this chapter makes an overview of the crowdsourcing translation practices in contemporary China, classifies them into different categories, and traces their development trajectory. The crowdsourcing subtitles translation activities are discussed in detail, as an example indicating how the crowdsourcing translation communities have been developed from their fan translation predecessors in the legalization process of user-generated internet contents, among the clashes of different discourses.

Conclusion

It is hoped that the chapters in this book shed new light on the significance of the human factor in machine translation at the present level of translation technology. The rapid advances in the fields relevant to translation technology will certainly push the field further ahead in a way that is beyond what we can imagine today.

1 Localizing websites using machine translation
Exploring connections between user eXperience and translatability

Lynne Bowker and Jairo Buitrago Ciro

1 Introduction

Over the past two decades, the World Wide Web and its associated navigation tools have developed into a resource that is currently unmatched as a means of providing users across the globe with access to information. Companies and organizations of various types create websites to promote and sell a wide range of products and services, and a significant factor in determining whether or not these efforts are successful is something that has come to be known as the User eXperience (UX).

Hassenzahl (2013) describes UX as an "evasive beast", noting that experience is an almost overwhelmingly rich concept, with a long history of debate and many attempts to define it. UX is a slippery concept because it focuses on the total subjective experience of the user – such as whether using a product or service produces a positive, a negative, or a middle-of-the-road reaction – and on whether the product or service meets the user's needs. According to Garrett (2011: 6), if someone asks you what it is like to use a product or service, they are asking about your user experience. This could include questions such as whether it is hard to do simple things, whether the product is easy to figure out, or how it feels to interact with the product (e.g. awkward, or satisfying). Every product that is used by someone – from a toothbrush to a digital camera, from a microwave oven to a pair of shoes, from a book to a website – creates a user experience. Designing for a positive UX has become an important aspect of website development. As more and more companies and organizations compete for business online, users have many possible websites to choose from. Providing a positive UX on a website is therefore becoming increasingly important as a means of attracting and retaining customers.

To date, much of the emphasis of website design has been placed on the visual aspects of a site, such as font size, icons, or colours, as well as on the navigational aspects, including screen layout, scrollability, and hyperlinks, among others (e.g. Lindgaard et al. 2011). Commonly asked questions that relate to UX include whether the site is easy to use, attractive, and appropriate. However, in the context of UX, relatively little attention has been paid to the textual content, even though much web content is text-based.

Some organizations have developed style guides for content creators that suggest the particular tone and voice that should be adopted to appeal to site users (e.g. MailChimp Style Guide, Microsoft Style Guide, WebAIM). However, to the best of our knowledge, a question that has not yet been deeply explored is how the UX of a website's text influences the translatability of that text, and vice versa. In other words, if a source text generates a positive UX for a reader, how easy is it to translate that text? And if the text is written in such a way as to make it more translation-friendly, how does that affect the UX for both the source- and target-language readers? Bowker (2015) reports on an initial exploration into the relationship between UX and translatability. The results of that study, which involved one text and one language pair (English and Spanish), suggest that UX and translatability have the following relationship: as translatability increases, the UX of source-language readers begins to decrease, while the UX of target-language readers begins to increase (Bowker 2015: 25).

This question of the relation between UX and translatability becomes important for organizations that wish to localize their websites into multiple languages in order to better market their products and services to customers in other countries or regions, where linguistic and cultural differences may come into play. Presumably these organizations would like their websites to generate a positive UX for both the source-language audience and the target-language audience. However, in business, there is also a need to be mindful of the bottom line. Translation and localization have the potential to be time-consuming and expensive undertakings, which means that organizations are also interested in seeking ways to minimize these costs (Lefeuvre 2012; Nantel and Glaser 2008; Spates 2014).

A strategy that can be used to reduce translation costs is to have the goal of translation in mind when creating the textual content of a website in the first place. So-called "writing for translation" or "controlled authoring" involves reducing linguistic ambiguities and simplifying structures in the source text so that it can be more easily translated (Ó Broin 2009; Sichel 2009). This approach is particularly attractive if the source text is to be translated into multiple target languages because eliminating a potential problem (e.g. an ambiguous construction) in the source text is much faster and cheaper than having to address the resulting problem in each of the different target texts (Brown 2003). Meanwhile, another strategy to reduce translation costs for website localization is to integrate the use of technology, such as a machine translation system, into the translation process (Garcia 2010; Jiménez-Crespo 2013). Machine translation systems attempt to automatically translate a text from one language to another; however, professional translators may also play a role, such as post-editing the machine translation output (i.e. revising the draft translation that was produced by the machine translation system). Indeed, these two cost-saving strategies can even be combined. A text that has been authored using a controlled language can often be processed more easily by a machine translation system and will typically result in higher quality machine translation output than would a text that has not been written in a controlled fashion (Clark 2009; Ferreira 2017).

In keeping with this volume's theme – the human factor in machine translation – this chapter seeks to build on the initial findings of Bowker (2015) with regard to the relationship between UX and translatability when machine translation is used to translate the textual content of a website. UX is an important human factor to consider when contemplating the use of machine translation, and so this chapter begins with a brief overview of UX, examining some definitions from the literature, and focusing in particular on the role of text as part of the UX of a website. Next, the notion of "writing for translation" is presented, including a very brief overview of controlled language and machine translation. Once the key concepts have been explained, we then present the results of a multilingual recipient evaluation. In this study, a group of English speakers act as source language recipients who weigh in on the UX of two different versions of a text that has been written to encourage students to apply to a graduate programme in information studies. Next, machine translations of these two versions of the source text are evaluated by target-language groups with different user profiles, including French-speaking undergraduate students, Italian-speaking professors and graduate students, and Spanish-speaking university library employees. The final part of the investigation introduces post-editing, which is another type of human factor in machine translation. In fact, O'Brien et al. (2014: vii) have described post-editing as "possibly the oldest form of human-machine cooperation for translation, having been a common practice for just about as long as operational machine translation systems have existed." In the present study, the French versions of the machine translated text are post-edited to see how this might affect the UX of a website.

2 User eXperience

The International Organization for Standardization (ISO DIS 9241–210:2010) provides the following definition for UX: "A person's perceptions and responses that result from the use or anticipated use of a product, system or service." This seems to be a reasonable high-level explanation. However, as emphasized by Law et al. (2009: 719), there is no universally accepted definition of UX because this concept is associated with a broad range of fuzzy and dynamic notions, including emotional, affective, experiential, hedonic, and aesthetic variables. Inclusion and exclusion of particular variables in the evaluation of UX is inconsistent and appears to depend largely on the researcher's background and interest. Law et al. (2009: 719) also observe that the unit of analysis for UX is very malleable, ranging from a single aspect of an individual end-user's interaction with a standalone application to all aspects of multiple end-users' interaction with the company and its merging of services from multiple disciplines.

Two other factors that make it challenging to provide a firm and consensus-based definition of UX are that it is subjective and dynamic. UX is subjective in nature because it is about an individual's perception and reaction with respect to a product or service. Moreover, it is dynamic because it is modified over time as circumstances change (e.g. the user becomes more accustomed to a product, or new features are added).

According to Garrett (2011: 7–8), a distinguishing feature of UX design is that it goes beyond aesthetics or function to deal with questions of context. Often when people think about product design, they first think of it in terms of aesthetic appeal: a well-designed product is one that looks or feels good. Another common way that people think about product design is in functional terms: a well-designed product is one that does what it promises to do. Garrett (2011: 7–8) clarifies that products might look good and work well functionally, but UX design seeks to ensure that the aesthetic and functional aspects work in the context of the rest of the product and in the context of what the user is trying to accomplish. He gives the example of a coffeemaker, noting that aesthetic design makes sure that the button on the machine is an appealing shape and texture, while functional design ensures that this button triggers the appropriate action on the device. Meanwhile, UX design makes sure that the aesthetic and functional aspects work in the context of the rest of the product and the intended task by addressing questions such as whether the button is the right size relative to the importance of its function, or whether it is in the right place relative to the other controls that the user would be using at the same time.

2.1 UX and websites

User experience is a vital part of any product, and this includes websites (Hartmann, Di Angeli and Sutcliffe 2008). Every organization that has a website creates an impression through UX. Increasingly organizations are recognizing that providing a quality UX on a website is an essential, sustainable competitive advantage. As explained by Garrett (2011: 12), UX forms the customer's impression of an organization's offerings, differentiates an organization from its competitors, and determines whether the customer will return.

Hassenzahl and Tractinsky (2006: 95) observe that conventionally, UX design has been largely focused on preventing usability problems. However, they go on to make a convincing case for considering a high quality UX of a website as being not merely one where there is an absence of problems, but rather as one where users have an overtly positive experience when interacting with the site.

2.2 Text as an element of UX

A main goal of almost every website is to communicate the information content of the site as effectively as possible. It is not sufficient to simply put the information online; it must be presented in a way that helps people to absorb and understand it. If the information is not conveyed effectively, users might not be able to establish that an organization offers the service or product that they are looking for, or if they only manage to find this information after a challenging exploration of the site, they might determine that if the site is difficult to work with, then the organization might be too. Effective communication is therefore a key factor in the success of the product or service. Creating an information-rich UX is about enabling people to find, absorb, and make sense of the information that is provided on a website.

According to Garrett (2011: 32), information content is an important factor that contributes to shaping the UX of a website, and he goes on to add that developing and maintaining valuable and effective content is hard work (73). It was noted above that when many people think about the effectiveness of a website, they think first of colours, images, typography, or layout. While these visually-oriented aspects are important, the UX of a site extends beyond the visual to include other factors, such as language, and in particular, language quality (van Iwaarden et al. 2004: 957; Nantel and Glaser 2008: 114).

Clearly, the set of conceptual associations or emotional reactions that a website generates is important because this inevitably creates an impression about the organization in the mind of the user. A website that contains typographical errors or poor grammar might cause a user to think that the organization could be equally careless in its operations, while a site whose information is presented in an inappropriate register could give a user the impression that the product or service is targeting a different type of customer.

2.3 UX and translation

If language is an important factor in website development, it is also critical in website localization. In the global economy, products are designed in a given country to be sold and used in countries around the world. Dray and Siegel (2006: 281) emphasize that when designing products, services, and websites for international users, it is important to start with a deep understanding of *all* users – domestic and international. This includes understanding how they are similar – and different – in different parts of the world, and then using that knowledge to create a website or websites that will work for each of them.

Hillier (2003: 2) makes a similar observation when he notes that designers of a website will have created the original website drawing on their cultural norms, of which the text will form a part of an integrated whole. If the text is then translated into another language, then the overall design may also need to be changed because the usability of the site will also change. The usability will change due to the users having different culturally based expectations. Hillier therefore argues that a relationship exists between language, cultural context, and usability.

Nantel and Glaser (2008: 114) also identify a link between a website's usability and linguistic and cultural factors, noting that one dimension of service that influences the usability of a site considerably is the quality of its language and ultimately its compliance with the culturally determined metaphors, attitudes, and preferences of its target groups. Translations of content, culture, and context play a significant role in the way users perceive a website.

Both Hillier (2003) and Nantel and Glaser (2008) remark that there has been relatively little research carried out on the usability implications of translating websites or on the impact of translations on the user-friendliness of websites, though Jiménez-Crespo (2013) has since gone some way towards filling this gap. Nevertheless, to the best of our knowledge, a question that has not yet been explored in any detail is the relationship between the UX of a website's source-language text and the translatability of that text, which in turn has an effect on the UX of the target-language text. In particular, we are interested in exploring this relationship between UX and translatability in the context of machine translation.

As mentioned briefly above, website localization can be time-consuming and expensive, which means that organizations are also interested in seeking ways to minimize these costs. Jiménez-Crespo (2013: 197–199), among others, has observed that there has been an increase in the use of machine translation (MT) tools to help with website localization, and that this can involve either the use of raw machine translation output, or machine translation combined with some degree of pre- and/or post-editing.

To better understand the relationship between the UX and the translatability of a website, we undertook a study, which will be described in detail. This study took the form of a recipient evaluation, which means that we asked the intended users or recipients of a text to provide feedback on their user experience with that text.

As pointed out by a number of researchers (e.g. van Iwaarden et al. 2004: 949; Dray and Siegel 2006: 282; Nantel and Glaser 2008: 114–115; Garrett 2011: 42), there has been an historic tendency to develop websites that reflect the mindset of the producers, rather than that of users. However, to achieve customer satisfaction, it is necessary to take the users' viewpoint into account. Indeed, as Garrett (2011: 45) reminds us: "Not only will different groups of users have different needs, but sometimes those needs will be in direct opposition." Meanwhile, Nantel and Glaser (2008: 114–115) indicate that this may have special implications in the context of website localization:

> Website usability enhances customer satisfaction, trust and ultimately loyalty. In a multicultural and multilingual world, it could therefore be argued that sites that address different populations should reach them in a manner that reflects their respective cultural contexts and linguistic preferences.

Lefeuvre (2012) makes a similar observation, noting that "When we pledge to embrace the adaptable nature of the web – to make our websites responsive and even future-ready – we're typically talking about diversity of devices. But the web's diversity also comes in the form of different languages and cultures." He then goes on to specify that "Translation affects users' experiences – and our organizations' success. It's time we [website developers] consider translation part of our jobs, too."

However, Lefeuvre (2012) then goes on emphasize that, although it is costly, website translation requires professional translation; he dismisses machine translation as a quick-and-dirty solution that is not an appropriate option in this context. Spates (2014) takes a more measured view, noting that when it comes to translating a website, "there is no one-size-fits-all solution," and the possibilities may range from raw machine translation through post-edited machine translation to varying levels of professional translation. Indeed, other investigations have demonstrated that there are contexts where raw machine translation output (Thicke 2013) and post-edited machine translation (Bowker and Buitrago Ciro 2015) can be useful to and even highly appreciated by website users. Therefore, as suggested by Nantel and Glaser (2008: 120–121), organizations will need to make decisions about their approach to website translation as part of a larger cost-benefit analysis.

3 Experiment

Bowker (2015) reported on an initial study conducted with heterogeneous groups of English source-language speakers and Spanish target-language speakers. To further our understanding of the relationship between UX and translatability, and to explore whether those findings appear to hold true over a wider range of languages, user profiles, and texts, we conducted the present follow-up study which expands on Bowker (2015) in a number of ways. First, the study is multilingual and involves English source-language speakers and three different groups of target-language speakers: (a) French Canadian undergraduate students, (b) Italian professors and graduate students, and (c) Spanish-speaking employees of a university library in Colombia. This study also used a different source text. In addition, while the first three phases of the investigation adopted the same methodology that was used in Bowker (2015), we expanded the study by adding a fourth phase that introduces post-editing:

1. evaluating UX in the source language (English);
2. evaluating translatability with a machine translation system (Google Translate™);
3. evaluating UX in three target languages (French, Italian, and Spanish);
4. evaluating UX with post-edited versions of the target text (French).

The methodology and findings for each of these phases will be described in more detail in an upcoming section. First, however, we will describe the text selection and pre-processing that was carried out to prepare for the study.

3.1 Preparatory work: text selection and pre-processing

As emphasized in Brouwer (2017), Canada is becoming a destination of choice for international graduate students. As part of its strategic plan, *Destination 2020*, the University of Ottawa has identified internationalization as one of its main strategic goals. Accordingly, the University is seeking to "welcome a greater number of international students and faculty to our campus" (p. 8). More specifically, the University of Ottawa sets out an ambitious goal that states:

> Between now and 2020, we will double the number of international graduate students (from 700 to 1,400) and increase the number of international undergraduate students by 50% (from 1,500 to 2,250), for a total of 3,650 international students, or 9% of the entire student body.
>
> (p. 8)

Although it might be reasonable to expect that any student wishing to come and study in English at the University of Ottawa would already be proficient in this language, there had been numerous discussions at the Faculty of Arts Council meetings about the fact that not all members of a potential student's support network are necessarily comfortable in English. The Faculty had been discussing the possibility of translating parts of the website into a range of foreign languages in order to provide potential international students and their support network members with some fundamental information about the university and its programmes. It was suggested that this strategy might allow people such as family members, friends, peers, and local university professors or mentors – who are often an important part of a student's decision-making and support network – to be more engaged in and comfortable with the process. While there was widespread support in principle for providing foreign-language versions, the issue of budgetary constraints came into play, and the question of whether machine translation could be used as a partial solution was raised. It was also noted that, even if the University of Ottawa does not provide official translations of its website, the prevalence of free online machine translation systems, such as Google Translate™ among others, means that foreign readers might choose to use such tools to translate sections of the University of Ottawa's website themselves. Therefore, it could be beneficial to ensure that the text contained on the university's website is (machine) translation-friendly.

For these reasons, the question of the relationship between UX and translatability is a pertinent one. If a text is constructed in order to produce a positive UX for source language readers, how well will this text translate into the target language? Will the resulting translation produce a correspondingly positive UX for target language readers? Conversely, if the source text is written in such a way as to improve its translatability – and particularly its translatability by a machine translation system – will this adversely affect the UX for source language readers? Will it positively affect the UX for target language readers? To find answers to these questions, two different versions of the English-language source text were produced.

3.1.1 Source text selection

For this study, we selected a source text that appeared on the website of the University of Ottawa. It consisted of a 130-word extract from a portion of the website that is intended to entice potential graduate students to apply for a newly established Master of Information Studies programme at the University of Ottawa. The programme has the potential to attract a wide range of students – both domestic and international – because it is open to graduates who have a bachelor's degree in *any* discipline. This text had been prepared in English by the university's Marketing and Communication team with a view to attracting students to the programme, but it had not been written specifically with the question of translatability in mind.

3.1.2 Pre-processing: writing for the web vs writing for translation

Writing for the web requires a style that is different from writing for print publications. Many different style guides have appeared to help writers produce texts that are suitable for this medium, and Jiménez-Crespo (2010) contains a useful overview and review of several different categories of digital style guides. For this study, we focused more specifically on guidelines that are intended to help writers produce a positive UX for readers (e.g. USDHHS 2006; Baldwin 2010; Kiefer Lee 2012). Based on these guidelines, we compiled a list of frequently made recommendations. Examples of guidelines that are intended to produce a positive UX for readers are listed in the left-hand column of Table 1.1.

Table 1.1 Examples of UX-oriented guidelines and translatability-oriented guidelines

UX-oriented guidelines	*Translatability-oriented guidelines*
<ul><li>Be as simple and concise as possible</li><li>Use headings and lists</li><li>Use familiar, commonly used words; avoid jargon</li><li>Use the active voice</li><li>Use short paragraphs (maximum of 5 sentences, ideally 2–3) and short sentences (maximum 20 words)</li><li>Use personal pronouns (e.g. you, we)</li><li>Use dashes and semicolons to break up phrases</li><li>You may start a sentence with "but", "and", or "or" if it clarifies the sentence</li><li>Start with the most important information at the beginning, then add more details as the text progresses</li><li>Think about your target audience</li></ul>	<ul><li>Avoid idioms and regionalisms</li><li>Avoid abbreviated forms</li><li>Use optional pronouns (that and who) and punctuation (commas)</li><li>Avoid modifier stacks</li><li>Use the active voice</li><li>Keep adjectives and adverbs close to the words they modify, and far from others they could potentially modify</li><li>Use standard English grammar, punctuation, and capitalization, even in headings</li><li>Use short sentences (maximum 25 words), but avoid very short sentences and headings and sentence fragments</li><li>Use parallel sentence construction</li><li>Avoid words ending in -ing, and if they must be used, make the meaning as clear as possible</li><li>Make sure words ending in -ed are clear (e.g. add an article to show it is an adjective not a verb)</li><li>Avoid linking more than three phrases in a sentence by coordinating conjunctions</li><li>Use precise and accurate terminology</li><li>Do not use non-English words or phrases</li><li>Use a word only for its primary meaning</li><li>Avoid phrasal verbs</li></ul>

Next, we consulted several sets of guidelines that have been developed with a view to helping writers produce a text that can be effectively translated and particularly with the help of a machine translation system (e.g. Kohl 2008; Ó Broin 2009; Sichel 2009; Microsoft 2012). We also included the guidelines for writing clearly and simply that were produced as part of the WebAIM (Web Accessibility in Mind) initiative. Although the latter set of guidelines focuses on ensuring that web content is accessible, it has been reported by Rodríguez Vásquez (2013: 101) that these guidelines can also contribute to successful website localization. From these various sets of guidelines, we extracted a list of the most commonly recommended tips. Examples of guidelines that aim to increase the translatability of a text are presented in the right-hand column of Table 1.1.

In looking at the two lists presented in Table 1.1, we can observe that there are some recommendations that are common to both, such as using the active voice and using short sentences. However, there are other recommendations that are in opposition to one another, as illustrated in Table 1.2. It is also interesting to note that some of the UX-oriented guidelines are quite general (e.g. "Think about your target audience"), whereas the list of translatability-oriented guidelines is much longer and more precise, and it includes recommendations to avoid particular structures (e.g. -ed, -ing, phrasal verbs, modifier stacks, abbreviations, regionalisms, and idioms) that are known to cause difficulties for translators, both human and machine. In general, it appears that UX-oriented writing guidelines place an emphasis on making a text engaging, while the machine translation-oriented writing guidelines focus more on textual precision. The main tension is between being ***catchy*** (UX) and being ***precise*** (MT).

Once the two sets of recommendations had been drawn up, we applied each set independently to the original text. This resulted in two different presentations of

Table 1.2 Some elements of overlap and contradiction between UX-oriented guidelines and translatability-oriented guidelines

	UX-oriented guidelines	*Translatability-oriented guidelines*
Similar	• Use the active voice • Use short paragraphs (maximum of 5 sentences, ideally 2–3) and short sentences (maximum 20 words)	• Use the active voice • Use short sentences (maximum 25 words)
In opposition	• Be as simple and concise as possible • Use headings and lists • You may start a sentence with "but", "and", or "or" if it clarifies the sentence • Use familiar, commonly used words; avoid jargon	• Use optional pronouns (that and who) and punctuation (commas) • Avoid very short sentences and headings and sentence fragments • Use standard English grammar, punctuation, and capitalization • Use precise and accurate terminology

that text, though the core meaning was preserved. In fact, the original text, which had been prepared by the university's Marketing and Communication team, already conformed quite closely to the UX-oriented guidelines: the sentences were relatively short and in the active voice, there were headings and a list, and the words were familiar. Therefore, relatively few changes were made to this text.

A greater number of changes resulted from the application of the translatability-oriented guidelines. In this case, sentence fragments were replaced with complete sentences, nouns were repeated, complex sentences were split into shorter and simpler sentences, long pre-modifier stacks were eliminated, and -ed and -ing constructions were clarified or replaced. Table 1.3 presents examples of some of the resulting differences.

Table 1.3 Examples of differences in the texts when the two different sets of guidelines are applied

Following application of UX-oriented guidelines	*Following application of translatability-oriented guidelines*	*Explanation of differences*
Complete work placements	Students will complete work placements.	Fragments converted to complete sentences
Encompassing the collection, organization, storage and retrieval of information – in all its varied forms – information studies is undergoing unprecedented growth and rapid change as our society adapts to the digital information age.	The domain of information studies encompasses the collection, the organization, the storage and the retrieval of information in all its many forms. As our society adapts to the digital information age, the domain of information studies is in a state of remarkable growth and of rapid evolution.	Complex sentences split into shorter sentences
. . . a choice of course-based, co-op and thesis options . . .	. . . may choose the course-based option, the co-op option, or the thesis option . . .	Nouns repeated
. . . registered students will . . .	. . . students who are registered will . . .	-ed and -ing constructions clarified or replaced
. . . Encompassing the collection, organization . . .	. . . The domain of information studies encompasses the collection, organization . . .	
Master of Information Studies Program Overview . . . emerging technologies librarians . . .	An overview of the Master of Information Studies . . . librarians who specialize in new technologies . . .	Pre-modifier stacks eliminated

3.2 Phase I: comparing users' experience of the two source-language texts

Once the two English-language versions of the text had been prepared, we conducted a recipient evaluation to try to determine whether readers felt that one text provided a better overall user experience than the other, and if so, what contributed to this experience. The recipient evaluation was carried out with the help of an online survey tool called FluidSurveys, which allows participants to respond to an online questionnaire. In addition, this tool permits randomization, which meant that we could change the order in which the texts were presented to control for potential order effect. FluidSurveys can also generate a variety of reports to facilitate data analysis.

After asking participants to provide some basic demographic information, we provided the following instructions, along with the two English-language versions of the text (i.e. the UX-oriented version and the translatability-oriented version), which were unlabelled and presented in a random order.

> **Instructions:** Please read the following TWO versions of the text. If you were looking for information for yourself or for someone you know about pursuing a master's degree in information studies at the University of Ottawa, which of these two texts would you prefer to read on a website? Please briefly explain the reasons for your choice.

3.2.1 Phase I: findings and discussion

A total of 47 completed responses were received. All of the respondents were Canadian and were native speakers of English. With regard to the key question – which version of the text was preferred – 30 (63.8%) of the respondents chose the UX-oriented version, while 17 (36.2%) selected the translatability-oriented guidelines. These findings are largely in line with those reported in Bowker (2015), where 61% of respondents preferred the UX-oriented version of the text, and 39% expressed a preference for the version that had been written according to translatability-oriented guidelines.

Respondents had an opportunity to explain the reasons for their preferences, and once again, there is considerable overlap with the reasons reported in Bowker (2015). For instance, among the English-language respondents who preferred the text that had been written according to the UX style guidelines, the most commonly cited reasons for this preference included that it flowed better, was more concise and less repetitive, and was more engaging.

Although the text written according to the translatability-oriented guidelines was preferred by fewer participants, the ones who did select it commented that they found its meaning to be clearer and that it came across as being informative, rather than as a sales pitch.

3.3 Phase II: comparing translation quality of the two target-language texts

In the next phase, the two different English-language versions – the UX-oriented version and the translatability-oriented version – were translated into French, Italian, and Spanish using the free online machine translation system Google Translate™.

The resulting translations, along with their corresponding source texts, were presented to professional translators in order to determine whether the version that had been written with adherence to the translatability-oriented guidelines did in fact produce a noticeably better translation. At this stage, neither of the target texts were revised or post-edited in any way; the texts presented to the translators consisted of raw machine translation output.

For each language – French, Italian, and Spanish – two professional translators were consulted. All six of the translators had received formal training in translation and had a minimum of four years of professional experience. In all cases, the translators were advised that both translated texts had been produced automatically using machine translation, and that it was possible that neither would be considered "good." The translators were not given any information about the guidelines that were used to produce the texts, and the texts were *not* labelled as being UX-oriented or translatability-oriented.

The translators were instructed that the goal was simply to look at each target text in relation to its corresponding source text, and to rank the two according to which was a better translation using the criteria of *fidelity* and *intelligibility*, which are commonly used measures in machine translation evaluation (e.g. White 2003). Fidelity is a measure of accuracy that aims to determine how well the contents of the translation reflect the contents of the original text. In other words, it considers whether the information been translated correctly with regard to its meaning. Intelligibility is a stylistic measure that seeks to determine how readable each text is in comparison to the other. In making their assessment, translators were also instructed to consider how much post-editing would likely be required to repair each target text.

3.3.1 Phase II: findings and discussion

In all cases, the translators identified the target text that corresponded to the translatability-oriented source text as being the "better" translation with regard to both fidelity and intelligibility. Nonetheless, for each of the target languages, all translators emphasized that *both* translated versions had multiple errors. Some of the problems noted by the translators included misplaced adjectives, homographs (e.g. words with multiple grammatical categories being erroneously translated as the wrong part of speech), difficulties recognizing the scope of modifiers in cases of noun stacking, problems with register (e.g. too formal), and omissions (e.g. missing definite articles).

Nevertheless, all six translators were clear that, of the two texts, the one that had been written according to translatability-oriented guidelines produced a somewhat higher quality raw machine translation output that would require less work to revise during a post-editing phase. These findings are completely in line with the results reported in Bowker (2015), where all the translators in that study also identified the translatability-oriented source text as the one that resulted in a higher quality machine translation.

3.4 Phase III: comparing users' experience of the two target-language texts

During the next phase of the project, we conducted recipient evaluations among three different target language groups: French, Italian, and Spanish speakers. In addition to belonging to different language groups, the three groups of participants had different profiles to represent different groups who might potentially be consulted by students who are considering applying to a graduate programme in information studies.

- **French**: the participants in this group were Francophone Canadian undergraduate students at the University of Ottawa who were completing their bachelor's degrees in a range of disciplines. These students, or their peers, might conceivably be thinking about pursuing graduate studies in a programme such as the Master of Information Studies.
- **Italian**: the participants in this group were university professors and doctoral students from different units at the Università di Verona in Italy. As people who have direct experience with graduate studies, members of this mentoring group might be consulted by local undergraduate students who are looking for advice or guidance about undertaking a master's degree abroad.
- **Spanish**: the participants in this group were employees of the library at the Universidad Simón Bolívar in Colombia. As people who are already working in the field of library and information science, members of this group might be consulted by students who are looking to break into this profession by pursing a graduate programme in information studies abroad.

In each case, the goal of the recipient evaluation was to try to determine whether one of the two target texts provided a better overall user experience than the other, and if so, what contributed to this experience. These recipient evaluations were identical to the one carried out in Phase I except that they were carried out using the machine-translated versions of the texts. Participants were presented with the following instructions (in their language), along with the two translated texts, which were presented in a random order.

Instructions: Please read the following TWO versions of the text. If you were looking for information for yourself or for someone you know about pursuing a master's degree in information studies at the University of Ottawa, which of these two texts would you prefer to read on a website? Please briefly explain the reasons for your choice. [NOTE: Both texts were produced by a machine translation system, and it is possible that both texts may therefore contain some erroneous or unusual constructions.]

3.4.1 Phase III: findings and discussion

The results obtained for each of the three target-language recipient evaluations are summarized in Table 1.4. We can see that in each case, more than three-quarters of the respondents preferred the translation of the text that had been written using translatability-oriented guidelines. These numbers represent an increase from the study reported in Bowker (2015), where 62% of the target-language of respondents preferred the translation of the text that had been written using translatability-oriented guidelines. However, in both studies, it is clear that the majority of respondents showed a preference for the translatability-oriented version.

Respondents had an opportunity to explain the reasons for their preferences, though not all respondents chose to do so. The main reasons provided by the Francophone respondents for preferring the translatability-oriented version are that it was clearer, easier to read, and was more grammatically correct. Meanwhile, the Italian-speaking participants who preferred the translatability-oriented version indicated that it contained better lexical choices, more normal sentence structure, more idiomatic expressions, better flow, more coherence, and fewer errors. Finally, among Spanish-speaking respondents, reasons given for preferring the translatability-oriented text included the following: easier to understand, less ambiguous, flowed better, better grammar, and fewer errors. Clearly, there is significant overlap in the reasons provided by all three target language groups, all of whom emphasize clarity, readability, and grammatical correctness. Moreover,

Table 1.4 Comparison of the preferences of different groups of target language respondents

	Total number of respondents	Number who prefer UX-oriented version	Number who prefer translatability-oriented version
French-speaking undergraduate students	31 (100%)	7 (22.6%)	24 (77.4%)
Italian-speaking professors and doctoral students	57 (100%)	12 (21.1%)	45 (78.9%)
Spanish-speaking university library employees	28 (100%)	5 (17.9%)	23 (82.1%)
TOTAL	116 (100%)	24 (20.7%)	92 (79.3%)

these cited reasons are also very similar to the ones provided in the initial study (Bowker 2015), where respondents mentioned the fact that the translatability-oriented version was easier to understand, contained fewer grammatical errors and better lexical choices, and that it was more concrete and detailed.

Following on from Bowker (2015), the findings from the present study provide a broader confirmation that a majority of target language users – in this case, French (77.4%), Italian (78.9%) and Spanish (82.1%) speakers – appear to have a better user experience when presented with the version that has been (machine) translated using the translation-oriented text as the source text. Additionally, the findings from the present study suggest that this seems to hold true for different profiles of users. In this case, undergraduate students (French), professors and graduate students (Italian), and university library employees (Spanish) all showed a similar tendency to prefer the (machine) translation that was based on the translatability-oriented source text.

As pointed out in Bowker (2015), these findings are not particularly surprising. However, it is useful to have confirmation of this tendency among a wider variety of user types and languages.

3.5 Phase IV: comparing users' experience of post-edited target language texts

In her concluding remarks, Bowker (2015: 26) suggested that a logical next step would be to explore post-editing and its potential effect on UX. Post-editing is a field that has begun to attract significant attention in the translation and localization communities (e.g. O'Brien et al. 2014; Koponen and Salmi 2015; Koponen 2016). We therefore decided to add an additional exploratory phase to the present study in order to conduct a preliminary investigation into the relation between post-editing and UX; however, owing to limited resources, this step was taken only for the French-language texts.

Post-editing is the act of revising raw machine translation output, which can be more or less heavily edited based on user requirements. Allen (2003) distinguishes between two levels of intervention: Maximal Post-Editing (MPE) and Rapid Post-Editing (RPE). MPE addresses both content and style with the goal of editing the machine translation output to a level that closely resembles a professional human translation, whereas RPE addresses only the accuracy of the content, but not readability or stylistic issues. As pointed out by Spates (2014), it is possible to present users with differing levels of translation quality on a website, but both Spates (2014) and Lefeuvre (2012) suggest that lower linguistic quality may alienate website users. Similarly, both Castilho et al. (2014) and Doherty and O'Brien (2014) observe that post-editing raw machine translation will improve user satisfaction. Therefore, we opted to proceed with MPE for this investigation. The Translation Automation User Society (TAUS) has developed guidelines for applying MPE to machine translation output (TAUS 2014), and these were provided to the translators.

The two French translators who participated in the initial machine translation evaluation exercise (see section 3.3) were also hired to perform the post-editing task. Both translators had a similar educational background and level of professional experience, including some post-editing experience. One translator was given the UX-oriented source text and the corresponding machine-translated version, while the second translator was given the translatability-oriented source text and its corresponding machine translation. Using the TAUS guidelines, each translator was instructed to post-edit the machine-translated text to a level that would resemble the quality of a human translation. The translators were also asked to keep a record of the time required to post-edit their text.

The next step was to repeat the recipient evaluation that was conducted in phase III of this investigation (see section 3.4), but to substitute the post-edited versions for the raw machine translations. Although the invitation to participate in this recipient evaluation of post-edited texts was distributed through the same channels as the invitation to participate in the evaluation of the raw machine translation output, we have no way of knowing whether any of the same respondents participated because participation in both evaluations was voluntary and anonymous.

3.5.1 Phase IV: findings and discussion

The translator who post-edited the translation of the UX-oriented source text indicated that this task took approximately 12 minutes. Meanwhile, the translator who post-edited the machine translation of the translatability-oriented source text noted that approximately 9 minutes were required to complete the task. In other words, it took 25% longer to post-edit the UX-oriented version of the translation than it did to post-edit the translatability-oriented version. As the volume of text to be post-edited increases – whether because a website contains more text, has frequent updates, or is being translated into a greater number of languages – the difference in the time required for post-editing becomes increasingly important because it will add to the cost of the project. As noted above, cost can be a crucial factor in deciding whether or how to localize a website.

Meanwhile, with regard to the recipient evaluation of the post-edited texts, 37 responses were received from French-speaking undergraduate students. These respondents expressed their preference as follows: 22 respondents (59.5%) preferred the post-edited version of the UX-oriented source text, while the remaining 15 (40.5%) selected the post-edited version of the translatability-oriented text.

Reasons given by those who preferred the post-edited version based on the UX-oriented source text included the following: more inviting, friendlier, less clunky, and less stiff. Meanwhile for those who preferred the post-edited version based on the translatability-oriented source text, the cited reasons included clear and straightforward.

As shown in Table 1.5, the results of phase III (raw machine translation) and phase IV (post-edited machine translation) illustrate opposing tendencies.

Table 1.5 Comparison of user preferences for raw machine translation and post-edited machine translation

	Total number of respondents	Number who prefer UX-oriented version	Number who prefer translatability-oriented version
Raw machine translation (French)	31 (100%)	7 (22.6%)	24 (77.4%)
Post-edited machine translation (French)	37 (100%)	22 (59.5%)	15 (40.5%)

In other words, when the machine translation output has been post-edited to resemble a human-quality translation, the majority of respondents prefer the version that is based on the UX-oriented text. This is in contrast to the situation where the machine translation was unedited; when faced with raw machine translation, the majority of respondents tended to prefer the version that was based on the translatability-oriented text.

An observation worth mentioning is that the results of the recipient evaluation that used raw machine translation output are more lopsided than the results of the evaluation that used post-edited texts. For the raw machine translation, the results showed a split that was approaching 80/20, whereas in the case of the post-edited machine translation, the split was much closer to 60/40. Perhaps the results were less balanced in the case of the raw machine translation because one text was clearly more correct than the other. In contrast, in the case of the post-edited machine translation, both texts were edited so that they were correct, so the choice was more likely to be based on which text the reader found to be more subjectively pleasing.

Another interesting observation, as summarized in Table 1.6, is that when the machine translation output has been post-edited, the user preferences strongly resemble the preferences put forward by the source language users who participated in phase I (see section 3.2.1). In other words, the majority of users prefer the UX-oriented version. This suggests that regardless of language, the majority of readers lean towards a preference for a UX-oriented text. However, as noted above, post-editing a UX-oriented text is likely to take longer and therefore to be more expensive. In the case of the French-language respondents who participated in the post-edited recipient evaluation, the number who preferred the UX-oriented version was not quite 60%. Given that it was not a large majority who preferred this version, it could be interesting to explore the feasibility of conducting rapid post-editing (RPE), rather than maximal post-editing (MPE). Other studies (e.g. Bowker and Buitrago Ciro 2015) have demonstrated that RPE is more cost-effective than MPE, and this could be a factor that comes into play in a cost-benefit analysis for an organization wishing to localize a website.

Table 1.6 Comparison of user preferences for source text and post-edited machine translation

	Total number of respondents	Number who prefer UX-oriented version	Number who prefer translatability-oriented version
Source text (English)	47 (100%)	30 (63.8%)	17 (36.2%)
Post-edited machine translation (French)	37 (100%)	22 (59.5%)	15 (40.5%)

4 Concluding remarks

In summary, we can see that the results of this multilingual study appear to confirm the tentative conclusion reached by Bowker (2015) with regard to the relationship between UX and translatability:

1 as translatability increases, the UX of source-language readers begins to decrease, but
2 as translatability increases, the UX of target-language readers begins to increase.

The English-speaking users in this follow-up study showed a marked preference (63.8%) for the text that was developed using UX-oriented guidelines. However, when faced with raw machine translation output, more than three quarters of the French-, Italian-, and Spanish-speaking respondents preferred the version that was based on the translatability-oriented source text (see Table 1.7). Moreover, this was true not only for the three different languages, but also for three different user profiles: undergraduate students, professors and graduate students, and university library employees.

However, when the experiment was repeated using maximally post-edited rather than raw machine translation, the French-speaking target-language respondents showed a similar preference pattern to the English-speaking source-language participants: approximately 60% of the respondents in each of these two groups preferred the text that was based on the UX-oriented guidelines. Of course, this investigation into the effect that post-editing might have on the user experience was merely exploratory. A more comprehensive investigation would need to be carried out in order for these tendencies to be confirmed.

Nevertheless, since the UX-oriented texts were preferred by only a modest majority, it could be worth investigating whether the more economical approach of rapid post-editing, rather than the costlier maximal post-editing, could meet users' needs. This approach may be of particular interest to companies wishing to undertake a large volume of website localization website (e.g. a site with a lot

Table 1.7 General comparison of the preferences of the source- and target-language respondents, which demonstrate opposing tendencies

	Source-language respondents (English)	Target-language respondents (French, Italian and Spanish combined)
Preference for UX-oriented version	63.8%	20.7%
Preference for translatability-oriented version	36.2%	79.3%
TOTAL	100%	100%

of content, frequent updates, or multiple language versions) because it will be increasingly important to keep localization costs at a manageable level. Although more work is needed to confirm whether such an approach would be viable, this exploratory study does suggest that it merits further investigation as part of a future study on the human factors of machine translation.

Acknowledgments

Part of this research was supported by a CooperInt grant for Lynne Bowker's visiting professorship at the Università di Verona, Italy. We are grateful to all the survey respondents, as well as to the translators, for their participation.

References

Allen, Jeffrey (2003) "Post-editing", in Harold Somers (ed.) *Computers and Translation: A Translator's Guide*, Amsterdam and Philadelphia: John Benjamins Publishing Company, 297–317.

Bowker, Lynne (2015) "Translatability and user experience: Compatible or in conflict?" *Localisation Focus* 14(2): 13–27.

Bowker, Lynne and Jairo Buitago Ciro (2015) "Investigating the usefulness of machine translation for newcomers at the public library", *Translation and Interpreting Studies* 10(2): 165–186.

Brouwer, Brenda (2017) "Why Canada has become a destination of choice for international graduate students", *University Affairs* 58(6), available from www.universityaffairs.ca/opinion/in-my-opinion/canada-become-destination-choice-international-graduate-students/.

Brown, M. Katherine (2003) "Trends in writing for translation", *MultiLingual Computing and Technology: Supplement on Writing for Translation* 59 (October/November): 4–8.

Castilho, Sheila, Sharon O'Brien, Fabio Alves, and Morgan O'Brien (2014) "Does post-editing increase usability? A study with Brazilian Portuguese as target language", in *Proceedings of the 2014 Conference of the European Association for Machine Translation (EAMT)*, 17–19 June 2014, Dubrovnic, Croatia, available from http://doras.dcu.ie/19997/.

Clark, Ken (2009) "Elements of style for machine translation", *MultiLingual – Getting Started Guide: Writing for Translation* (October/November): 8.

"Destination 2020: The University of Ottawa's strategic plan", available from www.uottawa.ca/about/sites/www.uottawa.ca.about/files/destination-2020-strategic-plan.pdf.

Doherty, Stephen and Sharon O'Brien (2014) "Assessing the usability of raw machine translated output: A user-centered study using eye tracking", *International Journal of Human-Computer Interaction* 30: 40–51.

Dray, Susan M. and David A. Siegel (2006) "Melding paradigms: Meeting the needs of international customers through localization and user-centered design", in Keiran J. Dunne (ed.) *Perspectives on Localization*, Amsterdam and Philadelphia: John Benjamins Publishing Company, 281–306.

Ferreira, Alberto (2017) *Universal UX Design: Building Multicultural User Experience*, Amsterdam: Elsevier.

Garcia, Ignacio (2010) "Is machine translation ready yet?" *Target* 22(1): 7–21.

Garrett, Jesse James (2011) *The Elements of User Experience: User-Centered Design for the Web and Beyond* (2nd ed.), Berkeley, CA: New Riders.

Hartmann, Jan, Antonella Di Angeli, and Alistair Sutcliffe (2008) "Framing the user experience: Information biases on website quality judgement", in *CHI'08: Proceedings of the SIGCHI Conference on Human Factors in Computing Systems*, New York: ACM, 855–864.

Hassenzahl, Marc (2013) "User experience and experience design", in Mads Soegaard and Rikke Friis Dam (eds.) *The Encyclopedia of Human-Computer Interaction* (2nd ed.), Interactive Design Foundation, available from www.interaction-design.org/literature/book/the-encyclopedia-of-human-computer-interaction-2nd-ed/user-experience-and-experience-design.

Hassenzahl, Marc and Noam Tractinksky (2006) "User experience: A research agenda", *Behaviour and Information Technology* 25(2): 91–97.

Hillier, Mathew (2003) "The role of cultural context in multilingual website usability", *Electronic Commerce Research and Applications* 2: 2–14.

ISO DIS 9241–210:2010 (2010) *Ergonomics of Human System Interaction – Part 210: Human-Centred Design for Interactive Systems (Formerly Known as 13407)*, Geneva: International Organization for Standardization (ISO).

Jiménez-Crespo, Miguel A. (2010) "Localization and writing for a new medium: A review of digital style guides", *Tradumàtica* 8, available from www.fti.uab.es/tradumatica/revista/num8/articles/08/08.pdf.

Jiménez-Crespo, Miguel A. (2013) *Translation and Web Localization*, London and New York: Routledge.

Koponen, Marit (2016) "Is machine translation post-editing worth the effort? A survey of research into post-editing and effort", *The Journal of Specialised Translation (JoSTrans)* 25: 131–148, available from www.jostrans.org/issue25/art_koponen.php.

Koponen, Marit and Leena Salmi (2015) "On the correctness of machine translation: A machine translation post-editing task", *The Journal of Specialised Translation (JoSTrans)* 23: 118–136, available from www.jostrans.org/issue23/art_koponen.php.

Law, Effie L-C., Virpi Roto, Marc Hassenzahl, Arnold P.O.S. Vermeeren, and Joke Kort (2009) "Understanding, scoping and defining user experience: A survey approach", in *Proceedings of the SIGCHI Conference on Human Factors in Computing Systems*, New York: ACM, 719–728.

Lefeuvre, Antoine (2012) "Translation is UX", *A List Apart*, available from https://alistapart.com/article/translation-is-ux.

Lindgaard, Gitte, Cathy Dudek, Devjani Sen, Livia Sumengi, and Patrick Noonan (2011) "An exploration of relations between visual appeal, trustworthiness and perceived usability of homepages", *ACM Transactions on Computer-Human Interaction* 18(1): 1–30, available from doi:10.1145/1959022.1959023.

Nantel, Jacques and Evelyne Glaser (2008) "The impact of language and culture on perceived website usability", *Journal of Engineering and Technology Management* 25: 112–122.

O'Brien, Sharon Laura Winther Balling, Michael Carl, Michel Simard, and Lucia Specia (eds.) (2014) *Post-Editing of Machine Translation: Processes and Applications*, Newcastle-upon-Tyne: Cambridge Scholars Publishing.

Ó Broin, Ultan (2009) "Controlled authoring to improve localization", *MultiLingual – Getting Started Guide: Writing for Translation* (October/November): 12–14.

Rodríguez Vásquez, Silvia (2013) "Making localised web content accessible: A collaborative task between the developer and the localiser", in P. Sánchez-Gijón, O. Torres-Hostench, and B. Mesa-Lao (eds.) *Conducting Research in Translation Technologies*, Bern: Peter Lang, 93–115.

Sichel, Barb (2009) "Planning and writing for translation", *MultiLingual – Getting Started Guide: Writing for Translation* (October/November): 3–4.

Spates, Carrie (2014) "Website translation: Deciding how and what to translate", *User Experience Magazine* 14(4), available from http://uxpamagazine.org/website-translation/.

Thicke, Lori (2013) "Revolutionizing customer support through MT", *MultiLingual* (March): 49–52.

Translation Automation User Society (TAUS) "Post-editing guidelines", 2014, available from https://evaluation.taus.net/resources/guidelines/post-editing/machine-translation-post-editing-guidelines.

van Iwaarden, Jos, Ton van der Wiele, Leslie Ball, and Robert Millen (2004) "Perceptions about the quality of web sites: A Survey amongst students at Northeastern University and Erasmus University", *Information and Management* 41: 947–959.

White, John S. (2003) "How to evaluate machine translation", in Harold Somers (ed.) *Computers and Translation: A Translator's Guide*, Amsterdam and Philadelphia: John Benjamins Publishing Company, 211–244.

Style Guides

Baldwin, Scott (2010) "Plain language tenets in UX", *UX Magazine*, Article 572 (October 27, 2010), available from http://uxmag.com/articles/plain-language-tenets-in-ux.

Kiefer Lee, Kate (2012) "Tone and voice: Showing your users that you care", *UX Magazine*, Article 868 (September 17, 2012), available from http://uxmag.com/articles/tone-and-voice-showing-your-users-that-you-care.

Kohl, John (2008) *The Global English Style Guide: Writing Clear, Translatable Documentation for a Global Market*, Cary, NC: SAS Institute Inc.

"MailChimp Style Guide", available from http://mailchimp.com/about/style-guide/.

"Microsoft manual of style" (2012) (4th ed.), available from http://ptgmedia.pearson cmg.com/images/9780735648715/samplepages/9780735648715.pdf.

U.S. Department of Health and Human Services (USDHHS) (2006) *The Research-Based Web Design and Usability Guidelines, Enlarged/Expanded Edition*, Washington, DC: U.S. Government Printing Office, available from www.usability.gov/sites/default/files/documents/guidelines_book.pdf.

2 Norms and controlled language for machine translation

Sylviane Cardey

1 Introduction

Is there a relationship between machine translation and sense mining? Looking closely, we see that both share the same model but that their respective processes are reversed. When translating, we start with a surface structure to which a meaning is attached. This meaning can be paraphrased in different surface representations not only in the source language but also in the target language(s). On the contrary, in sense mining, we start with a meaning and look in texts, which may be in different languages, for its surface representations. It is therefore interesting to see how such a relationship can be applied, on which domains, from one domain to another, but also from one language to another, however different the languages may be. We know with certainty that machine translation is not simple, and this explains the problems with current systems. To deal with these difficulties, we use a norms-oriented approach. We have conducted a comparative study on norms between several languages such as Arabic, Chinese, English, French, Japanese, Russian and Thai which has led to the generation of and use of controlled language for applications in machine translation for safety critical domains in avoiding the pitfalls of translation and without post-edition. We see how and why we use systemic linguistic analysis theory which has its roots in systemic and indeed micro-systemic analysis and in discrete mathematics in view not only to (1) analyse languages but also to (2) generate languages. The two resulting methodologies give rise to three applications, (1) controlled languages, (2) machine translations and (3) sense mining, all three for use in safety and security mission-critical domains which means that any work undertaken must ensure reliable results.

2 The theoretical point of view

2.1 *Parts of speech*

Nearly all the theories currently used for written text analysis and generation rely, for their first segmentation and tagging, on the traditional parts of speech which for certain Western languages have their roots in Greco-Latin antiquity.

The Arabic grammarians too based their description of Arabic on a word classification in parts of speech (generally three: *nouns, verbs, particles*). It is the Latin grammarian Aelius Donatus (fourth century CE) to whom we owe the parts of speech: *noun, pronoun, verb, participle, conjunction, adverb, preposition, interjection*. This classification has been much discussed but the interesting question to be posed is 'what condition ought this classification satisfy for it to be valid?'

It is this question which interests us all the more so seeing that our applications ought to allow going from one language to another, and it is just here the source of problems.

It is true that it is possible to describe French, Latin and even Greek with these cited categories in making certain adjustments. Even for one and the same language the criteria used for the classification are not homogeneous; sometimes morphology is used, and at another time we use syntactic function, and even the location occupied on the syntagmatic axis (for example for French prepositions that one says ought to precede). The syntactic criteria *verb* and *noun* do not provide a better aid, seeing that in some languages an *adjective* can be the subject of a *verb*. There have also been proposals for a classification in *morphemes*. We find also the opposition *theme/rheme* reused by Japanese linguists, the former serving for designating objects, and the latter for affirming something concerning these objects. We find this opposition in the somewhat similar distinction *argument/predicate*. However, here we cannot talk anymore of the original classification of words nor of parts of speech because the function of *rheme* can be accomplished in many other ways than the use of a *verb* in the grammatical sense. We will not present here all the problems nor all the possibilities that have been proposed, but what this does shows us is that an analysis of some language based on parts of speech is only rarely transposable to other 'barbarous' (as was said in ancient times) languages.

2.2 Syntactic analysis

We shall talk here only about the two methods currently used.

For current analysers, from this parts of speech analysis, can be derived variously:

i   an immediate constituents analysis (Chomsky 1957) which attempts to render the functions linking the words together visible;

ii   an analysis based on valence theory (Tesnière 1959), the valence of a verb being the number of its complements needed to construct a single complete utterance where these complements are attached either directly to the verb or to the whole sentence. One can thus classify the verbs of a language according to their valence.

These two theories seem to be different at first sight, but what is interesting is the easy passage from one to the other as is illustrated in Figure 2.1.

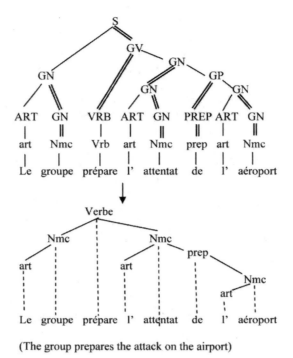

Figure 2.1 Chomsky Type Schema with double arcs which if suppressed lead us to Tesnière

In a general manner, there are two ways to make an utterance's cohesion appear, the latter of which is supposed to represent the unity of some thought or of the communicative act. One way consists in describing the sentence as a nest of constituents (in generative terms, one engenders the sentence starting from a unique symbol by means of rules which are independent of the words and morphemes of which the sentence is made). The other way consists in showing a sort of attraction that the lexical elements exercise between themselves (the idea underlying Tesnière's stemma). Neither way involve semantics, or if so, very little.

2.3 Semantic analysis

Semantics, which is involved with sense in general, is found at different levels. For example, Tesnière said that one finds semantics at the level of the links. In fact, semantics has been really studied only very recently. These studies above all have been lexical (homonymy, polysemy). However, syntax, flexions and word order are elements which also participate in respect of sense, just as do phenomena such as anaphora, dislocation and many others.

2.4 Systemic linguistic analysis theory

2.4.1 From the linguistic point of view

Systemic linguistic analysis and its theory (both of these having been created and developed at Centre Tesnière (Cardey and Greenfield 2006, Cardey 2015)), and which, contrary to what has been said, has no ambition to describe a language in its whole with a global representation of its different 'layers': lexis, syntax, morphology and semantics, and these separately. Rather, systemic linguistic analysis recommends firstly the identification of the problem or the analysis needs for some particular application. Depending on the needs, a dedicated system capable of representing and resolving the problem is constructed. This system can be manipulated and represented contrarily to the language in its globality which is impossible to either delimit or manipulate. Thus, only those elements which are necessary be these lexical, morphological or syntactical in nature will be represented in a single unique system, this system being able to enter in interrelation with others. Here, semantics is not even mentioned because whatever the operations are, they are for providing access to the sense. Thus, we do not need a complete description of the language or languages concerning their lexis, their morphology, as is habitually practised, and this allows us to resolve problems by means of analyses which are much lighter in weight in terms of quantity and duration.

Several Arabic utterances from the simplest to the most complex and providing important semantic elements for example can be simply represented by the structure shown in Figure 2.2. We do not need a transformational analysis to enable us, amongst other things, to pass from an affirmation to a negation. One can observe that syntax, morphology and certain categories that have been defined according to the needs are presented all together in this structure. This structure can be linked to micro-systems that have been defined for the type of problem to be processed.

2.4.2 From the calculability and computational point of view

As we have already said, systemic linguistic analysis is based on discrete mathematics and in particular on constructive logic and model theory, set theory, relations and partitions. This basis also serves as the language of communication between the linguist and the software engineer as, independent of applications, it is understood by both. In respect of the calculations to be performed for some

$$\text{opt}(\text{particule}(s)) + (...) + \text{verbe} + \text{opt}(\text{particule}(s)) + (...) + \text{sujet}$$
$$+ \text{opt}(\text{particule}(s)) + (...) + \text{cod} + \text{opt}(\text{particule}(s)) + (...)$$

Figure 2.2 Structure covering several Arabic utterances from the simplest to the most complex

application, a representation such as that presented in Figure 2.2 can be interpreted by a computer program that has been specified and implemented according to the linguistic model. Thus the linguist does not have to be concerned with the computer programming; instead it is the software engineer who, according to the linguistic model, constructs the computational model and the subsequent program. The advantage here is that instead of having some predefined computational model, which unfortunately in practice is in reality nearly always the case, and with which the linguist(s) must either 'bend' linguistics or 'bend' the language(s), each linguist performs *linguistic programming* by entering his or her data in, for example, a spreadsheet table (see Figure 2.3), this latter being then read by the computer program produced by the software engineer, the only constraint being that of consistency. Another advantage is that one can add as many languages as one wishes, and also as many linguists as is necessary.

2.4.2.1 REPRESENTATION FOR MACHINE TRANSLATION

A spreadsheet file serves as the link between the linguist who is a specialist in the source and target languages, and the software engineer. This file is designed so as to enable simple and rapid formalisations; additions and modifications are carried out on the different tables making up the file.

Take for example the French (source) sentence from the aeronautical domain *maintenir le train d'atterrissage en position DOWN* (keep the landing gear on DOWN position) so as to show the data input process for its translation to English (target). As already mentioned, the spreadsheet file includes several tables which correspond to the formalisation model, this having been established during the 'LiSe' project.[1] The linguist enters the source language *verb* together with its target language translation in the verbal group table *anC_groupesVerbaux_frC* (*an*glais – English). Identifiers with a numerical component are associated with each verb according to its macro-structure. The French verb *maintenir* will be ascribed by the linguist *fr*C_7 which refers to a particular structure in French. For this identifier, the linguist will make another identifier correspond which represents the target structure, which for this example is *an*C_1.7. A second table *anC_groupes* retakes the two micro-structures (source and target) with the identifiers already attributed. Once this second table has been completed, the other tables which depend on it will be filled by the linguist according to the content of the two macro-structures. The structure of our verb *maintenir* imposes going to the table *anC_args_frC*, which lists all the possible micro-structures with all the transfer rules which are associated with them. In our example, the particular micro-structures are respectively one which represents *le train d'atterrissage* as arg1 and *position DOWN* as arg2 which will be entered in this table. It is important to underline that another table – *anC_comps_frC* – could intervene if our structure includes complements. Two other tables exist which make an inventory, for example, of all the parts of speech according to the source language and the target language, and which data is necessary respectively for segmentation and generation. The final table is *anC_dictionnaireLexical_frC* which contains the dictionary; this table is invoked during the construction of the target sentence.

ACRONYMS_Legal_Sequences_Graphemes					
Start_References					
Ø	COMPETENCE				Nov - Dec 2007
M	www.merriam-webster.com				Nov - Dec 2007
. . .	. . .				. . .
X	HAPAX				Jan - Feb 2008
End_References					
Maximum_Length				6	
Start_Attestations					
2 Letters	plus Ø	plus A	plus B	. . .	plus Z
AA	Ø	Ø	Ø	. . .	Ø
AB	STAB	ABATE-D	ABBEY	. . .	Ø
. . .	. . .	. . .	. . .	. . .	. . .
AI	CHAIN	NAIAD-M-X	Ø	. . .	BAIZE-M-X
. . .	. . .	. . .	. . .	. . .	. . .
ZZ	NOZZLE	PIZZA	Ø	. . .	Ø
End_Attestations					

Legend

Attestation cell content	Meaning
Ø	Indicates no attestation
WORD	Indicates by its presence an attestation. Must be capital letters. Must be < or = Legal_Sequences_Graphemes_ Maximum_Length
WORD with no suffix	Attested by competence
WORD with a suffix ' – ' followed by a letter other than X	The letter is a reference. Must appear in the Reference cells
WORD with a suffix ' – X'	The word is a hapax attested by competence
WORD with a suffix ' – ' followed by a letter other than X followed by ' – X'	The letter is a reference and the word is a hapax

Figure 2.3 Example of our linguistic programming using a spreadsheet table

2.4.2.2 REPRESENTATION FOR SENSE MINING

In Figure 2.3 we show as an example an extract from a spreadsheet table which has been programmed by the linguist; this table is part of a system for the automatic recognition of acronyms which has been implemented during a project with Airbus France in the context of safety/security critical technical documentation (Cardey et al. 2009).

To avoid confusing acronyms and conventional lexis, it seemed judicious that the controlled acronyms do not contain certain sequences of graphemes present in the host language, namely American English. Our technique, as mentioned at the beginning of this chapter, is based on systemic linguistic analysis which furthermore is based on a formal (mathematical) model (Cardey and Greenfield 2005; Cardey 2013). We observe here that in terms of legal sequences of graphemes in English, we have partitioned the English lexis over sequences of 2 and of 3 letters contained in each lexical unit; thus each non-empty cell (not containing 'Ø') which contains a couple (sequence of letters, attestation) gives rise to a distinct equivalence class of English lexical units which share this same sequence, the couple being in effect the name of the equivalence class. In particular, the hapax attestations correspond to equivalence classes with unit cardinality. As traceability is mandatory due to the safety/security critical nature of the domain, the attestations act not only as a static trace of justification, but also as decisive elements during the algorithmic interpretation of the table by the automatic recognition program in producing a dynamic trace.

The significant difference and supplementary quality thus obtained is that, independently of the application, all the operations done are traceable (see Figure 2.4, here for machine translation) which is never the case for statistically based systems. This advantage enables us to correct errors very rapidly during testing. A tracing system is often mandatory in safety/security critical domains and this is certainly the case in the aeronautical domain.

3 Methodologies

We now explain the two methodologies: analysis and generation.

3.1 Analysis

We describe analysis from the standpoint of sense extraction whether for machine translation or for sense mining, the methodology being the same for both. The descriptive model uses the same rule format. The general methodology can be effectively used for diverse applications.

In Figure 2.5 we show 2 rules, the first being for machine translation and the second for sense mining. The formal representation is the same.

3.2 Generation

Here generation concerns the utterances output by the machine translation system and the utterances produced by the controlled language, both of these being intimately linked because the translation results depend not only on the quality of the translation model but also on the quality of the control applied to each of the

```
    RegroupageEnSyntagms_LS =
    [["",neg1],["",neg2],[maintenir,vinf],['le       train
d'atterrissage',arg1],[en,prep_v],['position
DOWN',arg2],[comp(",")comp1],[comp(",")comp2],['.',pt]]
    LS = frC, LC = anC
    LC_GroupeVerbal_LS =
    [maintenir,frC_7,",arg,",en,pos,",",",",",",keep,'anC_1
.7',",on,prep_v,",",",",",",]
    Regroupage_En_Arguments_LS =
    [neg1          -          [],neg2          -          [],vinf  -
[[maintenir,frC_7,keep,'anC_1.7']],arg1       -
([[le,adms,the,ad,",",",",],['train
d'atterrissage',nms,'landing         gear',ns,",",",]]  -
[[art,n],[art,n],",",",]]),prep_v                         -
[[en,prep_v,on,prep_v]],arg2                              -
([[position,nfs,position,ns,",",",],['DOWN',adjs,'DOWN',
adj,",",",]] - [[n,adj],[adj,n],",",",]]),comp1 - ([]   -
[]),comp2 - ([] - []),pt - [['.',pt,'.',pt,",",",]]]
    Unites_Source = frC
    [maintenir - frC_7,le - adms,'train d'atterrissage'     -
nms,en - prep_v,position - nfs,'DOWN' - adjs,'.' - pt]
    Regroupage_En_Arguments_LC =
    [neg1          -          [],neg2          -          [],vinf  -
[[maintenir,frC_7,keep,'anC_1.7']],arg1                   -
([[le,adms,the,art],['train d'atterrissage',nms,'landing
gear',n]]      -       [[art,n],[art,n],",",",]]),prep_v -
[[en,prep_v,on,prep_v]],arg2                              -
([['DOWN',adjs,'DOWN',adj],[position,nfs,position,n]]     -
[[n,adj],[adj,n],",",",]]),comp1   -    ([]  -  _9884308),comp2 -
([] - _9926514),pt - [['.',pt,'.',pt,",",",]]]
    Unites_Cible = anC
    [keep - 'anC_1.7',the - art,'landing gear' - n,on       -
prep_v,'DOWN' - adj,position - n,'.' - pt]
    Traduction = 'keep the landing gear on DOWN position.'
```

Figure 2.4 Trace for the machine translation of *maintenir le train d'atterrissage en position DOWN* (Keep the landing gear on DOWN position) to English

two languages, source and target. This particular aspect is discussed later in the chapter. Concerning the control itself, the goal is to improve not only the quality of the messages, but also and above all their understandability by suppressing, amongst others, any ambiguities.

Machine translation:
```
opt(neg1) + lexis('يجب') + opt(neg2) + nver + arg1(acc) +
opt(opt(prep_comp1),comp1(n))+ opt(opt(prep_comp2),comp2(n)) + pt
```
Sense mining:
```
l(d) + '['(_) + 从 + l(chiffres) + 到 / 至 + l(chiffres) +
l(temps) + ']'(_) + l(f)
```

Figure 2.5 Example of rules for machine translation and sense mining

3.2.1 Lack of precision and controlled language

The following example is extracted from the *Guide des premiers secours à la maison de la Croix-Rouge* (Red Cross First Aid Guide for Use at Home).

Starting text:

> *Disposez le lien en double sous le membre blessé alors que vous maintenez le point de compression.*

Due to the various uses of certain terms, the lack of precision and the non respect of chronology, this extract is difficult to understand, even in training situations, but particularly so when what it says has to be executed in real situations. Tests carried out on this same text have enabled verifying the improvements due to the CL (controlled language) for which we have established the lexis and the syntax. In the experiment that we have conducted, the participants have stated that they had to reread the above extract several times in order to understand it and also to establish the chronology to be respected. These problems were absent with the text reformulated in the 'LiSe' controlled language:

Reformulated text:

> Pendant la pose du garrot:
>   Maintenir le point de compression.
> Pour poser le garrot:
>   Plier le lien en 2.
>   *But : obtenir une boucle.*
> Passer le lien sous le membre inférieur de la victime.

3.2.2. Interferences

One of the rules of our controlled language is the attribution of a unique sense to each lexical entry. However, certain polysemic terms can occur in the everyday lexicon as well as in one or even several specialty domains; we call such a phenomenon 'domain interference'. A strict application of our aforementioned rule results in reducing the scope of the 'LiSe' controlled language to a particular domain. So as to ensure our controlled language's application to diverse domains, specific senses can be attributed to the same lexical entry according to the application domain or the intended audience (general public, professional etc.). Thus the term *plateau* will be generally used with its most common meaning *support plat* (serving to put or transport objects) which is translated in English by tray, in Arabic by طبق and in Chinese by 盘子. In a medical protocol addressed at specialists, this same term *plateau* could designate the support upon which one places the instruments required for carrying out an operation, tray in English, صينية in Arabic and 托盘 in Chinese. However, when *plateau* is qualified as *technique* (e.g. *plateau technique de radiologie*), the set of equipment needed to perform an examination is translated by technical wherewithal in English, معدات تقنية in Arabic and 器械盘 in Chinese. If we pass to the aeronautical domain, here the term *plateau* will designate a relatively flat area of country which dominates its surroundings, plateau in English, هضبة in Arabic and 高原 in Chinese.

3.3 *Our methodology/other methodologies*

We will only briefly recall here the often discouraging results from online machine translation systems which, if we require the very reliable results needed for safety/security critical domains, render them inadequate. Concerning sense mining, current methodologies, whatever they may be, all use statistics which results in only using keywords, and this is insufficient if we require reliable results. As for controlled languages, up to the present only the source language has been controlled; we have also controlled the target languages in order to obtain better results.

3.3.1 *Our methodology for machine translation*

Our methodology requires no pre-edition in the conventional sense of the term.

As we use a controlled language which firstly serves to provide a good interpretation of the information to be transmitted by suppressing any ambiguities and everything which is detrimental to the intelligibility of the information, the writing guide that we have developed and which is incorporated into the user interface, is an aid to the user when entering the sentence to be translated (see Figure 2.6). However, we quickly discovered that even in controlling the source language, the results were still far from what we had hoped. We therefore decided to control also the target languages; this signifies that a very fine comparative analysis of the target languages and French, the source language, was undertaken. We were thus able to extract mega and micro structures which were similar not only for French and the target languages, but also between the target languages. We have constructed our translation system from these resemblances, each divergence being subsequently treated at the specific transfer level for each language (see also section 2.4.2.1).

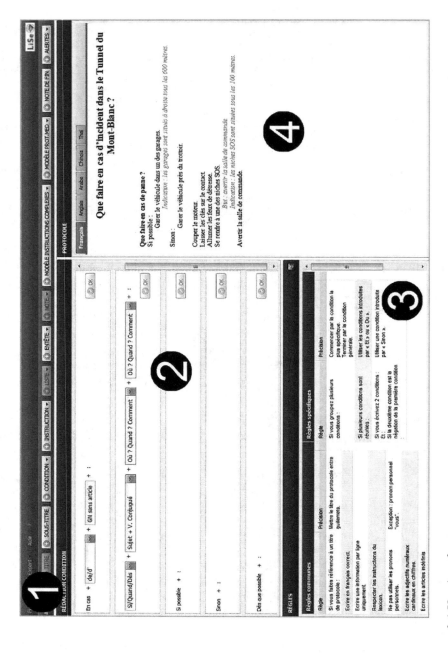

Figure 2.6 User interface

The following example shows how and why this control is necessary. We take the non-controlled sentence:

Refroidir immédiatement la brûlure, en l'arrosant avec de l'eau froide durant 5 minutes.

(example taken from Cassan and Cross [2005])

After controlling, we obtain:

Verser de l'eau froide sur la brûlure immédiatement durant 5 minutes.

The reasons for the control are as follows:

1. The sentence contains two distinct pieces of information: (1) the injunction *arroser* and (2) the explanation *refroidir*. It seems more logical to state first the action to be done and only afterwards the motives for this action. Furthermore, in order to ensure understandability as well as obtaining a good translation, the controlled language imposes a unique verb for each sentence, and also forbids the use of the gerundive, here *arrosant*.
2. The control is required also as a result of the three target languages, Arabic, Chinese and English because of the verb *arroser*. These three target languages use this verb only when it is followed by an argument which is of vegetable type.
3. So as to avoid any error in identifying a pronoun's antecedent, pronouns are forbidden in the 'LiSe' controlled language.

Controlling resolves numerous linguistic problems; nevertheless, problems are still observed when controlled sentences are translated by machine translation systems which are available on the market. In the examples that follow, elements exhibiting problems are underlined.

Chinese Reverso:

在 5 分钟期间在烧伤上立刻倒冷水 (preposition在 5 min <u>pendant brûlure</u> maintenant verser froide eau)

The problem with the Chinese is at the structural level, and there is also a lexical inexactitude concerning *pendant*.

"在 . . . 期间" can only be used for a duration much longer than 'minute', for 'année' (year) for example. For the error concerning *brûlure* (burn), in this context one would use rather *blessure* (wound) in Chinese.

Arabic Reverso:

الدفع (صب) بعض الماء البارد على أن تحترق بعد 5 دقائق (poussée (verser) quelque eau froide pourvu que tu brûles après 5 minutes) (pushed (pour) some water cold provided you burn after 5 minutes)

English Reverso:

Cool <u>at once</u> the burn, by spraying <u>him(it)</u> with some cold water for 5 minutes.

There are two problems in the English – the location of the complement *at once* which is understandable but non standard, and the problem of the pronoun. We give below the results produced by our LiSe machine translation system:

Chinese LiSe:

立刻在伤口上浇冷水5分钟，

Arabic LiSe:

يجب صبّ الماء البارد على الحرق فورا لمدّة 5 دقائق .

English LiSe:

Pour cold water on the burn immediately for 5 minutes.

3.3.2 Our methodology for sense mining

Contrary to data mining, which consists in searching for words in a sentence or indeed a text so as to identify the important points, we work at the level of sense in general, that is to say with all the various elements: morphemes (syntactic or derivational flexions [lexical], simple or compound lexes etc.) and with their organisation and distribution in the sentence, or in the lexes for the morphemes. Thus, our methodology is not that of the 'semantic web' which is based on the same principle as data mining where currently there are two major methodologies: (1) keywords and (2) statistical. That the technique used be Boolean retrieval (extended or not), vector space model, fuzzy set model, or network model, all these are based on keywords, and therefore just on a part of the lexis, and not the lexis in its totality. Thus, lists of 'non important words' are created (also called 'empty words') so as to enable recognising only the words (terms) called 'important' words or 'keywords'. The problem is, what is an 'important word'? The principal question is what is a word? Take the example: *Ce produit était parfait* (This product was perfect), where there is the understatement *il ne l'est plus* (it is not so anymore). So, if we keep only the keywords *parfait* and *produit*, we obtain a bad interpretation. The same bad interpretation occurs in Arabic if we only consider the two words 'المنتوج/produit' and 'ممتاز/parfait'. The statistical method has its limits too. It is based on counting the number of occurrences of a word (or pairs of consecutive words – digrams, . . . , n-grams) and this does not take into account the context which therefore leads inevitably to bad interpretations. Furthermore, one finds the same problem as in the keyword methodology because the words that are counted are 'important' words. If we know that there are

Norms and controlled language   43

languages such as Japanese that are agglutinative and are therefore languages which concatenate words that are 'full' or 'important' and words that are 'empty' or 'non-important', this creates a real problem for those methods based on keywords. To this it is necessary to add that these very methods require training and/or pre-edition, and this is not possible in crisis situations due to the lack of time.

Our methodology, sense mining, uses the lexicon in its totality, principally its morphology but also and most importantly syntax and of course semantics together with their intersections: morpho-syntaxictic, lexico-syntactico-semantic etc., represented by rules and structured sets functioning in interrelation. Sense mining interprets a text even if it contains no keyword, and it analyses all the text.

We give an example of the extraction of sense (semes) by means of rules. When the seme is found in the text, it is compared with the current knowledge that one has concerning this same seme.

Chinese example:

Relation_Seme_Name: 年代, année
Text Before: "
Matched Text: " 从80到90，年代"
Text After: 劳动是朝鲜研制的中程弹道导弹。该导弹是前苏联地对地导弹"飞毛腿C"(射程500公里) 的改良型，射程约1300公里。"
Informations_Compared: [从,80,到,90,年代]
Structure used:
1. l(d) + '['('_) + 从 + l(chiffres) + 到/至 + l(chiffres) + l(temps) + ']'('_) + l(f)

With the same structure, one can also find the following Chinese sentences:

从60到90年代,
从60至80年代,
从六十至八十年,
etc.

Arabic example:

The first piece of information found:

المجموعة حضّرت الاعتداء في لبنان → Le groupe a préparé l'attentat au Liban (The group prepares the attack in Lebanon)

The structure which enables finding this piece of information is as follows:

opt(Part. interrog) + opt(Part. nég) + opt(Part.prob) + Primat + opt(Part. prob) + Prédicat + opt(Pronom.connect) + opt(Cod1>>Cod2>>Cod3) + opt(Prép) + opt(Coi) + opt(opt(Prép) +Ccirt) + opt(opt(Prép) + Ccircl) + opt(opt(Prép) + Cman)

With this same structure we can find other types of information:
Information 2 found:

العصابة سرقت المخزن بالأمس → la bande a volé le magasin hier (the gang stole from the shop yesterday)

Information 3 found:

المجرم قتل الشرطي في العاصمة → le criminel a tué le policier dans la capitale (the criminal has killed the policeman in the capital)

4 Global result

4.1 Schema

Figure 2.7 shows a schema of the LiSe project.

4.2 Norms

The idea at the outset was to extract and apply norms in order to use them in our methodologies, both for analysis and generation, in the particular applications of machine translation and sense mining. A sense can effectively be expressed by means of various written or spoken sequences (synonymous structures and lexica).

A writing guide was created together with a user interface, of which the latter facilitates entering normalised text. For example, there are different ways of expressing an injunction, both in the same language and in different languages (Dziadkiewicz 2007). In French, if the imperative and the infinitive are frequently used as written injunctive moods, our study of the corpus has enabled us firstly to note that, paradoxically, the passive is often used when it is a question of indicating some action to be executed, and secondly, we found numerous other injunctive constructions, of which we give some examples: *il convient de, il est recommandé, il n'est pas nécessaire de*, etc. However, an injunction in the passive voice often induces confusion with a purely informative type of content, and the other injunctive constructions for which we have given examples cast doubt on the real need to execute an action, and often perturb the reading of the text. It is for these reasons that we authorise only the infinitive mood for expressing injunctions.

We then tried to put the norms of each of the languages that we treat in relation with each other and we kept only those which enabled us to obtain the best translations (Cardey et al. 2008). For example:
For the French:

Réduire la vitesse en dessous de 205/.55.

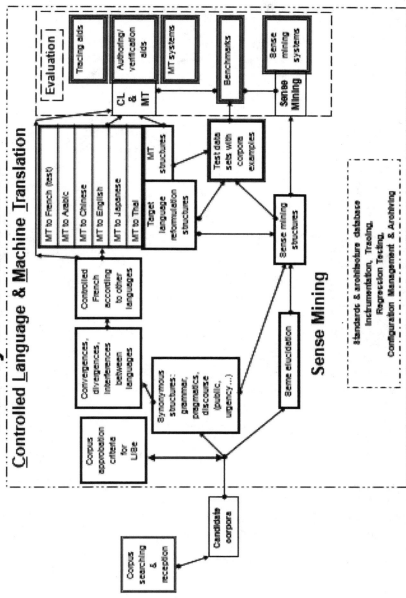

Figure 2.7 Schema of the LiSe Project

we have the structure:

*fr*C_7
opt(neg1) + opt(neg2) + vinf + arg1 + prep_v + arg2 + opt(opt(prep_comp), comp1(n)) + opt(opt(prep_comp), comp2(n)) + pt

and the corresponding sentence in Arabic:

يجب تقليص السرعة تحت 205/. 55 .

with its structure:

*ar*C_7.a
opt(neg1) + lexis('يجب') +opt(neg2) + nver + arg1(acc) + prep_v + arg2(acc) + opt(opt(prep_comp1), comp1(n)) + opt(opt(prep_comp2),comp2(n)) + pt

For the French sentence:
Signaler le cas à l'Institut de Veille Sanitaire immédiatement.

we have the same structures as before:

*fr*C_7
opt(neg1) + opt(neg2) + vinf + arg1 + prep_v + arg2 + opt(opt(prep_comp), comp1(n)) + opt(opt(prep_comp), comp2(n)) + pt

However for the translation in Arabic:

يجب إعلام مركز المراقبة الصحية بالحالة فورا .

we have a different structure:

*ar*C_7.b
opt(neg1) + lexis('يجب') +opt(neg2) + nver + arg2(acc) + prep_v + arg1(acc) + opt(opt(prep_comp1), comp1(n)) + opt(opt(prep_comp2), comp2(n)) + pt

By means of these two examples, we thus observe that the same French structure *fr*C_7 which refers to the two French verbs *réduire* and *signaler* gives two different Arabic structures *ar*C_7a and *ar*C_7b. If the structure of the first verb *réduire* is nearly identical to that of the Arabic, the same structure *fr*C_7 of the verb *signaler* requires a permutation of the two arguments arg1 and arg2 in Arabic which gives the Arabic structure *ar*C_7b which is totally different from the French one.

Concerning the application of sense mining, here the norms and the divergences are retained in the same structure because the goal is to find all the different ways to say the same thing.

4.3 Applications and application domains

We now present extracts of results from various applications in the domains of aeronautics, medicine and civil security (Cardey 2009).

The user interface has 4 parts, which are indicated in Figure 2.6:

1   enables making various choices which influence the form of the output
2   guides the user in entering his or her text
3   gives explanations as to the choice of rules provided by the user guide
4   presents the output, and thus the alert or protocol.

In part 4, if one clicks on one of the languages, one obtains the translation in the chosen language, as shown in Figure 2.8.

Figure 2.8 Translations Output

48 *Sylviane Cardey*

> **PROTOCOLE**
> Français | Anglais | Arabe | Chinois | Thaï
> Maintenir le train d'atterrissage en position DOWN.

> **PROTOCOLE**
> Français | Anglais | Arabe | Chinois | Thaï
> keep the landing gear on DOWN position.

Figure 2.8 (Continued)

4.4 Applicability: examples of supplementary applications

So as to demonstrate both the strength and the potential of our theory and the methodologies which result from it, we show here two supplementary applications.

The first supplementary application concerns an extension of sense mining to search for words, terms. Starting from a definition, either invented by the user or from a definition in a dictionary, the system searches for the terms which this definition expresses (DeVitre 2009). In Figure 2.9 the user has entered *signal that warns of danger* and the system has found *alert, n* (noun).

For the second supplementary application, we have tested adding target languages to our controlled language machine translation system in order to show its flexibility and its scalability. Take as an example Thai, which is a language which is distant from French, the source language, and which has as a characteristic the presence of classifiers (the function of a classifier is for example to qualify a noun (human, pointed object, a fruit etc.). Normally these classifiers are obligatory but they can be avoided in certain contexts. Thus, the Thai structures corresponding to the sentence *Ne pas brancher plusieurs prises* (Do not connect many plugs) are for example:

a) อย่า เสียบ ปลั๊ก หลาย อัน
    NegV   N   Adj   cl. du N
    (Ne pas brancher prises plusieurs + classifier for objects in general)

b) อย่า เสียบ ปลั๊ก หลาย ปลั๊ก
    NegV   N   Adj   cl. du N
    (Ne pas brancher prises plusieurs + 'prises' as classifier)

c) อย่า เสียบ ปลั๊ก จำนวนมาก
    NegV   N   Adj
    (Ne pas brancher prises plusieurs)

```
Enter in free text a conceptual description of the
word that you are looking for:
|: signal that warns of danger
sortie_1(alert)
sortie_2(n)
```

Figure 2.9 System for extracting terms represented by a user-entered definition

For this case, we control the Thai by choosing c) as the canonical transfer structure because it is closer to the French sentence structure. In this manner we have eliminated the classifier variants which eventually can provoke ambiguities, whilst having an exact translation which is not ambiguous, neither lexically nor syntactically.

In respect of our controlled language machine translation system, its methodology has also been applied to Japanese and to Russian, and Russian has been added to the system as a target language (Jin and Khatseyeva 2012).

5 Conclusion

To conclude, we can say that without the theoretical support provided by systemic linguistic analysis, and the diverse methodologies which all respect the same formal model, it would have been impossible to have obtained such reliable results and, furthermore, to have been able to extend the methodologies and the application domains.

Note

1 Projet LiSe Linguistique et Sécurité ANR-06-SECU-007.

References

Cardey, Sylviane (2009) Proceedings of ISMTCL, Presses universitaires de Franche-Comté, Ed. S. Cardey, ISSN 0758 6787, ISBN 978-2-84867-261-8.

Cardey, Sylviane (2013) *Modelling Language*, Amsterdam and Philadelphia: John Benjamins Pubishing Company.

Cardey, Sylviane (2015) "Translation technology in France", in Chan Sin-wai (ed.) *The Routledge Encyclopedia of Translation Technology*, London and New York: Routledge, 279–291.

Cardey, Sylviane, Dilber DeVitre, Peter Greenfield, and Laurent Spaggiari (2009) "Recognising acronyms in the context of safety critical technical documentation", in Sylvaine Cardey (ed.) *Proceedings of the International Symposium on Data and Sense Mining, Machine Translation and Controlled Languages, and Their Application to*

Emergencies, and Safety Critical Domains (*ISMTCL*), France: Presses universitaires de Franche-Comté, 56–61.

Cardey, Sylviane and Peter Greenfield (2005) "A core model of systemic linguistic analysis", in *Proceedings of the International Conference RANLP-2005: Recent Advances in Natural Language Processing*, Bulgaria: Borovets, 21–23 September, 134–138.

Cardey, Sylviane and Peter Greenfield (2006) *Systemic Linguistics with Applications*, Newcastle upon Tyne: Cambridge Scholars Press, 261–271.

Cardey, Sylviane, Peter Greenfield, Raksi Anantalapochai, Mohand Beddar, Dilber DeVitre, and Gan Jin (2008) "Modelling of multiple target machine translation of controlled languages based on language norms and divergences", in *Proceedings of the Second International Symposium on Universal Communication* (ISUC2008), Osaka, Japan, 15–16 December, 2008, the IEEE Computer Society, 322–329.

Chomsky, Noam (1957) *Aspects of the Theory of Syntax*, Cambridge, MA: MIT Press.

DeVitre, Dilber (2009) "Constructing an English electronic reverse dictionary using a seme-matching methodology", in *Proceedings of the 11th International Symposium on Social Communication*, Santiago de Cuba, Cuba, 19–23 January 2009, 261–265.

Dziadkiewicz, A. (2007) "Vers une reconnaissance et une traduction automatique de phraséologismes pragmatiques (application du français vers le polonais)", PhD thesis, Centre Tesnière, Besançon.

Jin, Gan and Natallia Khatseyeva (2012) "A reliable communication system to maximize the communication quality", in *Proceedings of the 8th International Conference on Natural Language Processing* (JapTAL 2012), Kanazawa, Japan, 22–24 October 2012, Berlin and Heidelberg: Springer-Verlag, 52–63.

Tesnière, Lucien (1959) *Eléments de syntaxe structurale*, Paris: Klincksieck.

3 Caught in the web of translation
Reflections on the compilation of three translation encyclopedias

Chan Sin-wai

Introduction

This article deals with the human factor in machine translation from a personal and encyclopedic perspective, reflecting the importance of this factor through contributions to machine translation by specialists in the context of the three encyclopedias compiled by the author in the field of translation and interpreting.

The year 2015 is of great significance to the author. It marks the thirtieth anniversary of my teaching career at the Department of Translation of The Chinese University of Hong Kong, as I joined the Department in 1985. It also marks the twentieth anniversary of the publication of the first encyclopedia in the field of translation which was co-edited by David Pollard and myself and published by The Chinese University Press in 1995. It marks the publication of the first encyclopedia of translation technology edited by myself and published by Routledge. It also marks the preparation of the encyclopedia of practical translation and interpreting, edited by me and to be published by The Chinese University Press in 2018.

In the past three decades, besides writing monographs, translating books, and editing anthologies, I have devoted myself to the compilation of these three translation encyclopedias, covering virtually all the areas in the field. My life as a translation teacher and researcher has been, like that of many other fellow scholars in the field, caught in the web of translation – to borrow partly the title of the book written by Elizabeth Murray, *Caught in the Web of Words* (Murray 1977), which describes how her father James Murray prepared the *Oxford English Dictionary*.

1995: *Encyclopedia of Translation*

The idea of publishing an encyclopedia of translation, with special reference to translation between Chinese and English, had been on my mind since I started to teach the course "Translation Theory" at The Chinese University many years ago. Before my goal could be achieved, however, I needed to know what had been written before and by whom. I therefore started to collect bibliographical information on translation studies in order to work out a list of scholars who could contribute to the planned encyclopedia. This resulted in the publication of the book entitled *A Topical Bibliography of Translation and Interpretation* (1995).

This is probably the first comprehensive topical bibliography that specializes in works on translation written in English and Chinese. It has 169 topics, covering most aspects of translation and interpreting. The entries in the book are "the printed literature on translation and interpretation, such as monographs, anthologies, journals, and theses. Articles, chapters or prefaces which deal specifically with certain aspects of translation and interpretation have been treated as separate entries" (Chan 1995(1): xi). This bibliography formed the basis on which the decisions on which scholars should be invited to contribute to the planned encyclopedia.

The actual work of preparing the first *Encyclopedia of Translation* started sometime in 1992. Shortly after, Professor David Pollard joined the Department and together we co-edited this encyclopedia, which was completed in 1995 with the contributions of 89 experts. Most of the general topics were written by European and American scholars, while language-specific and culture-specific entries were provided by colleagues in China, Hong Kong, and Sinological circles worldwide. A breakdown of the contributors is given in Table 3.1.

The above shows that a total of 89 scholars contributed to this encyclopedia, covering 95 topics. These contributors were from Asia, Europe, and North America, but none of them was from Africa, Australia, or South America. Asian scholars included those from China (22), Hong Kong (24), Israel (1), Singapore (1), and Taiwan (3), totaling 51, European contributors included those from Austria (2), Belgium (1), Croatia (1), Denmark (1), Germany (4), Slovenia (1), Spain (1), and United Kingdom (11), totaling 22, and American experts included those from Canada (2) and the United States (14), totaling 16. In terms of percentage, Asia had the highest with 57.30%, Europe came second with 24.71%, and North America had the lowest with 17.98%.

The number of Hong Kong contributors was the highest for several reasons: (1) this encyclopedia focuses on translation between Chinese and English, and Hong Kong is about the only place in the world where the teaching of translation is confined to the only language pair of Chinese and English; (2) seven out of nine universities in Hong Kong offer translation as an undergraduate discipline and five out of the seven programmes offer translation as a postgraduate programme; Hong Kong therefore has the highest concentration of translation programmes in the world and a large number of scholars and researchers working on topics in the field; (3) of all the cities in China, Hong Kong, which was under the British colonial rule for 150 years, is the only actual bilingual city, as both Chinese and English are recognized as official languages; and (4) both editors were familiar with the specializations of their local co-workers in the field.

Scholars in China also made great contributions to this encyclopedia. Their entries shed light on specific areas, such as the translation of political writings, children's literature, and English poetry, and the study of the history of translation in China, Chinese-English dictionaries, and conference translation. Their articles were illustrated with useful examples and insights gained from practical

Table 3.1 List of Contributors (1995 encyclopedia)

Country/Place	Name	Topic
Austria (Europe)	Qian, Feng 钱峰	Computational Linguistics
Austria (Europe)	Snell-Hornby, Mary	Lexicography and Translation
Belgium (Europe)	Delabastita, Dirk	Mass communication
Canada (America)	Pong, Lam Shuk-lin 庞林淑莲	Simultaneous Interpreting Training of Conference Interpreters
Canada (America)	Schlepp, Wayne	Sanqu
China (Asia)	Cheng, Zhenqiu 程镇球	Political Writings
China (Asia)	Dai, Liuling 戴镏龄	Children's Literature
China (Asia)	Dong, Zhendong 董振东	Transtar
China (Asia)	Guo, Jianzhong 郭建中	Translatability
China (Asia)	He, Ziran 何自然	Pragmatics
China (Asia)	Huang Jianhua 黄建华	Conference Translation
China (Asia)	Huang Yushi 黄雨时	Form and Spirit
China (Asia)	Jin, Di 金堤	Equivalent Effect
China (Asia)	Liu, Bingshan 刘炳善	Translation of English Essays
China (Asia)	Liu, Zhongde 刘重德	English Attributive Clauses
China (Asia)	Ma, Zuyi 马祖毅	History of Translation in China
China (Asia)	Shen, Dan 申丹	Literalism
China (Asia)	Wang, Zongyan 王宗炎	Linguistic Aspects of CE/EC Translation
China (Asia)	Wang, Zuoliang 王佐良	Translation Standards
China (Asia)	Wu, Jingrong 吴景荣	Chinese-English Dictionaries
China (Asia)	Yan, Qingjia 杨庆甲	Scientific Translation
China (Asia)	Yang, Guobin 杨国斌	English Poetry
China (Asia)	Yu, Lisan 余立山	Rhetoric
China (Asia)	Yu, Yungen 俞云根	Onomatopoeia

(*Continued*)

Table 3.1 (Continued)

Country/Place	Name	Topic
China (Asia)	Zeng, Xiancai 曾宪才	Semantics
China (Asia)	Zhang, Liangping 张良平	Practical Considerations of Machine Translation
China (Asia)	Zhang, Peiji 张培基	English Letters
Croatia (Europe)	Ivir, Vladimir	Formal Correspondence
Denmark (Europe)	Gottlieb, Henrik	Subtitling
Germany (Europe)	House, Juliane	Translation Quality Assessment
Germany (Europe)	Lorscher, Wolfgang	Psycholinguistics
Germany (Europe)	Neubert, Albrecht	Textlinguistics
Germany (Europe)	Wilss, Wolfram	Cognitive Aspects of the Translation Process
Hong Kong (Asia)	Almberg, S.P.E 吴兆朋	Retranslation
Hong Kong (Asia)	Chan, Man Sing 陈万成	Arthur Waley
Hong Kong (Asia)	Chau, Simon S. C. 周兆祥	Translation Education
Hong Kong (Asia)	Cheng, Y. P. 郑仰平	Interpreting
Hong Kong (Asia)	Deeney, John	Biculturalism Transcription
Hong Kong (Asia)	Fong, Gilbert C. F. 方梓勋	Translated Literature in Pre-modern China
Hong Kong (Asia)	Dent-Young, John	Chinese Fiction
Hong Kong (Asia)	Fung, Mary M. Y. 冯张曼仪	Translation of Metaphor
Hong Kong (Asia)	Ho, Wai Kit 何伟杰	Media Translating
Hong Kong (Asia)	Hung, Eva 孔慧怡	Translation Editing
Hong Kong (Asia)	Jin, Serena S. H. 金圣华	Colour Terms
Hong Kong (Asia)	Lai, Jane Chui Chun 黎翠珍	Drama Translation
Hong Kong (Asia)	Lie, Raymond S. C. 李成仔	Commercial Translation
Hong Kong (Asia)	Liu, Ching-chih 刘靖之	Western Music
Hong Kong (Asia)	Liu, Miqing 刘宓庆	Aesthetics and Translation Grammar and Translation Translation Theory from/into Chinese
Hong Kong (Asia)	Pfister, Lauren F.	James Legge

Country/Place	Name	Topic
Hong Kong (Asia)	Pollard, David E.	Body Language
		Empty Words
Hong Kong (Asia)	Shih, Hsio-yen	Chinese Calligraphy and Painting
Hong Kong (Asia)	Sinn, Elizabeth 洗玉仪	Yan Fu
Hong Kong (Asia)	Tsai, Frederick 蔡思果	Book Titles
		English Fiction
		Europeanized Structure
Hong Kong (Asia)	Witzleben, John L.	Chinese Music
Hong Kong (Asia)	Wong, Ian P. K. 黄邦杰	Empty Words
Hong Kong (Asia)	Wong, Kin Yuen 王建元	Hermeneutics and Translation
Hong Kong (Asia)	Wong, Siu Kit 黄兆杰	Arthur Waley
Israel (Asia)	Blum-Kulka, Shoshana	Discourse Analysis
Singapore (Asia)	Tan, Cheng Lim	Language Teaching and Translation
Slovenia (Europe)	Duff, Alan McConnell	Over-translation
		Under-translation
Spain (Europe)	Golden, Sean	Translator and Interpreter Training
Taiwan (Asia)	Huang, I-min 黄逸民	Puns
Taiwan (Asia)	Hwang, Mei-shu 黄美序	Allusions
Taiwan (Asia)	Loh, I-Jin 骆维仁	Chinese Translations of the Bible
United Kingdom (Europe)	Bassnett, Susan	Translation Theory in the West
United Kingdom (Europe)	Cayley, John	Chinese Classical Poetry
United Kingdom (Europe)	Hartmann, Reinhard R. K.	Bilingual Lexicography
United Kingdom (Europe)	Hutchins, W. J.	Machine Translation
United Kingdom (Europe)	James, Carl	Transfer
United Kingdom (Europe)	Jones, Francis Redvers	Translation in Language Teaching
United Kingdom (Europe)	Lang, Margaret F.	Discourse Analysis
United Kingdom (Europe)	Lam, Jacqueline K. M. 林锦薇	Thinking-aloud Protocol
United Kingdom (Europe)	McDougall, Bonnie S.	Contemporary Chinese Poetry
United Kingdom (Europe)	Newmark, Peter	Translation Procedures
United Kingdom (Europe)	Nkwenti-Azeh, Blaise	Terminology
United States (America)	Ames, Roger	Translating Chinese Philosophy

(*Continued*)

Table 3.1 (Continued)

Country/Place	Name	Topic
United States (America)	Birch, Cyril	Yuan *Zaju*
United States (America)	Brislin, Richard W.	Back-translation
United States (America)	Feleppa, Robert	Cultural Description
United States (America)	Freimanis, Carolina	Back-translation
United States (America)	Kao, George 高克毅	Humorous Writings
United States (America)	Knechtges, David R.	Han Rhapsody
United States (America)	Larson, Mildred L.	Factors in Bible Translation
United States (America)	Lau, Joseph S. M. 刘绍铭	Author as Translator
United States (America)	Lee, Thomas H. C. 李宏祺	Western History
United States (America)	Lefevere, Andre	Factors of Poetic Translation
United States (America)	Nida, Eugene	Dynamic Equivalence
United States (America)	Rose, Marilyn Gaddis	Text Typology
United States (America)	Watson, Burton	Chinese History

experience. Taiwan scholars deserve a special mention for their contributions to the translation of puns, allusions, and the Bible.

As aforementioned, Western scholars from Europe wrote on more theoretical or general topics, including mass communication, psycholinguistics, discourse analysis, and back-translation. It cannot be denied that many of the ideas and concepts in translation have originated in Europe, and translation theory is largely Eurocentric. The American scholars were equally impressive in their contribution. Most of them were Sinologists specialized in Chinese literature and other cultural aspects, who wrote chapters on topics such as the translation of Chinese philosophy, Han rhapsody, and Yuan *zaju*. Eugene Nida, an American scholar generally known as the "father of translation theory", however, wrote a chapter on his concept "dynamic equivalence", which was applied to the translation of *The Good News Bible*.

2015: *The Routledge Encyclopedia of Translation Technology*

The second translation encyclopedia that I edited was *The Routledge Encyclopedia of Translation Technology* (Chan 2015), which was published in January 2015. It has taken me years to accumulate experience in the area of translation technology, mainly through programme administration, teaching, publication, and collection of bibliographical data, to lay the foundations for the publication of the first encyclopedia in this area.

As far as administration is concerned, I started to plan the establishment of the world-first Master of Arts in Computer-aided Translation (MACAT) Programme in 2000. It took me one year to work out a curriculum to be approved by the relevant authorities, and the MACAT Programme accepted the first batch of students in 2002. During the process of curriculum design and course offering, my understanding of the scope of translation technology was widened, which was helpful to work out the topics for the encyclopedia.

With the establishment of the MACAT Programme, I began to focus on the teaching of translation technology. I then realized that as the students who enrolled in the Programme were mostly graduates of the humanities and social sciences, they needed to have a solid foundation of the knowledge and skills of translation technology. This led to the publication of *A Dictionary of Translation Technology* (Chan 2004), authored by myself and published by The Chinese University Press in 2004. Actually, I started this dictionary project even before I planned the MACAT Programme. As I said in the Preface (p. xx):

> *A Dictionary of Translation Technology* is possibly the first dictionary in the field that serves as a comprehensive reference for general readers, as far as key terms in translation studies are concerned, with a new orientation to serve specialists in computer translation and translation technology.

It provides a glossary of terms in translation technology, an introduction to commercial translation software, a bibliography of electronic and paper references for translation technology, and a history of machine translation in the world. This dictionary laid a good foundation for me to work on an encyclopedia of translation technology.

The last publication that helped me prepare for the planned encyclopedia was the book *A Topical Bibliography of Computer(-aided) Translation* (Chan 2008), which was actually an exercise in the collection of bibliographical data. This bibliography, which divides its entries into 39 parts, contains 8,363 entries of works written either in English or Chinese by 5,404 authors between 1948 and 2006, a period of 58 years. It was with the help of this bibliography that I prepared the list of topics to be included in the encyclopedia and the scholars to be invited to contribute to this work.

The Routledge Encyclopedia of Translation Technology, which was released in 2015, is aimed at providing a state-of-the-art survey of the field of computer-aided translation. It is the first definitive reference to provide a comprehensive overview of the general, regional, and topical aspects of translation technology. This work is divided into three parts: Part 1 represents general issues in translation technology, Part 2 discusses national and regional developments in translation technology, and Part 3 evaluates specific topics in the field.

The following are the topics and scholars with their countries of institutional affiliations in the encyclopedia.

Several observations can be made from the preceding table. First, as Europe was the cradle of translation technology, 18 contributors out of 49 have institutional affiliations in Europe, accounting for 36.73%. Second, as Asia is fast becoming a prosperous emerging market for translation technology, it has the same number of contributors as Europe, accounting for another 36.73%. Third, scholars from America, comprising those from Canada and the United States, are smaller in number, nine altogether, accounting for 18.37%. Fourth, Europe and America, the two continents which lead the world in technology, take up 55.1% of the total number of contributors, which shows the prominence of Western scholars in the area of translation technology. Fifth, Africa, with two contributors, accounts for 4.08%. This shows that scholars from Europe and Asia take up 73.46% of the total number of contributors, a strong indication of the fast development of translation technology in these two areas. Lastly, I consider myself fortunate to be able to edit this first encyclopedia of translation technology.

Table 3.2 List of contributors (2015 encyclopedia)

Country/Place	Name	Topic
Australia (Asia)	Garcia, Ignacio	Computer-aided translation Systems
Australia (Asia)	Schwitter, Rolf	Controlled Language
Canada (America)	Bowker, Lynne	Translator Training
Canada (America)	Macklovitch, Elliott	Translation Technology in Canada
Canada (America)	Nie, Jian-yun 聂建云	Information Retrieval and Text Mining
China (Asia)	Bai, Xiaojing 白小晶	Rule-based machine translation
China (Asia)	Liu, Yang 刘阳	Statistical machine translation
China (Asia)	Qian, Duoxiu 钱多秀	Translation Technology in China
China (Asia)	Yu, Shiwen 俞士汶	Rule-based machine translation
China (Asia)	Zhang, Min 张闽	Statistical machine translation
China (Asia)	Zhang, Yihua 章宜华	Computational Lexicography
France (Europe)	Cardey, Sylviane	Translation Technology in France
Germany (Europe)	Lommel, Arle	Bitext
Hong Kong (Asia)	Chan, Sin-wai 陈善伟	Development of Translation Technology Major Concepts of Computer-aided Translation Translation Technology in Hong Kong
Hong Kong (Asia)	Chow, Ian Castor 周志仁	Translation Technology in Hong Kong

Country/Place	Name	Topic
Hong Kong (Asia)	Kit, Chunyu 揭春雨	Evaluation in machine translation and computer-aided translation Information Retrieval and Text Mining
Hong Kong (Asia)	Kwong, Oi Yee 邝凯儿	Natural Language Processing
Hong Kong (Asia)	Lee, Tan 李丹	Speech Translation
Hong Kong (Asia)	Li, Lan 李兰	Corpus
Hong Kong (Asia)	Warburton, Kara	Terminology Management
Hong Kong (Asia)	Wong, Tak-ming 黄德铭	Example-based machine translation Evaluation in machine translation and computer-aided translation Translation Technology in Hong Kong
Hong Kong (Asia)	Webster, Jonathan J.	Example-based machine translation
Hong Kong (Asia)	Wong, Shuk Man 黄淑雯	Teaching of machine translation
Italy (Europe)	Gaspari, Federico	Online Translation
Italy (Europe)	Zanettin, Federico	Concordancing
Japan (Asia)	Isahara, Hitoshi	Translation Technology in Japan
Netherlands, The (Europe)	van den Bosch, Antal	Translation Technology in the Netherlands and Belgium
Netherlands, The (Europe)	van der Beek, Leonoor	Translation Technology in the Netherlands and Belgium
South Africa (Africa)	Griesel, Marissa	Translation Technology in South Africa
South Africa (Africa)	Van Huyssteen, Gerhard B.	Translation Technology in South Africa
Spain (Europe)	Farwell, David	Pragmatics-based machine translation
Spain (Europe)	Forcada, Mikel L.	Open-source machine translation
Spain (Europe)	Sanchez-Martinez, Felipe	Part-of-speech Tagging
Sweden (Europe)	Ahrenberg, Lars	Alignment
Switzerland (Europe)	Vazquez, Lucia Morado	Bitext

(*Continued*)

Table 3.2 (Continued)

Country/Place	Name	Topic
Taiwan (Asia)	Shih, Chung-ling 史宗铃	Translation Technology in Taiwan
United Kingdom (Europe)	Choi, Freddy Y.Y.	Segmentation
United Kingdom (Europe)	Diaz Cintas, Jorge	Subtitling
United Kingdom (Europe)	Declercq, Christophe	Translation Technology in the United Kingdom Editing in Translation Technology
United Kingdom (Europe)	Hutchins, John	Machine Translation: History and Applications
United Kingdom (Europe)	Liu, Qun 刘群	Machine Translation: General
United Kingdom (Europe)	Shuttleworth, Mark	Translation Management Systems
United Kingdom (Europe)	Zhang, Xiaojun 张小军	Machine Translation: General
United States (America)	DeCamp, Jennifer	A History of Translation Technology in the United States
United States (America)	Dunne, Keiran J.	Localization
United States (America)	Helmreich, Stephen	Pragmatics-based machine translation
United States (America)	Melby, Alan K.	Bitext Translation Memory
United States (America)	Wright, Sue Ellen	Language Codes and Language Tags Translation Memory
United States (America)	Zetzsche, Jost	A History of Translation Technology in the United States

Forthcoming: *An Encyclopedia of Practical Translation and Interpreting*

It was no mere coincidence for me to propose a publication project on an encyclopedia of practical translation and interpreting when I was urged by the staff of The Chinese University Press to prepare a sequel to the *Encyclopaedia of Translation* that was published in 1995, twenty-three years ago. It first occurred to me that the proper course to take was to revise and expand the 1995 encyclopedia. But this is not possible for two reasons. On the one hand, the cost of typesetting the revisions would be enormous. A supplement would thus be more economical. On the other hand, as some of the contributors, such as Eugene Nida, Andre Lefevere, Wang Zuoliang, and Jin Di, are no longer with us, it would not be possible to do revisions on their contributions. Eventually, it was decided that a separate volume would be the best option.

This separate volume, after much deliberation, is to be entitled *An Encyclopedia of Practical Translation and Interpreting*. The aim of preparing this encyclopedia, which is the first of its kind, is to provide a general and authoritative reference for translation teachers, professionals, and practitioners, and students working in the area of practical domains, with special reference of the language-pair of Chinese and English. It will cover more than 30 topics in the areas of practical translation and interpreting, to be written by prominent scholars and researchers and experts and up-coming specialists in the field and industry.

The choice of these two areas is obvious. First, all the published dictionaries and encyclopedias in the field, including those by Shuttleworth and Cowie (1997), Baker (1998), and Millan-Varela and Bartrina (2013), are mainly on concepts and ideas of translation theory, culture, and literary translation, neglecting translation practice and interpreting. Second, practical translation, which takes up over 90% of the annual translation output in a country, such as China, has not received the attention it deserves, while literary translation, which has a small percentage in terms of translation output, has been much studied. This encyclopedia thus serves the purpose of readdressing the imbalance between practical translation and literary translation. Third, scholars in the areas of practical translation are far fewer than those of translation studies, and this poses difficulties in soliciting the assistance of scholar-translators in practical translation to write on topics proposed for this encyclopedia. Fourth, practical translation, by its nature, is both general and language-specific: general as there are universal concepts that apply to all languages, and language-specific as there are specific considerations when translating or interpreting between two or more languages. It is therefore necessary to invite scholars to write on general topics, as well as specialists in translation between Chinese and English to write on language-, culture-, and text-specific topics.

The proposed contents for this encyclopedia are as follows.

As this is an encyclopedia of practical translation and interpreting, the emphasis is to have scholars and experts sharing their practical experience with the readers. As practical experience is more important than an academic discussion, a number of contributors have been invited on the merits of their length of service in the profession of translation rather than their experience in teaching courses in practical translation.

Conclusion

To be caught in the web of translation is a source of great pleasure to me. I have enjoyed and benefitted in several ways from compiling and editing all the three encyclopedias that have been or will be published.

First, these three encyclopedias have widened my intellectual horizons. Through the compilation of these works, I gained a comprehensive knowledge of the topics in translation. The 163 topics in these three encyclopedias cover most of the subjects in the four major areas of translation studies, translation technology, practical translation, and interpreting.

62 *Chan Sin-wai*

Table 3.3 List of contributors (2018 encyclopedia)

Country/Place	Name	Topic
Australia	Taylor-Bouladon, Valerie	Conference Interpreting
China (Asia)	Qian, Duoxiu 钱多秀	Translation Technology
China (Asia)	Wu Zhiwei	Interpreting between Mandarin and English
France (Europe)	Serban, Adriana	Translation of Religious Texts
France (Europe)	Hassen, Rim	Translation of Religious Texts
Hong Kong (Asia)	Chan, Sin-wai 陈善伟	Translating Chinese Famous Quotes into English
Hong Kong (Asia)	Cheng, Eos 郑晓彤	Translation of Songs
Hong Kong (Asia)	Chung, Lung-shan 钟龙山	Public Administration Translation
Hong Kong (Asia)	Li, Kexing 李克兴	E-C Translation of Practical Writings
Hong Kong (Asia)	Daisy Ng Sheung Yuen	Legal Interpreting in Hong Kong
Hong Kong (Asia)	Sin, King Kui 冼景炬	Legal Translation: Sociolinguistic Aspects
Hong Kong (Asia)	Wang, Ling 王凌	Legal Translation: Cultural Aspects
Italy (Europe)	Russo, Mariachiara	Liaison Interpreting
United Kingdom (Europe)	Banos, Rocio	Technology and AV Translation
United Kingdom (Europe)	Desblache, Lucile	Translation of Music
United Kingdom (Europe)	Liao, Min-Hsiu	Tourism Translation
United States (America)	Daniel Gile	Simultaneous Interpreting
United States (America)	Mikkelson, Holly	Court Interpreting
United States (America)	Mossop, Brian	Editing in Translation

Second, these works have provided me with a very large context to see each topic in translation in a proper perspective. A topic in translatology is like a tree in a forest. We have to see the trees as well as the forest. A quotation of a poem by the Song poet Su Shi (1037–1101) can best illustrate how limited is our scope.

横看成岭侧成峰 From the front of a range, from the side of a peak,
远近高低各不同 Unlike from near or far, or high or low,
不识庐山真面目 I do not know the true face of Mount Lu,
祇緣身在此山中 as it is only by chance that I am on this mountain.

This poem tells us that we have to know the world of translation from a global perspective so as to be able to see one's specialized area(s) in a better light.

Third, they have enlarged my academic network. Through the publication of these encyclopedias, I came to know 159 co-workers in the field, some of whom are leading scholars, others, up-comers, and still others, devoted practitioners known in their own circles. Their support and contributions have given me encouragement to achieve the goals I set, which demanded continuous and systematic efforts.

It should also be emphasized that nothing can be achieved by coincidence. It is clear that the compilation of my encyclopedias is always preceded by the production of a reference work and a bibliography. This was the case with my first encyclopedia, the *Encyclopedia of Translation: Chinese-English, English-Chinese*, which was preceded by *A Glossary of Translation Terms* (Chan 1993) and *A Topical Bibliography of Translation and Interpretation* (Chan 1995). This was also the case with my second encyclopedia *The Routledge Encyclopedia of Translation Technology*, which was preceded by *A Dictionary of Translation Technology* (Chan 2004) and *A Topical Bibliography of Computer(-aided) Translation* (Chan 2008).

Looking into the future, we should acknowledge that this trilogy of encyclopedias on the theory and practice and knowledge and skills of translation in a large number of aspects does not mean that there will be no topics and subjects to be covered in the future. Future changes in the field, like what we have done before, need to be studied in the more general forms, such as dictionaries and encyclopedias, or in the more focused ways, such as articles and monographs. We will stay with translation for a long time to come. In other words, we will continue to be caught in the web of translation.

References

Baker, Mona (1998) *Routledge Encyclopedia of Translation Studies*, London and New York: Routledge.
Chan, Sin-wai (1993) *A Glossary of Translation Terms*, Hong Kong: The Chinese University Press.
Chan, Sin-wai (1995) *A Topical Bibliography of Translation and Interpretation*, Hong Kong: The Chinese University Press.
Chan, Sin-wai (2004) *A Dictionary of Translation Technology*, Hong Kong: The Chinese University Press.
Chan, Sin-wai (2008) *A Topical Bibliography of Computer(-aided) Translation*, Hong Kong: The Chinese University Press.
Chan, Sin-wai (2015) *The Routledge Encyclopedia of Translation Technology*, London and New York: Routledge.Millan-Varela, Carmen and Francesca Batrina (eds.) (2013) *The Routledge Handbook of Translation Studies*, London and New York: Routledge.
Murray, K.M. Elisabeth (1977) *Caught in the Web of Words: James A.H. Murray and the Oxford English Dictionary*, New Haven: Yale University Press.
Shuttleworth, Mark and Moira Cowie (1997) *Dictionary of Translation Studies*, Manchester: St. Jerome Publishing.

4 A comparative study of term extraction methods in translation

Jiang Cheng and Wang Min

1 Introduction

Since 1978, China has been undergoing a process of rapid social, economic and cultural transition due to its practice of reform and opening up to the outside world. Translation, as an important means of communication, serves as a bridge to link China with the international community. China's entry into WTO, new international contacts, foreign investments, as well as investments in foreign markets, has caused an enormous increase in the volume of translation produced and required, particularly that in the field of localization(Yang Yingbo, Wang Weihua and Cui Qiliang 2011)in recent years.

In order to accomplish the translation tasks with maximum quality and efficiency, translators employ all kinds of translation technologies. Terminology management systems have proved very useful in supporting translators' work. As Alan Melby (2010: p. 2) points out, "A translation project can be thought of as sitting on a tripod whose three legs are the source text, the specifications, and the terminology. If any of the three legs is removed, the project falls down." The importance of term in the field of translation is illustrated in Melby's saying. For collaborative translation projects, unified terminology (Cohen 1995) can guarantee consistency of the terms, ensuring the translation quality and the smoothness of relative professional communication. Unfortunately, for a specific localization project the translators are not likely to find reliable terminological resources for a specific translation project.

A possible solution is the creation of a domain-specific termbase (Makoto et al. 2009; Zhai and Baisong 2010) to ensure the consistency of specialized terms in translation, which is directly related to term extraction (Abasi and Ghaznavi-Ghoushchi 2012). Term extraction is the main research topic of automatic knowledge acquisition and information processing, widely used in the research field of natural language processing like information extraction, knowledge presentation, data mining (Palshikar 2007), information retrieval and machine translation. Extracted terms can also be used to build a glossary or termbase in the field of computer-aided translation. Term extraction, if done manually, is quite time-consuming. The current term extraction can be completed automatically by term extraction tools, thus eliminating the time-consuming issue by manual term extraction. However, the term extraction accuracy is not always satisfactory. For example, "use Moses" is not a term, but it is extracted by a certain tool as a term because of its high frequency in the source text. The possible reason is that the term extraction algorithm adopted by the term extraction tool is statistically based. The workload from manual modification after extracting terms is relatively large and time-consuming, which sometimes completely annihilates the usefulness of automatic term extraction tools.

The objective of research presented in this chapter was to make a comparative study of the performances of four different term extraction algorithms for bilingual text (English and Chinese) through an experiment, hoping to provide insight for improving the performance of term extraction tools.

2 Term extraction method for the research

Past research on term extraction methods mainly fall into two types: linguistic and statistical, which are two mainstream approaches to extracting terms. A linguistic approach to term extraction tries to identify terms by capturing their syntactic properties. A statistical approach to term extraction is to identify the candidate term by frequency. However, term-extraction tools that use a linguistic approach or statistical approach have drawbacks of one kind or another during the process of term extraction (Bowker 2002). So is it possible to find out a solution to the problems in extracting terms?

This chapter aims to investigate the term extraction performance of a method that combines several algorithms in identifying terms in an English-Chinese translation project (hereafter it is referred to as the hybrid method). We compared the hybrid method with three others in measuring their precision, recall and F index so as to verify whether the hybrid method outperforms the others in extracting terms. The three methods (or algorithms) for comparison are the bonding strength and character filtering-based method (hereafter referred to as BSCF) (Xu et al. 2013), C-value (Frantzi, Ananiadou and Mima 2000; Liang, Wenjing and Youcheng 2010) and TF-IDF (Rezgui 2007; Gu and Hao 2011). C-value and TF-IDF are commonly used statistical automatic term recognition algorithms (Cen, Zhe and Peipei 2008; Keim, Oelke and Rohrdantz 2010; Su 2012). Through comparative analysis of the strengths and weaknesses of the methods selected for the experiment, we hope to find out the more effective one for term extraction tools, thus improving the efficiency and reliability of term extraction.

3 Term extraction in experiment

3.1 Research hypothesis

This research mainly focuses on the evaluation of the precision, recall and F index of the four term recognition methods. This chapter presents the following three assumptions:

1 The precision rate of the BSCF method is higher than that of C-value and TF-IDF. The precision rate of the hybrid method is higher than that of a single method.

2 The recall rate of BSCF is higher than that of C-value and TF-IDF. The recall rate of the hybrid method is higher than that of a single method.
3 The F index of BSCF is higher than that of C-value and TF-IDF. The F index of the hybrid method is higher than that of a single method.

3.2 Corpus and instruments

The corpus includes 95 source texts in English and 95 target texts in Chinese in the field of semiconductor chips from a language service company. The extracted articles cover various sectors of the semiconductor like microcontrollers, sensors and power devices. The total number of words in the Chinese version is about 420,000 words. A reference list of 1568 is available for the research. We also selected 200 irrelevant articles as a background corpus for the TF-IDF method.

PDF texts are converted to Word files or to. txt format files for subsequent processing. NLPIR Chinese Word Segmentation (ICTCLAS 2014, http://ictclas.nlpir.org) is used to do text segmentation and POS tagging for term extraction.

3.3 Experimental procedures

3.3.1 Text format processing

Of all the 95 texts materials in this corpus, most of them are in PDF format. To facilitate the subsequent processing, the PDF text needs to be converted to. txt format. Therefore, PDF Convertor Enterprise is used to convert all PDF files to text files. The title, content and summary of each text are extracted and saved as. txt format files.

3.3.2 Text segmentation and POS tagging

The converted texts need segmentation, adding POS tagging. The segmentation tool used for this experiment is NLPIR Chinese Word Segmentation (ICTCLAS 2014). The text imported is required to be. txt format, and the imported text will be displayed in the small window at the top of the interface of the tool. After clicking on "Ordinary Segmentation", text after segmentation and POS tagging will be displayed in the small window at the bottom of the interface of the tool (as shown in Figures 4.2 and 4.3. And specific words will be displayed in different colours (Figure 4.1).

3.3.3 Stop words deleting

There is still some high frequency words in the text after segmentation and POS tagging: although those words frequently appear in the text, they cannot reflect knowledge about chips, like high frequency words "的", "地", interjection, function words and words reflecting the grammatical structure. Likewise, for the

Figure 4.1 Specific words and corresponding colours

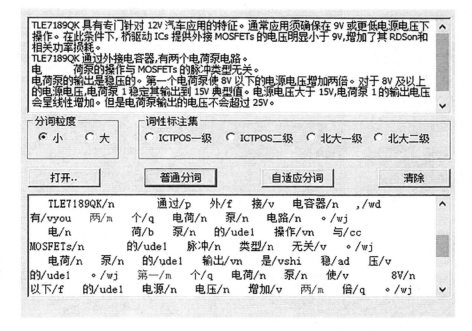

Figure 4.2 Results of Chinese text segmentation and POS tagging

English text, high frequency words like "in", "at", and "for example" should be deleted. These words are not supposed to appear as candidate terms; therefore, they are not seen as objects in this experiment. Remove stop words by comparing the segmented text with the stop list.

3.3.4 Word merging

Finally, the word merging (Zhai Dufeng and Liu Baisong 2010) is done to deal with moot strings after semantic splitting for the texts in Chinese. There are two situations: if three one-character Chinese words appear one after another in a string, like "电/n 荷/b 泵/n", then these words need to be merged into new units as "电荷", "荷泵". When a one-character word appears between two

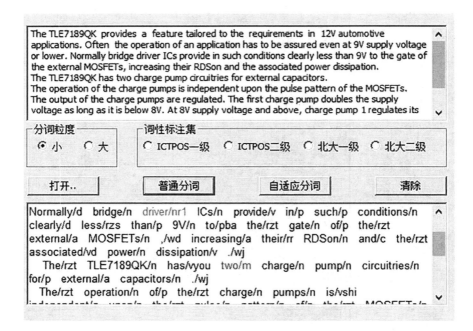

Figure 4.3 Results of English text segmentation and POS tagging

candidate terms, and if it can form new candidate terms with the one before and after it, then the character should be merged with the candidate terms before and after it, like the string "电荷/n泵/n电路/n". After word merging, we can get two new candidate terms: "电荷泵", "泵电路". Before the application of any term extraction method, it is necessary to make a linguistic analysis of the text. This step is to help select all the admissible candidate terms.

3.3.5 *Term extraction*

(1) EXTRACTING CANDIDATE TERMS BY C-VALUE

The C-value algorithm measures the frequency of the candidate term based on the idea of the TF algorithm, but it also considers the impact of term length and nested words, i.e. the longer the term, the less likely it appears, so there will be a corresponding weighting in the frequency of the longer candidate term. Because some words in the candidate terms can cumulate frequency several times, but have little meaning, it is necessary to give appropriate penalties to get the final score. When calculating the C-value, we should consider three factors: extract higher frequency terms, give a penalty to the embedded term which is the substring of a longer candidate term, and consider the length of the candidate term.

1   If there is no possibility for the word "a" in a document to be merged with another word or candidate term to form a new candidate term, then its C-value is calculated as follows:

$$C\text{-}value(a) = \log_2 g(a) \times f(a) \quad \dfrac{\Sigma_{b \in T_a} f(b)}{} \tag{1}$$

2   If there is any possibility for the word "a" in a document to be merged with other words or a candidate term to form a new term, then its C-value is calculated as follows:

$$C\text{-}value(a) = \log_2 g(a) \times \left(f(a) - 1/p(T_a) \times \Sigma_{b \hat{i} T_a} f(b) \right) \tag{2}$$

Whereby, "a" is a word, $g(a)$ is the number of one-character words in word "a", (a), $ff(a)$ is the frequency of candidate term "a" in the text corpus, T_a refers to the longer merged word containing word "a", $p(T_a)$ is the number of new merged words combined with word "a" and another one-character word, $\Sigma_{b \in T_a} f(b)$ is the total number of frequency of the new words merged by word "a" and another one-character word.

According to the C-value algorithm, we conduct statistical analysis on the number of candidate terms appearing in the preprocessed text and the number of phrases containing those candidate terms, and the C-value for each candidate term after the corresponding entry into the formula can be calculated. Take candidate term "诊断电流" for example, it can form new merged terms with other terms, so formula (2) is adopted, i.e. $C\text{-}value(a) = \log_2 g(a) \times \left(f(a) - 1/p(T_a) \times \Sigma_{b \hat{i} T_a} f(b) \right)$, whereby, a = 诊断电流, b = 诊断电流信号, here $g(a) = 2$, $f(a) = 28$, $p(T_a) = 6$ $\Sigma_{b \in T_a} f(b) = 24$, take the previous values into formula (2), the C-value (诊断电流) = 48。 Given the limited space, only the results of six candidate terms are listed in the Table 4.1:

Table 4.1 Sample candidate terms extracted by C-value

Candidate Term	$p(T_a)$	$\sum_{b \in T_a} f(b)$	$f(a)$	C-value
诊断电流	6	6	28	48
诊断电流信号	0	0	18	46.51
器件	23	25	40	38.91
该器件	0	0	30	47.52
文档	20	30	38	43.5
本文档	0	0	20	31.68

In this experiment, when the value of the candidate term is less than 17.45, they are meaningless, so the C-value threshold is set at 17.45. From Table 4.1, we can see that the values of candidate terms are much bigger than the threshold value. Therefore, they are extracted as the final terms.

(2) EXTRACTING CANDIDATE TERMS BY TF-IDF

The TF-IDF algorithm considers the distribution of terms on the basis of the TF algorithm. Under a fixed frequency, a candidate term appears in some documents, but does not exist in other documents, which indicates the candidate term is more discriminative and suitable for classification. IDF, i.e. inverse document frequency, refers to the number of documents containing candidate terms divided by the total number of documents. TF, term frequency, is the number of candidate terms appearing in the corpus. The expression of the TF-IDF algorithm is:

$$TF\cdot IDF(i) = TF(i) \times IDF(i) = \begin{cases} \sum_{n}^{j=1} tf_{ij} \times \log\left(\dfrac{D}{df_i}\right) & if\ df_i \neq 0 \\ \sum_{n}^{j=1} tf_{ij} \times m & if\ df_i = 0 \end{cases}$$

Whereby, tf_{ij} is the frequency of word "I" in domain text j, df_i is the number of documents containing the word "I" in the background corpus, D is the number of text in the background corpus; if the frequency of a candidate term appearing in the background corpus is 0, i.e. $di = 0$, it indicates that this term is representative for the testing field and likely to be the real term in this field. Through the TF-IDF(i) calculation, words carrying the features of the professional field can obtain a higher weight. Therefore, we set the IDF value of the term as a constant "m". To meet the convenience of calculation while improving the weight, "m" is set to be the constant 10.

The higher the TF of the candidate term is, the more likely it is distributed in the corpus, while the lesser its IDF will be, which can suppress the score of this term. To get a high score, the candidate term needs to be in few documents with a high frequency, which is suitable for the introduction and description of the domain corpus.

By the TF-IDF algorithm, we get the statistical results of the number of the candidate terms in the foreground corpus and the number of documents containing the candidate term in the background corpus. Then follow the TF-IDF formula to calculate the TF-IDF value of the candidate term. The results of six candidate terms are shown in Table 4.2:

Table 4.2 Sample candidate terms extracted by TF-IDF

Candidate Term	Number of Text	df_i	$\sum tf_{ij}$	TF-IDF
诊断电流	200	0	28	280
诊断电流信号	200	0	18	180
器件	200	0	40	400
该器件	200	0	30	300
文档	200	50	18	36
本文档	200	30	13	36.19

Sort the TF-IDF value of candidate terms and set a threshold value, wherein the candidate term whose TF-IDF value is bigger than the threshold value is extracted as the final candidate term. The threshold value in this experiment is 40; therefore, candidate terms except for "文档" and "本文档" in Table 4.2 are final candidate terms.

(3) EXTRACTING CANDIDATE TERMS BY BONDING STRENGTH AND CHARACTER FILTERING-BASED METHOD

For a better understanding of how this method is applied to extract candidate terms, it is necessary for us to define the following three terms.

String border is the single word corresponding to the beginning or the end of the string.

Border binding refers to the bonding strength between the borders of two adjacent ordered strings in the same text.

Edge binding refers to the bonding strength between the word formed by two adjacent ordered strings and the above or below of the adjacent border.

To extract candidate terms, the first step is to calculate the border binding. In a text, words or phrases with the occurrence frequency ≥ 2 are denoted as $E = E_1E_2$, where $E_1 = F_aF_b \ldots F_n$, $E_2 = F_AF_B \ldots F_N$. The calculation formula for border binding $i_c(E_nE_A)$ between strings E_1 and E_2 is shown in expression (1)

$$i_c(E_nE_A) = MAX\left\{\frac{S(E_nE_A)}{S(E_n)}, \frac{S(E_nE_A)}{S(E_A)}\right\} \qquad (1)$$

If $i_c(E_nE_A)$ is too large, it indicates that words E_n and F_A are closely bound, reflecting to some extent the close binding between strings E_1 and E_2; on the other hand, if $ic(E_nE_A)$ is too small, it indicates to a certain extent that strings E_1 and E_2 are not closely bound.

The second step is to calculate the edge binding, which is conducted as follows:

As in step one, words or phrases with the occurrence frequency ≥ 2 are denoted as $E = E_1E_2$, where $E_1 = F_aF_b \ldots F_n$, $E_2 = F_AF_B \ldots F_N$. The calculation formula for edge binding $i_E(E_n\ E_A)$ between strings E_1 and E_2 is shown in expression (2)

$$i_E(E_nE_A) = MAX\left\{\frac{S(E_nE_A)}{S(E_1)}, \frac{S(E_nE_A)}{S(E_2)}\right\} \qquad (2)$$

If $i_E(E_nE_A)$ is too large, it indicates that string E_1 can be followed by word F_A, or word F_n can be followed by string E_2. Therefore, to a certain extent, it indicates the close binding between string E_1 and string E_2; on the other hand, if $i_E(E_nE_A)$ is too small, it indicates to some extent that strings E_1 and E_2 aren't closely bound.

The third step is to carry out double words filtering. By positive double words segmentation and reverse double words segmentation, the candidate terms we got by calculating the border binding and the edge binding can be verified through seven steps; the valid strings are the final terms.

Formulas (1) and (2) are used to calculate the bonding strength of words or phrases, and retain the words or phrases whose value is bigger than specified threshold value in the preliminary valid set. If the string length in the preliminary valid set is bigger than 1, then the first segment of the string is valid. Lastly, the double words filtering method is adopted to filter the string with a valid first segment. The valid strings remaining are taken as final terms. For example, by calculating the border binding and edge binding of candidate terms "诊断电流" and "信号" with formulas (1) and (2), it comes to the value $i_c(E_n E_A) = 0.63$, $i_E(E_n E_A) = 0.73$. The bonding strength between the two strings is bigger than the threshold value 0.5, so they should be kept in the valid set. Because the length of this candidate term is 4 characters, which is bigger than 1, so by double words filtering, "诊断电流" is the final term. The Table 4.3 shows the results of six candidate terms:

Table 4.3 Sample candidate terms extracted by BSCF

Candidate Term	$i_c(E_n E_A)$	$i_E(E_n E_A)$	Double Words Filtering
诊断电流	0.67	0.83	Effective
诊断电流信号	0.59	0.63	Effective
器件	0.73	0.94	Effective
该器件	0.70	0.87	Effective
文档	0.78	0.90	Effective
本文档	0.69	0.85	Effective

Table 4.3 shows that the string bonding strength of the candidate terms is bigger than the threshold value 0.5; after double words filtering, they are extracted as final terms.

(4) EXTRACTING CANDIDATE TERMS BY THE HYBRID METHOD

The hybrid method combines the C-value and TF-IDF methods. By taking advantage of these two algorithms, double assurance can be obtained in extracting candidate terms.

Term extraction by this method is carried out in the following steps: First, we calculate the C-value of the strings in the preprocessed text to get the candidate terms; next, we filter them with the TF-IDF algorithm. Those terms whose TF-IDF value is greater than threshold value are the final terms. Some sample candidate terms are shown in Table 4.4.

Table 4.4 Sample candidate terms extracted by the hybrid method

Candidate Term	C-value Method	TF-IDF Method
诊断电流	48	280
诊断电流信号	46.51	180
器件	38.91	400
该器件	47.52	300
文档	43.5	76
本文档	31.68	55.68

4 Analysis of results

4.1 *The evaluation of the term extraction algorithms*

The following three generic indicators are analyzed to evaluate the term recognition performance: they are Precision Rate (P), Recall Rate (R) and F index, whereby

$$Precision\ Rate = \frac{terms\ identified\ correctly}{terms\ identified} \times 100\%$$

$$Recall\ Rate \frac{terms\ identified\ correctly}{actual\ number\ of\ terms} \times 100\%\ .$$

$$F_{\beta=1} = \frac{(\beta^2+1) \times Precision\ Rate \times Recall\ Rate}{\beta^2 \times Precision\ Rate + Recall\ Rate} \times 100\%$$

ββ is the relative weight between the precision rate and the recall rate: when β = 1, it shows that P and R are of the same importance; when β>1, it means that the precision rate is more important; when β<1, the recall rate is more important. β is generally set to be 1, 1/2 and 2, but typically, β value is set to be 1.

The Precision Rate (P), Recall Rate (R) and F index of the C-value algorithm are calculated as follows:

$$P = \frac{terms\ identified\ correctly}{terms\ identified} \times 100\% = \frac{983}{1663} \times 100\% = 59.11\%$$

$$R = \frac{terms\ identified\ correctly}{actual\ number\ of\ terms} \times 100\% = \frac{983}{1568} \times 100\% = 62.69\%$$

$$F_{\beta=1} = \frac{(\beta^2+1) \times Precision\ Rate \times Recall\ Rate}{\beta^2 \times Precision\ Rate + Recall\ Rate} \times 100\%$$

$$= \frac{(1+1) \times 0.5911 \times 0.6269}{1 \times 0.5911 + 0.6269} 100\% = 0.61$$

Likewise, we can get the Precision Rate (P), Recall Rate (R) and F index of the other three algorithms.

For convenience, the number of terms correctly identified is expressed as Num(r), the number of terms identified is expressed as Num(s), actual number of terms is expressed as Num(a), then formulas of precision rate P, recall rate R and F index are expressed as follows:

$$P = \frac{Num(r)}{Num(s)} \times 100\%$$

$$R = \frac{Num(r)}{Num(a)} \times 100\%$$

To clarify, the Precision Rate (P), Recall Rate (R) and F index of term extraction by BSCF should be evaluated separately. There are 95 texts in the corpus and due to the limited space, the results of 12 texts are listed in Table 4.5.

To facilitate the comparison on term recognition performance among those algorithms, number of the extracted terms is divided into three orders of magnitude, i.e. 16, 156 and 1568 as a benchmark, since the total number of terms extracted manually from the translation project is 1568. We choose 16 for the first order of magnitude because from one of the text in the corpus, 16 terms were extracted; and 156 is the maximum number of terms extracted from another single text. By using the four term extraction algorithms, we calculate on preprocessed text and get the following results which are shown in Table 4.6.

Table 4.6 shows the number of terms extracted by the four methods. On average, the results are satisfactory when extracting 16 terms. Comparatively, the C-value and the TF-IDF did the best while BSCF did the worst since the total number of terms and the number of valid terms extracted by BSCF method is lower than that by the other three algorithms.

Table 4.5 Results of terms extracted by BSCF in 12 texts

No.	Num(r)	Num(s)	Num(a)	Ps	Rs	F-score-s
1	31	35	43	88.57%	72.09%	0.79
2	51	66	58	77.27%	87.93%	0.82
3	33	44	47	75.00%	70.21%	0.73
4	27	45	37	60.00%	72.97%	0.66
5	26	31	32	83.87%	81.25%	0.83
6	72	87	90	82.76%	80.00%	0.81
7	42	54	46	77.78%	91.30%	0.84
8	27	35	29	77.14%	93.10%	0.84
9	15	18	22	83.33%	68.19%	0.75
10	24	31	30	77.42%	80.00%	0.79
11	60	67	69	89.55%	86.96%	0.88
12	44	56	62	78.57%	70.97%	0.75

Table 4.6 Results calculated by four methods when order of magnitude is 16

Algorithm	Num(r)	Num(s)	Num(a)	Ps	Rs	F-score-s
C-value	14	15	16	93.33%	87.50%	0.90
TF-IDF	14	15	16	93.33%	87.50%	0.90
BSCF	11	13	16	84.62%	68.75%	0.76
Hybrid	14	14	16	100.00%	87.50%	0.85

Table 4.7 Results calculated by the four methods when order of magnitude is 156

Algorithm	Num(r)	Num(s)	Num(a)	P/PM	R/RM	F-score/F-score-M
C-value	128	150	156	85.33%	82.05%	0.84
TF-IDF	120	151	156	79.47%	76.92%	0.78
BSCF	124	150	156	82.67%	79.49%	0.81
Hybrid	130	150	156	86.67%	83.33%	0.85

Table 4.8 Results calculated by four methods when order of magnitude is 1568

Algorithm	Num(r)	Num(s)	Num(a)	P/PM	R/RM	F-score/F-score-M
C-value	983	1663	1568	59.11%	62.69%	0.61
TF-IDF	1098	1609	1568	68.24%	70.03%	0.69
BSCF	1263	1574	1568	80.24%	80.55%	0.80
Hybrid	1332	1570	1568	84.84%	84.99%	0.85

To further test their performances, we increase the number by about one order of magnitude to 156. The results are shown in Table 4.7.

From Table 4.7, we can see that the results are also satisfactory when order of magnitude is set to 156. But we find that the TF-IDF algorithm is not as good as the other three algorithms since the precision rate, recall rate and F index are lower than that of the other three algorithms.

To test their performances even further, we increase the number of candidate terms by another order of magnitude, the results are presented in Table 4.8.

The results in Table 4.8 show that the total number of terms extracted by the four algorithms varies from 1663 to 1570; and the number of validated candidate terms varies from 983 to 1332. C-value has extracted the most number of terms but has the least number of validated terms, which means that many of the terms are false ones. It is interesting to note that the number of terms extracted by each method is larger than that of the reference list. The statistics show that the C-value and the TF-IDF have the lowest Precision Rate (P), Recall Rate (R) and F index scores, which indicates the C-value and TF-IDF have the lowest term recognition performance when the order of magnitude is set to 1568, while the hybrid algorithm has an excellent performance in dealing with volume term extraction. It is worth noting that the total number of terms (Num(s)) extracted by each algorithms is more than 1568. To describe the performance of each individual algorithm in greater details, we can make a more careful study of the following bar graphs.

From Figure 4.4, it can be seen that the term recognition performance of the C-value algorithm drastically decreases with the increasing order of magnitude. And the gap between its precision rate and recall rate narrows down, ending with the recall rate higher than its precision rate when the magnitude amounts to 1568.

The bar graph in Figure 4.5 is the results of the Precision Rate (P), Recall Rate (R) and F index of the TF-IDF algorithm when order of magnitude is 16, 156 and 1568. It demonstrates that the term recognition performance of the TF-IDF algorithm also decreases with the increasing of magnitude, but not as much as that of the C-value algorithm. And the difference between its precision rate and recall rate declines too, resulting in the recall rate being higher than its precision rate when the magnitude reaches 1568.

Figure 4.6 illustrates the results of term extraction performance of the BSCF algorithm.

From Figure 4.6 it can be noticed that the Precision Rate (P) decreases slowly when increasing order of magnitude, while the Recall Rate (R) and F index

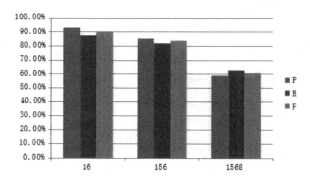

Figure 4.4 Results calculated by C-value

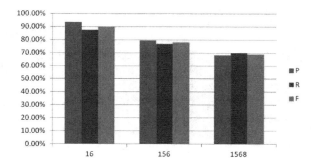

Figure 4.5 Results calculated by TF-IDF

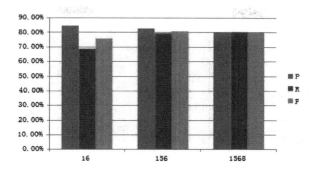

Figure 4.6 Results calculated by BSCF

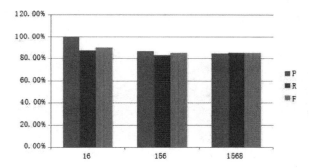

Figure 4.7 Results calculated by hybrid method

increase. The gap between the precision rate and recall rate is getting narrower and they are approximately the same when the magnitude arrives at 1568. It indicates that the performance of the BSCF algorithm remains relatively stable in term extraction.

The bar graph in Figure 4.7 shows the results of the term recognition performance of the hybrid algorithm. The Precision Rate (P) decreases from 100% to 86.67% and then to 84.84% when increasing the order of magnitude. Unlike the C-value and TF-IDF, it declines slowly and steadily with the increase of magnitude. The differences between the precision rate and recall rate decline as the magnitude increases, and they are almost of the same percentage when the magnitude reaches 1568.

4.2 Discussion

For a better comparison of the term extracting performance of the four methods, the results of precision at the different orders of magnitude of each are shown in a line graph in Figure 4.8.

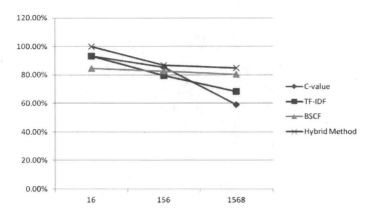

Figure 4.8 Precisions of the four methods at different orders of magnitude

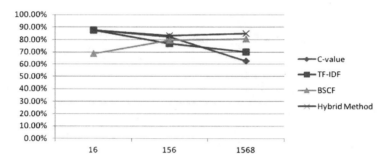

Figure 4.9 Recall of four methods at different orders of magnitude

With a first look at Figure 4.8, it can be noticed that all four methods have a decreasing trend in precision when increasing the order of magnitude for terms to be extracted. Precision of C-value drops significantly from 93.33% to 85.33% and then to 59.11%. TF-IDF comes in next, with its precision decreasing from 93.33% to 79.47% and then to 68.24%. Precision of BSCF remains relatively stable, decreasing from 84.62% to 82.67% and then to 80.24% but still remaining above 80%. Precision of the hybrid method remains the highest when increasing the order of magnitude for terms to be extracted, though it also has a decreasing trend, yet leads the other three.

Figure 4.9 compares the recall of the four methods. Considering the results of C-value and TF-IDF, it can be noticed that the two methods have a decreasing trend. Recall of C-value drops significantly from 87.5% to 82.5% and then to 62.69%. Recall of TF-IDF comes in next, decreasing from 87.5% to 76.92% and then to 70.03%. Recall of the hybrid method drops from 87.5% to 83.33% and then rises to 84.99%. Interestingly, only the recall of the BSCF method has an increasing trend, rising from 68.75% to 79.49% and then to 80.55%.

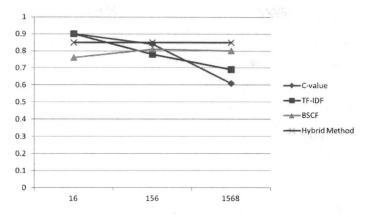

Figure 4.10 F indexes of four methods at different orders of magnitude

Figure 4.10 compares the F-index of the four methods in term extraction.

By a look at Figure 4.10, it can be noticed that the F varies in its trend. C-value and TF-IDF have a decreasing trend. F of C-value decreases significantly from 0.9 to 0.84 and then to 0.61. And F of TF-IDF drops from 0.9 to 0.78 and then to 0.69. Interestingly, it can be noticed that only the BSCF has a rising trend, with an increase from 0.76 to 0.8. Of all these methods, F of the hybrid method remains stable.

When considering all these measurable indicators, we have found if C-value and TF-IDF are employed separately in term extraction, the results of their performance are not satisfactory. Considering the results of precision, recall and F, the overall performance of BSCF is satisfactory. It is better than that of C-value and TF-IDF. When the C-value and TF-IDF are integrated for volume term extraction, the results of term extraction are significantly improved. It can be concluded that the hybrid method excels in contrast to any single method in terms of the Precision Rate (P), Recall Rate (R) and F index – the hybrid method leads the other three algorithms. The findings of the experiment verify and confirm our hypothesis of the research.

The reason why the C-value algorithm has a relatively poor performance in term extraction lies in the limitation of its algorithm. Lacking category processing of the candidate terms, it cannot exclude domain-independent words in the corpus, thus leaving a number of semantic-clear but domain-independent words in the corpus; the TF-IDF algorithm also extracts many redundant terms, but less than that of the C-value algorithm. Although its accuracy is higher than that of the C-value algorithm, it is still fairly low. Its drawbacks are also obvious because it does not consider word formation characteristics and it is likely to extract high-frequency function words. Statistics show BSCF leads C-value and TF-IDF in term recognition performance. But its shortcomings are also obvious. When checking the terms extracted by BSCF, we found there are a few false terms. Take "该", "器", "本" and "文" in the words "该器件","本文档"

for example; they are extracted as candidate terms due to their high frequency, and they are combined with great bonding strength, leading to erroneous identification. Another example is the verb-subject structure, like "操作器件", "检测电路"; although they have low frequency in the corpus, structures with strong bonding strength, are most likely to be recognized as candidate terms. So noise occurs. The method has relatively high accuracy compared with C-value and TF-IDF, but the operation is too complicated and time-consuming. By integrating the C-value and TF-IDF algorithms, the hybrid method has effectively improved the accuracy of term extraction and enhanced term recognition performance. The C-value in the hybrid method can overcome the shortcoming of TF-IDF in extracting low-frequency terms, while the TF-IDF algorithm can overcome the drawbacks of C-value.

4.3 Implications to developing term extraction tools

Now translation tools are widely used by translators to improve efficiency and quality, especially for translating technical documents. Some translation software provides a term extraction tool. However, in translation practice, project managers and translators are more likely to find the results of term extraction by the tool are not satisfactory. The problem lies in the algorithm on which the term extraction tool is based.

In view of the findings of the chapter, it is strongly recommended that a term extraction tool be based on multi-principles. Linguistic approaches can be integrated with statistical ones, or two more statistical methods can be integrated to guarantee the quality and efficiency of term extraction. The hybrid method in this experiment is one which makes comprehensive use of two statistical methods. The results show the hybrid method has advantages over a single method. As to what methods should be combined, it is necessary to weigh their merits and demerits so as to develop a term extraction tool with high performance and universal applicability.

5 Conclusion

The problems of term recognition of four term extraction algorithms have been fully discussed in this chapter by analyzing the data collected from an experiment. The overall performances of the hybrid method have been compared with other three methods. The experimental results show that the hybrid method is superior to the other three in terms of term recognition performance, universality and the amount of calculation. Therefore, it is strongly recommended that an integration of linguistic method, C-value algorithm and TF-IDF algorithm be used for the improvement of term extraction efficiency and quality in localization projects. For the solution of false recognition problems by BSCF, semantic analysis can be used to correctly identify the verb-object structure so as to improve the accuracy of term recognition. For improving the term extraction performance of the term extraction algorithm, there is still a long way to go. An integrated method or a hybrid approach may be a better solution. The authors hope that the findings of the chapter can be of some significance in developing term extraction tools and helping term extraction in localization projects.

References

Abasi, Mohsen and Mohammad Bagher Ghaznavi-Ghoushchi (2012) "Low-Power Themes Classifier (LPTC): A human-expert-based approach for classification of scientific papers/themes with low-power theme", *Intelligent Information Management* 4(6): 364–382.

Bowker, Lynne (2002) *Computer-Aided Translation Technology: A Practical Introduction*, Ottawa: University of Ottawa Press.

Cen, Yonghua, Han Zhe, and Ji Peipei (2008) "Chinese term recognition based on Hidden Markov Model", in Zhang Yanduo, Tan Honghua, and Luo Qi (eds.) *Proceedings: 2008 Pacific-Asia Workshop on Computational Intelligence and Industrial Application*, 172(12): 54–58.

Cohen, Jonathan D. (1995) "Highlights: Language- and domain-independent automatic indexing terms for abstracting", *Journal of the American Society for Information Science* 46(3): 162–174.

Frantzi, Katerina, Sophia Ananiadou, and Hideki Mima (2000) "Automatic recognition of multi-word terms: The C-value/NC-value method", *International Journal on Digital Libraries* 3(2): 115–130.

Gu, Jun and Wang Hao (2011) "Study on term extraction on the basis of Chinese domain texts", *New Technology of Library and Information Services* 204(4): 29–34.

ICTCLAS (2014) "NLPIR Chinese Word Segmentation", available from http://ictclas.nlpir.org/.

Keim, Daniel A., Daniela Oelke, and Christian Rohrdantz (2010) "Analyzing document collections via context-aware term extraction", in Helmut Horacek, Elisabeth Métais, Rafael Muñoz, and Magdalena Wolska (eds.) *Natural Language Processing and Information Systems*, Berlin and Heidelberg: Springer, 154–168.

Liang, Yinghong, Zhang Wenjing, and Zhang Youcheng (2010) "Term recognition based on integration of C-value and mutual information", *Computer Applications and Software* 27(4): 108–110.

Makoto, Nakatani, Adam Jatowt, Hiroaki Ohshima, and Katsumi Tanaka (2009) "Quality evaluation of search results by typicality and speciality of terms extracted from Wikipeida", in Chen Lei, Liu Chengfei, Liu Qing, and Deng Ke (eds.) *Database Systems for Advanced Applications*, Berlin and Heidelberg: Springer, 570–584.

Melby, Alan (2010) "Machine translation: The translation tripod", available from www.ttt.org/theory/mt4me/index.html.

Palshikar, Girish Keshav (2007) "Keyword extraction from a single document using centrality measures", in Ashish Ghosh, Rajat K. De, and Sankar K. Pal (eds.) *Pattern Recognition and Machine Intelligence*, Berlin and Heidelberg: Springer, 503–510.

Rezgui, Yacine (2007) "Text-based domain ontology building using TF-IDF and Metric Clusters Techniques", *The Knowledge Engineering Review* 22(4): 379–403.

Su, Chao (2012) "Rank aggregation-based automatic term recognition", *Computer Applications and Software* 29(1): 196–198, 223.

Xu, Chuan, Shi Shuicai, Fang Xiang, and Lü Xueqiang (2013) "Chinese patent terminology extraction", *Computer Engineering and Design* 34(6): 2175–2179.
Yang, Yingbo, Wang Weihua, and Cui Qiliang (2011) *A Guidance to Localization and Translation*, Beijing: Peking University Press.
Zhai, Dufeng and Liu Baisong (2010) "Automatic domain-specific term extraction in administrative-domain ontology", *New Technology of Library and Information Services* 4: 59–65.

5 Introducing corpus rhetoric into translation quality assessment

A case study of the white papers on China's national defense

Qian Duoxiu

1 Introduction

In 1998, China released its first White Paper on China's National Defense. Since then, this White Paper has been published regularly every two years. Due to the changes in international and national situations, each Paper has its own major concerns and addresses different issues. For example, the Paper in 2012 introduced the fundamental policies and principles followed by the diversified employment of China's armed forces.

The major topics for the White Papers include:

> safeguarding national sovereignty, security and territorial integrity, and supporting the country's peaceful development, formulating the concept of comprehensive security and effectively conducting military operations other than war, deepening security cooperation and fulfilling international obligations, and acting in accordance with laws, policies and disciplines.[1]

In order to make its policy accessible to the outside world, the Chinese government immediately releases the Paper in English and several other languages. In doing so, it is self-evident that the Chinese government wants to guarantee the accurate translation of the message to the global community and generate similar effects on the target readers in different languages exactly the way that the Chinese version of the White Papers has on the Chinese readers.

Based on the English translation of the Papers, the present paper will investigate how faithful the message has been to the original text in its rhetorical effect. It is the hope of the author that this case study will contribute to the assessment of translation from a new perspective, i.e. the persuasive effect of a translation in its call for similar actions when the message reaches the target audience.

2 Translation quality assessment: with a special view on the rhetorical "effect"

Translation quality assessment has been discussed from many perspectives. It has been particularly the concern of the linguistic approach to translation studies for a long time. Within this domain, this issue has been explored mainly at different levels to see how faithfully or creatively the linguistic features have been transferred across the language barrier into other languages.

Since the 1960s, the functional approach also has considered this as one of the most important issues. Reiss (1971/2000), House (1977, 1997) and many others have tried to tackle it based on criteria beyond the linguistic ones, such as pragmatic and text-typological measurements.

So far, however, there is still "no *operative* model of analysis for translation evaluation that is capable of bringing together textual, contextual and functionalist criteria, and that has been sufficiently validated by means of empirical experimental research" (Melis and Albir 2001: 274). Though some attempts have been made in domain-specific areas and some useful framework and steps have been provided (Qian 2006), more case studies are still needed to make translation quality assessment more accessible and more operative.

This is particularly true when people turn to the so-called "effect" of translation. Traditionally, "effect" in translation has been closely related to "equivalence." Much has been published on this subject. Nida and Taber (1969) stressed that a translation needs to be both dynamically and formally equivalent to the source text. They also clarified dynamic equivalence as being equivalent in effect which was initially rhetorically oriented. It was later elaborated and evolved into many different terms by other scholars from different perspectives (e.g., Newmark's communicative equivalence put forward in 1981 and 1988 respectively, Catford's shifts in 1965, Baker's pragmatic equivalence in 1992, and Pym's directional equivalence in 2010). The most recent attempts at effective translation were made by Boase-Beier (2006, 2011) from the stylistic approach. Boase-Beier (2006: 4) points out that "it is the style that enables [. . .] to express attitude and implied meanings, to fulfill particular functions, and to have effects on its readers." She argued that the evaluation of a translation should focus on examining whether it has achieved its intended conventional effects on readers. Further, Boase-Beier (2011) argued that, for a translator, understanding the style of the source text and being able to recreate similar stylistic effects in the target text are essential. In her words (2006: ii), style has a lot to do with issues such as "voice, otherness, foreignization, contextualization, and culturally-bound and universal ways of conceptualizing and expressing meaning."

It can be noted that the previous discussions are all about the equivalent effect of a translation on the target readers and have approached this topic mainly from the traditional linguistic viewpoints. Little has been done from the real rhetorical perspective, i.e., how successful a translation is in persuading its readers or arousing the same feelings in the readers and calling on them to take actions intended by the source text.

Therefore, this will be the research goal of the present chapter and the following sections will try to answer this question through a corpus-based rhetorical assessment of the English translation of the eight *White Papers on China's National Defense* published from 2000 to 2012.

3 Introducing corpus rhetoric into the study of the effect of translation

The study here will generally follow what has been done in corpus-based translation studies (cf. Baker 2000; Laviosa 1997, 1998a, 1998b; Olahan 2004).

A corpus will be built up and tools relevant to the research will be used. The results will be employed as auditing measures to see how faithful the translations are to the original texts in terms of the overall rhetorical effect, i.e., persuading readers or arousing similar feelings in them so as to call on them to take actions intended for the audience of the source text.

3.1 Corpus

Eight corpora in English are built up, consisting of the English version of the *White Papers on China's National Defense* published in 2000, 2002, 2004, 2006, 2006, 2008, 2010, and 2012, respectively. Altogether, there are 125,618 word tokens. Correspondingly, eight corpora in Chinese are also built up, consisting of 182,800 Chinese characters.

It is noted that the number of texts is too small a sample size for multivariate statistics with Minitab, which typically requires at least 30 observations per cell to approximate a normal distribution. Because of the large number of words per text, the eight English translations are split into 214 texts of approximately 550 words each. The eight original Chinese tests are retained for later comparison.

3.2 Tools to be used in rhetorical analysis

Two tools are used for the analysis of rhetorical features in the English translation and the evaluation of how faithful the translation has been to the original text in its overall rhetorical effect.

DocuScope is used for retrieving rhetorical features (words and phrases) in the translated text. The result will be exported to be further analyzed by Minitab for feature distribution and to see whether there are significant differences in each of the 17 variables identified by DocuScope.

DocuScope is a text analysis platform with a suite of interactive visualization tools for corpus-based rhetorical analysis. It was designed and developed by David Kaufer and Suguru Ishizaki at Carnegie Mellon University (Kaufer et al. 2004). The tool (Figure 5.1) has two main functions, MTV (Multiple Text Viewer, Figure 5.2) and STV (Single Text Viewer, Figure 5.3). They allow researchers to examine multiple texts and single text, respectively, for rhetorical features and identify the most frequently used words in English as well as the most frequently appearing 2–4 word combinations into strings classified by rhetorical effect. Each category of effect is broken down into specific functional features, called a "Language Action Type" (LAT). Each LAT is placed into a Dimension, which is further subsumed under a larger, superordinate cluster. Each LAT (Figure 5.3, Interactive) is underlined and color coded for analysis. In this way, researchers can use this tool for investigating the rhetorical effect of one single piece of text or for comparing the rhetorical effects of different groups of texts.

Its language measures cover a range of categories of rhetorical experience recognized by native speakers of English. These measures include the following 17 top-level categories (also see Figure 5.3):

> *Academic*: Texts high in this feature are full of specialized knowledge and abstract concepts.

Assertive: Texts high in this feature are full of confidence and power. First person pronouns are frequently used.

Descriptive: Texts high in this feature are full of visual and auditory language and appeal to the senses.

Directive: Texts high in this feature focus on directing others and are full of prescriptive or prohibitive language.

Elaborative: Texts high in this feature have in-depth exposition and/or are full of syntactic complexities.

Emotional: Texts high in this feature are full of positive or negative emotions.

Future: Texts high in this feature take a proactive attitude and are full of expressions with forward-looking implications.

Interactive: Texts high in this feature are full of inquiry, seek the audience's engagement, and need follow-up actions; second person pronouns are many. They often indicate intimacy with the audience.

Narrative: Texts high in this feature have chains of verbs and time expressions, building blocks of personal stories while providing background information.

Past: Texts high in this feature have the orientation focused on actions before the speech or text.

Persons: Texts high in this feature often refer to people; many personal pronouns, person-based descriptions and proper nouns are present.

Privy: Texts high in this feature tend to focus on inner thinking or feeling.

Public: Texts high in this feature focus on institutions, duty, order and responsibilities.

Reasoning: Texts high in this feature tend to be strong in logic and have many inferences between ideas.

Relations: Texts high in this feature focus on positive, negative and inclusive relationships.

Reporting: Texts high in this feature tend to use single verbs to indicate updates on the world at large.

Strategic: Texts high in this feature tend to demonstrate complex planning and to be keen on advantage-seeking.

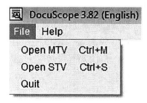

Figure 5.1 Main menu

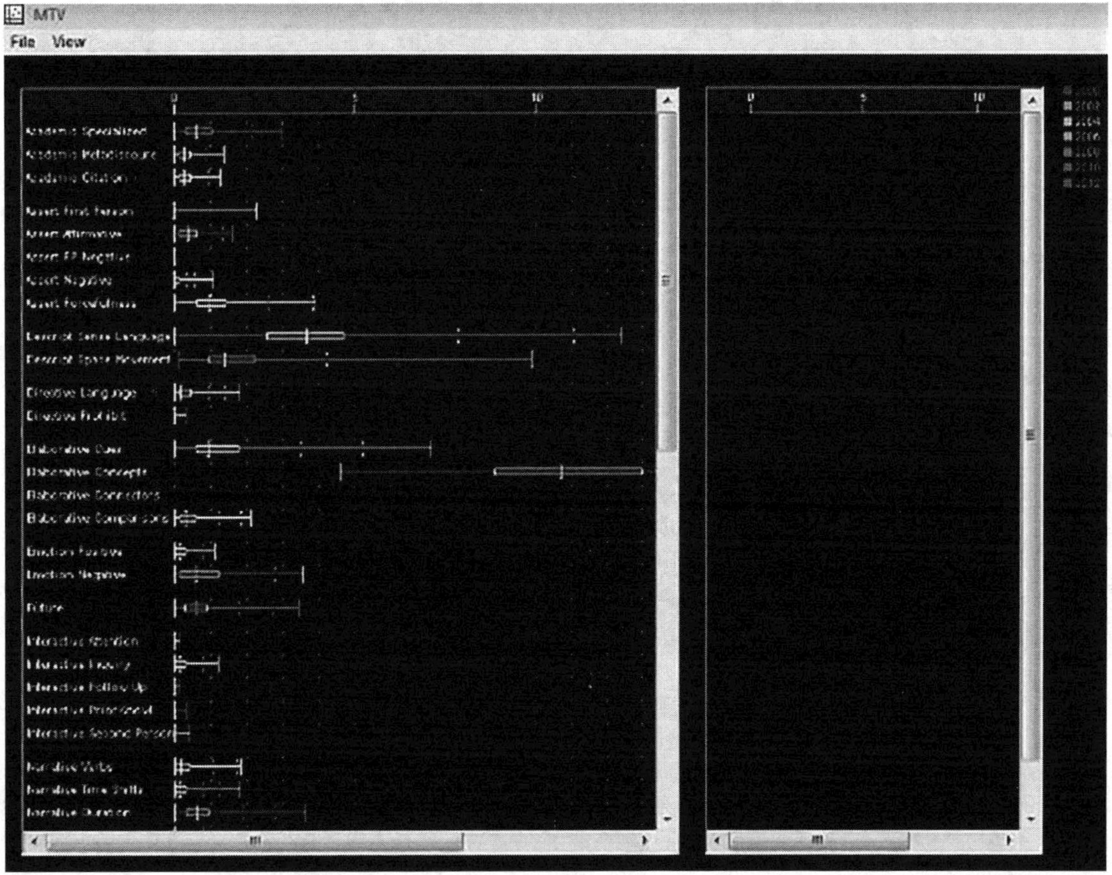

Figure 5.2 MTV

Figure 5.3 STV

The platform is supported by a dictionary consisting of over 40 million linguistic patterns of English classified into over 150 categories of rhetorical features. It has been used in a variety of studies in the rhetorical analysis of social-political texts (Collins et al. 2004; Kaufer and Ishizaki 2006; Kaufer and Hariman 2008; Kaufer and Al-Malki 2009; Ishizaki and Kaufer 2012). Hope and Witmore (2004) use this too to support peer-reviewed research on the rhetoric of Shakespeare and other modern texts, indicating this is also applicable in literary studies.

In Translation Studies, it has been used to analyze translated news stories from Arab journalism (Al-Malki et al. 2012). It proves very useful to track rhetorical effects in translated international news.

Another tool to be used is Minitab (Version 17) which has many statistical functions. In this study, ANOVA (one-way) and Multivariate Factor Analysis will be used to find out the most striking features in each category.

3.3 How to do the analysis

Using DocuScope, the 214 translated texts are tagged for rhetorical features drawn from the measures given previously and analyzed. Then DocuScope tags

Table 5.1 Factor analysis result and the relative strengths of positive and negative factors

Factors and square sums	Positive and square sums	Negative and square sums
Factor 1 2.63	Relations, Emotional, Assertive, Privy, Future 2.23	Past, Elaborative 0.40
Factor 2 1.63	Public, Elaborative 0.58	Past, Reporting, Narrative 1.05
Factor 3 1.01	Strategic, Descriptive, Directive 1.01	none 0

are exported to a statistical package for factor analysis, which organizes the texts of the corpus into "factors" or "rhetorical strategies." These factors or strategies are linear combinations of rhetorical variables that are highly inter-correlated within a factor but not across factors.

Factor analyzing the 214 texts yields three linear combinations of the measures, also known as factors or rhetorical strategies. The three rhetorical strategies consist of the factors below. Variables with positive values have a high positive loading on the factor, while variables with negative values have a high negative loading. Variables that share the same sign are positively correlated, while variables that have different signs are negatively correlated. The details are provided in Table 5.1.

This analysis consists of calculating the relative strengths of the factors by taking a total sum of squares of the coefficient weights loaded on each factor. This analysis finds that the total sums of squares of the three factors are 2.63, 1.63 and 1.01, respectively. The positives for the three factors are 2.23, 0.58 and 1.01, respectively. Therefore, a summary of the factors can be made below.

> Factor 1:Positive (Relations, Emotional, Assertive, Privy, Future) plays the leading role.
> Factor 2:Negative (Past, Reporting, Narrative) plays the leading role.
> Factor 3:Positive (Strategic, Descriptive, Directive) plays the only dominant role.

Since it's self-evident that the White Papers discussed in this chapter are mainly about things in the past, Factor 2 is of little significance and can be left aside. Further analysis of the variances and weights of the factors reveals that Factors 1 and 3 are the most important strategies to be explained and so they are the focus here.

3.4 Findings and interpretation

Based on the above factor analysis, it can be found that the White Papers are concerned about both international and domestic affairs, confident about the years before and ahead, with many expressions to either positively or negatively express the feelings of the Chinese people and to express a desire to concentrate on its own development without interfering in another's affairs (Factor 1). Another striking feature of the White Papers is that they are very forward-looking, full of plans for the coming years, and full of specifics of what should be done and what is going to happen (Factor 2).

The next sections will be an evaluation of how faithful the translation has been in arousing the feelings and calling on people for actions so that this evaluation can be used for further assessment of the translation.

3.5 Looking back at the Chinese text and its segmentation for rhetorical effect analysis

As in English, there are mainly three ways of segmenting Chinese into its smallest lexical unit. First, there are single characters that can be used only as bound morphemes, such as 化 (hua,[2] meaning "transform, -isation") in 全球化 (quan qiu hua, meaning "globalization") and 观 (guan, meaning "view") in 安全观 (an quan guan, meaning "security view") as suffixes. Second, there are single characters that can be used as free morphemes, such as 有 (you, meaning "have"), 将 (jiang, meaning "will"). Finally, there are multi-character compound expressions that can be used as free morphemes. A huge number of Chinese expressions belong to this type, such as 执行 (zhi xing, literally translated into English as "carry" and "practice", meaning "carry out"), 国防 (guo fang, literally translated into English as "nation" and "defense", meaning "national defense"), 加强 (jia qiang, literally translated into English as "add" and "strength", meaning "strengthen"), 军事 (jun shi, literally translated into English as "military" and "affairs", meaning "military affairs"), and 人民解放军 (ren min jie fang jun, literally translated into English as "human," "people," "free," "liberate," and "army," meaning "People's Liberation Army"). Below is one example to show how this works in both languages.

> 新 世纪 以来, 世界 发生 深刻 复杂 变化,
> New century since world take place profound complex change
> 和平 与 发展 仍然 是 时代 主题。
> Peace and development still is era theme
>
> (2012)
>
> (English version: Since the beginning of the new century, profound and complex changes have taken place in the world, but peace and development remain the underlying trends of our times.)

The rhetorical strategies used in this sample segment are analyzed by DocuScope in Figure 5.4.

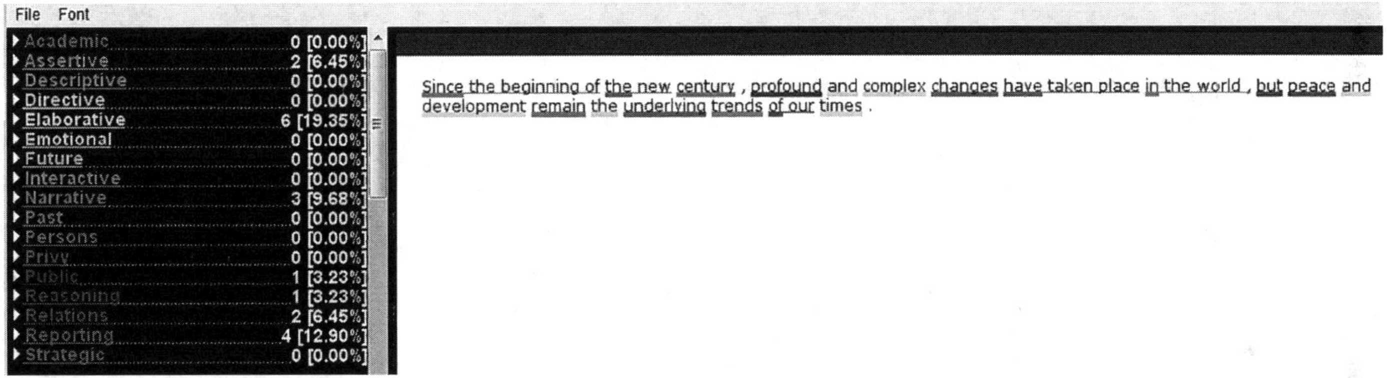

Figure 5.4 DocuScope STV sample analysis

As Figure 5.4 shows, there are 2 Assertive (in the world, trends), 6 Elaborative (and, complex, and, development, the, times), 3 Narrative (since, the century, remain), 1 Public (profound), 1 Reasoning (but), 2 Relations (peace, of our) and 4 Reporting (the new, changes, have, underlying) expressions.

3.6 Procedures of evaluating the translation's faithfulness in rhetorical effects

To be more specific, a demonstration of how DocuScope can be used as an auditing tool to evaluate the translation's overall rhetorical effect is provided.

There are basically three steps. Step 1 is to segment the Chinese text, followed by its English literal translation, with its rhetorical strategy identified using DocuScope coding scheme. Step 2 is to check whether the rhetorical strategies in both the translation and the original text correspond to each other. Step 3 is to arrive at a conclusion on the overall correspondence in the rhetorical effect of a segment in both texts.

Take one sentence in the segment which is of the highest value in Strategic (positive) as an example (2012).

> It is accelerating the development of army aviation troops, light mechanized units and special <u>operations</u> forces, and enhancing building of digitalized units, gradually making its units small, modular and multi-functional in organization so as to enhance their capabilities for air-ground integrated <u>operations</u>, long-distance <u>maneuvers</u>, rapid assaults and special <u>operations</u>.

In this sentence alone, words and expressions like "operation" and "maneuver" (underlined) appear several times to let the readers have ideas about China's strategic goals, acts and logistics in this very specific aspect.

Another example is taken from the same year (2012) for detailed analysis. For the convenience of presentation, it is split into two parts (Tables 5.2 and 5.3). The DocuScope rhetorical analysis of the two parts is in Figure 5.5, where it is shown that there are 7 Descriptive, 1 Directive, 25 Elaborative, 1 Emotional, 1 Future, 1 Privy, 8 Public, 1 Reasoning, 3 Relations, 4 Reporting and 7 Strategic expressions.

In this first part of a segment, the rhetorical effect of each constituent can be identified and helps to confirm that the identification process is similar to that in English as demonstrated by DocuScope. The second part of the segment is analyzed below in Table 5.3.

[Full English version of the whole segment: In line with the requirements of its offshore defense strategy, the PLAN endeavors to accelerate the modernization of its forces for comprehensive offshore operations, develop advanced submarines, destroyers and frigates, and improve integrated electronic and information systems. Furthermore, it develops blue-water capabilities of conducting mobile operations, carrying out international cooperation, and countering non-traditional security threats, and enhances its capabilities of strategic deterrence and counterattack.]

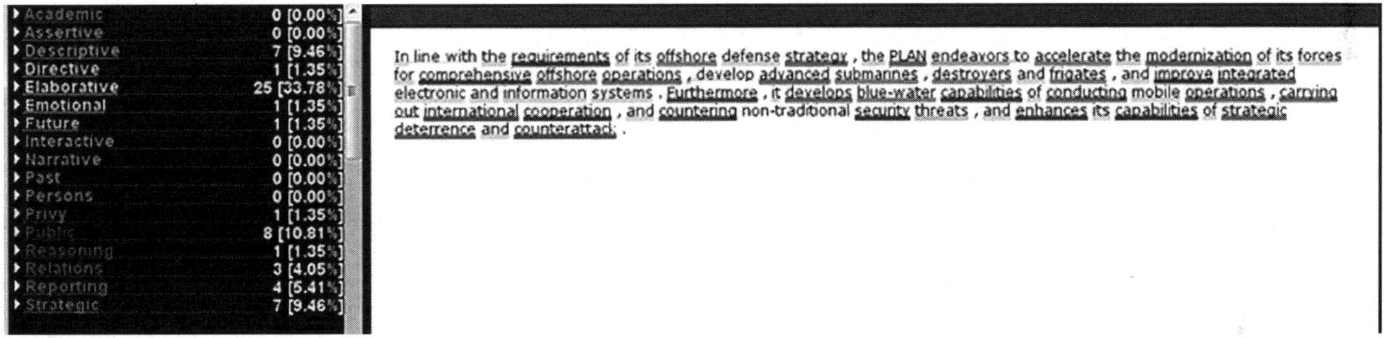

▲ Academic	0 [0.00%]
▲ Assertive	0 [0.00%]
▲ Descriptive	7 [9.46%]
▲ Directive	1 [1.35%]
▲ Elaborative	25 [33.78%]
▲ Emotional	1 [1.35%]
Future	1 [1.35%]
▲ Interactive	0 [0.00%]
▲ Narrative	0 [0.00%]
Past	0 [0.00%]
▲ Persons	0 [0.00%]
Privy	1 [1.35%]
▲ Public	8 [10.81%]
▲ Reasoning	1 [1.35%]
▲ Relations	3 [4.05%]
▲ Reporting	4 [5.41%]
▲ Strategic	7 [9.46%]

In line with the requirements of its offshore defense strategy, the PLAN endeavors to accelerate the modernization of its forces for comprehensive offshore operations, develop advanced submarines, destroyers and frigates, and moreover integrated electronic and information systems. Furthermore, it develops blue-water capabilities of conducting mobile operations, carrying out international cooperation, and countering non-traditional security threats, and enhances its capabilities of strategic deterrence and counterattack.

Figure 5.5 Sample demonstration of DocuScope identification

Table 5.2 Chinese segmented and rhetoric strategies explained (Part 1)

Chinese expression (pin-yin annotated)	English literal translation of each constituent	Rhetorical strategy using DocuScope coding scheme
按照 [an zhao]	in line with	Elaborative
近海 [jin hai]	offshore	Descriptive
防御 [fang yu]	defense	Elaborative
的 [de]	of	Elaborative
战略 [zhan lue]	strategy	Strategic
要求 [yao qiu]	requirements	Public
海军 [hai jun]	navy	Public
注重 [zhu zhong]	stress, endeavor	Future
提高 [ti gao]	enhance	Public
近海 [jin hai]	offshore	Descriptive
综合 [zong he]	integrated	Elaborative
作战 [zuo zhan]	combat, operation	Strategic
力量 [li liang]	forces	Elaborative
现代 [xian dai] 化 [hua]	modernization	Reporting
水平, [shui ping]	level, capability	Public
发展 [fa zhan]	develop	Reporting
先进 [xian jin]	advanced	Strategic
潜艇、[qian] [ting]	submarine boat	Descriptive
驱逐舰、[qu zhu] [jian]	drive away, dispel ship	Descriptive
护卫 舰[hu wei] [jian]	defense ship	Descriptive
等 [deng]	etc.	Elaborative
装备, [zhuang bei]	equipment	Descriptive

Table 5.3 Chinese segmented and rhetoric strategies explained (Part 2)

Chinese expression (pin-yin annotated)	English literal translation of each constituent	Rhetorical strategy using DocuScope coding scheme
完善 [wan shan]	improve	Public
综合 [zong he]	comprehensive	Public
电子 [dian zi]	electronic	Elaborative
信息 [xin xi]	information	Elaborative
系统 [xi tong]	system	Elaborative
装备 [zhuang bei]	equipment	Descriptive
体系 [ti xi]	overall system	Elaborative
提高 [ti gao]	enhance	Public
远海 [yuan hai]	international	Relations
机动 [ji dong]	mobile	Elaborative
作战 [zuo zhan]	combat, operation	Strategic
远海 [yuan hai]	international	Relations
合作 [he zuo]	cooperation	Public
与 [yu]	and	Elaborative
应对 [ying dui]	countering, in response to	Relations

Chinese expression (pin-yin annotated)	English literal translation of each constituent	Rhetorical strategy using DocuScope coding scheme
非 [fei] 传统 [chuan tong]	non-traditional	Academic
安全 [an quan]	security	Public
威胁 [wei xie]	threat	Emotional
能力 [neng li]	capability	Public
增强 [zeng qiang]	enhance	Public
战略 [zhan lue]	strategic	Strategic
威慑 [wei she]	deterrence	Privy
与 [yu]	and	Elaborative
反击 [fan ji]	counter-attack	Relations
能力。[neng li]	capability	Public

3.7 Further findings and discussion

After the analysis of Chinese source text and the explanation of the rhetorical strategies used, it can be safely concluded that this whole segment is on the whole, very strategic, descriptive and public. It takes a forward-looking attitude towards the modernization of its forces for both off-shore and international operations. In the meantime, it provides many specific details on what is to be done in various aspects to help the goals materialize. The English version closely corresponds to the original one in its rhetorical effect.

A simple statistic summary (Table 5.4) of the number of rhetorical strategies in the White Papers (2000–2012) and a close comparison of representative segments in the other 16 rhetorical categories further testify that as high as 95% of the rhetorical features in the English translation can find their correspondents in the original texts.

According to Xinhua News Agency, China's State Media, the White Paper on China's National Defense in 2012 says "China advocates a new security concept featuring mutual trust, mutual benefit, equality and coordination, and pursues comprehensive security, common security and cooperative security."[3]

Again, a simple statistical summary and a close reading of the White Paper in 2012 helps to find out that this view is a very true synopsis of the 2012 version (Figure 5.6).

Apart from Descriptive, Elaborative, Narrative, Past and Reporting, which are unsurprisingly frequently appearing expressions for white papers, there are 834 Descriptive, 375 Persons, 959 Public, 291 Relations and 427 Strategic expressions. The high frequency of such expressions guarantees the readers to have a strong feeling that this text is about detailed information exchange (Descriptive) on military affairs (Strategic) between different parties (Public, Relations) in a not so frigid manner (Persons). It is mainly concerned about international and strategic affairs (Public, Relations, Strategic). The numerous specifics provided (Descriptive) also allow the readers to have confidence about the information on China's national defense and thus create trust.

96 *Qian Duoxiu*

Table 5.4 Number of rhetorical devices in the White Papers (2000–2012)

Categorization	2000	2002	2004	2006	2008	2010	2012	Total
Academic	290	313	336	229	291	278	126	1863
Assertive	374	363	387	264	363	294	183	2228
Descriptive	855	1221	1328	1076	1391	1254	834	7959
Directive	55	61	51	62	97	64	55	445
Elaborative	5766	6515	7839	5687	7525	7126	3307	43765
Emotional	231	208	214	150	235	213	147	1398
Future	147	151	163	107	137	130	87	922
Interactive	44	60	68	33	68	41	23	337
Narrative	287	327	404	278	389	369	193	2247
Past	160	138	208	141	224	186	54	1111
Persons	494	578	1202	652	640	765	375	4705
Privy	143	156	136	89	140	114	73	851
Public	1509	1742	2130	1422	1879	2078	959	11718
Reasoning	111	99	148	62	87	65	69	641
Relations	425	436	373	279	413	524	291	2741
Reporting	1788	1973	2439	1770	2306	2158	1031	13465
Strategic	425	541	668	516	699	693	427	3969

```
China's National Defence-2012.txt
File  Font
▶ Academic ............................... 126 [1.08%]
▶ Assertive .............................. 183 [1.57%]
▶ Descriptive ............................ 834 [7.15%]
▶ Directive ............................... 55 [0.47%]
▶ Elaborative .......................... 3307 [28.36%]
▶ Emotional ............................ 147 [1.26%]
▶ Future ................................... 87 [0.75%]
▶ Interactive ............................. 23 [0.20%]
▶ Narrative .............................. 193 [1.66%]
▶ Past ...................................... 54 [0.46%]
▶ Persons ................................ 375 [3.22%]
▶ Privy ..................................... 73 [0.63%]
▶ Public .................................. 959 [8.23%]
▶ Reasoning ............................. 69 [0.59%]
▶ Relations ............................. 291 [2.50%]
▶ Reporting ........................... 1031 [8.84%]
▶ Strategic ............................. 427 [3.66%]
```

Figure 5.6 DocuScope analysis of the White Paper in 2012

As to the high degree of faithfulness, it can be explained by the fact that the translation is prepared each time by a panel of translators who work for the government's various translation agencies.[4] Because of the sensitivity of the information in the White Papers here, little is known about who is involved in the process. The speculation is that the translation is usually done by senior translators and then reviewed many times before its release.

4 Conclusion

In Translation Studies, quality assessment has always been one of the most debated topics. The overall rhetorical effect, that is, how successful the translation is in calling the audience for similar actions intended for the audience of the source text, has been particularly hard to understand and under-researched.

Based on what has been analyzed and discussed in the previous sections, the present study comes to the conclusion that the overall rhetorical effect of a translation as a text for intercultural communication can be quantitatively measured and evaluated. Though it is still elusive to gauge the effect a translated text has on its target readers, through this case study based on a small corpus, it is shown how translation, as a tool for inter-cultural communication, also enables the text to express attitudes, implied meanings, fulfill particular functions and have effects on the target readers (Boase-Beier 2006: 4).

The present study is an early attempt at exploring how a translation can accomplish the abovementioned goal. Rhetorically speaking, both language and translation are for effective communication. This method therefore could be applied in various linguistic and translational studies for rhetorical effect.

Future research can be conducted along the following lines. First, large-scale corpora can be built up for similar case studies to see whether regularities can be arrived at for at least some specific domains where effective communication and call for action is the focus. Second, like previous studies on translation, close reading and comparison of the texts involved should be advocated so as to have practical implications for translation and its evaluation. Third, pedagogical studies can be conducted to see how such findings can be applied in translator training to draw both trainer and trainee's attention to this much-neglected aspect so as to promote better inter-cultural communication.

Acknowledgements

The author wants to express thankfulness to China National Foundation for Social Sciences (award reference 11BYY015) and to Fulbright Program (2014–2015) for support. The author also feels indebted to David Kaufer of Carnegie Mellon University for the use of DocuScope.

Notes

1 http://news.xinhuanet.com/english/china/2013-04/16/c_132312555.htm, retrieved on 26 April 2015.
2 All Chinese characters are followed by full pinyin, literal translation into English, and meaning.
3 "China issues white paper on national defense", available from http://news.xinhuanet.com/english/china/2013-04/16/c_132313390.htm, retrieved on 1 May 2015.
4 There are several government agencies for the translation of government documents. They include Central Compilation and Translation Bureau, China Translation and Publishing Corporation, and the most recently (July 2014) established Chinese Translation Academy.

References

Al-Malki, Amal, David Kaufer, Suguru Ishizaki, and Kira Dreher (2012) *Arab Women in Arab News: Old Stereotypes and New Media*, Doha: Bloomsbury Academic.

Baker, Mona (2000) "Towards a methodology for investigating the style of a literary translator", *Target: International Journal of Translation Studies* 12(2): 241–266.

Boase-Beier, Jean (2006) *Stylistics Approaches to Translation*, Manchester: St. Jerome Publishing.

Boase-Beier, Jean (2011) "Stylistics and translation", in Yves Gambier and Luc van Doorslaer (eds.) *Handbook of Translation Studies*, Amsterdam and Philadelphia: John Benjamins Publishing Company, 2: 153–156.

Catford, John (1965) *A Linguistic Theory of Translation: An Essay in Applied Linguistics*, Oxford: Oxford University Press.

Collins, Jeff, David Kaufer, Pantelis Vlachos, Brian Butler, and Suguru Ishizaki (2004) "Detecting collaborations in text comparing the authors' rhetorical language choices in the Federalist Papers", *Computers and the Humanities* 38(1): 15–36.

Hope, Jonathan and Michael Witmore (2004) "The very large textual object: A prosthetic reading of Shakespeare", *Early Modern Literary Studies* 9.3 / Special Issue 12 (January 2004): 6.1–36, available from http://purl.oclc.org/emls/09-3/hope whit.htm.

House, Juliane (1977) *A Model for Translation Quality Assessment*, Tübingen: Gunter Narr Verlag.

House, Juliane (1997) *Translation Quality Assessment: A Model Revisited*, Tubingen: Gunter Narr Verlag.

Ishizaki, Suguru and David Kaufer (2012) "Computer-aided rhetorical analysis", in Philip M. McCarthy and Chutima C. Boonthum-Deneche (eds.) *Applied Natural Language Processing: Identification, Investigation, and Resolution*, Hershey, PA: Information Science Reference, 276–296.

Kaufer, David and Amal M. Al-Malki (2009) "The war on terror through Arab-American eyes: The Arab-American Press as a rhetorical counterpublic", *Rhetoric Review* 28(1): 47–65.

Kaufer, David and Robert Hariman (2008) "A corpus analysis evaluating Hariman's theory of political style", *Text and Talk* 28(4): 475–500.

Kaufer, David and Suguru Ishizaki (2006) "A corpus study of canned letters: Mining the latent rhetorical proficiencies marketed to writers in a hurry and non-writers", *IEEE Transactions on Professional Communication* 49(3): 254–266.

Kaufer, David, Suguru Ishizaki, Brian Butler, and Jeff Collins (2004) *The Power of Words: Unveiling the Speaker and Writer's Hidden Craft*, London and New York: Routledge.

Laviosa-Braithwaite, Sara (1997) "Investigating simplification in an English comparable corpus of newspaper articles", in Kinga Klaudy and Janos Kohn (eds.) *Transferre Necesse Est. Proceedings of the 2nd International Conference on Current Trends in Studies of Translation and Interpreting*, 5–7 September 1996, Budapest, Hungary, Budapest: Scholastica, 531–540.

Laviosa-Braithwaite, Sara (1998a) "The corpus-based approach: A new paradigm in translation studies", in Sara Laviosa (ed.) *L'Approche Basée sur le corpus/The Corpus-Based Approach*, Special Issue of *Meta* 43(4): 474–479.

Laviosa-Braithwaite, Sara (1998b) "Core patterns of lexical use in a comparable corpus of English narrative prose", in Sara Laviosa (ed.) *L'Approche Basée sur le corpus/The Corpus-Based Approach*, Special Issue of *Meta* 43(4): 557–570.

Melis, Nicole Martinez and Amparo Hurtado Albir (2001) "Assessment in translation studies: Research needs", *Meta* 46(2): 272–287.
Newmark, Peter (1981) *Approaches to Translation*, Oxford and New York: Pergamon Press.
Newmark, Peter (1988) *A Textbook of Translation*, New York: Prentice Hall.
Nida, Eugene A. and Charles R. Taber (1969) *The Theory and Practice of Translation, With Special Reference to Bible Translating*, Leiden: Brill.
Olohan, Maeve (2004) *Introducing Corpora in Translation Studies*, London and New York: Routledge.
Pym, Anthony (2010) *Exploring Translation Theories*, London and New York: Routledge.
Qian, Duoxiu (2006) "A computer-aided approach to accuracy in Chinese-English pharmacological translation: The pharmacopoeia of the people's republic of China as a case study", PhD Thesis, Hong Kong: The Chinese University of Hong Kong.
Reiss, Katherina (1971/2000) *Translation Criticism, The Potentials and Limitations: Categories and Criteria for Translation Quality Assessment*, translated by Erroll Franklin Rhodes, Manchester: St. Jerome Publishing.

WHITE PAPERS

China's National Defense in 2000, available from http://eng.mod.gov.cn/Database/WhitePapers/2000.htm
China's National Defense in 2002, available from http://eng.mod.gov.cn/Database/WhitePapers/2002.htm
China's National Defense in 2004, available from http://eng.mod.gov.cn/Database/WhitePapers/2004.htm
China's National Defense in 2006, available from http://eng.mod.gov.cn/Database/WhitePapers/2006.htm
China's National Defense in 2008, available from http://eng.mod.gov.cn/Database/WhitePapers/2008.htm
China's National Defense in 2010, available from http://eng.mod.gov.cn/Database/WhitePapers/2010.htm
China's National Defense in 2012, available from http://eng.mod.gov.cn/Database/WhitePapers/2012.htm

6 Evaluating term extraction tools

System performance vs user perception

Olivia Kwong Oi Yee

1 Introduction

Under the umbrella of translation technology, there is a category of tools, including terminology management software and term extraction systems, which aims at facilitating translators' work in handling the recognition and accurate translation of terminology (Bowker 2002). Terminology management software capitalises on database design principles for more systematic storage of terms with other relevant terminographic data in the form of termbases and to subsequently allow efficient retrieval and effective maintenance of the data. Term extraction systems make use of linguistic and/or statistical methods to extract potential terms from some given text, or corpus as more generally called these days, and possibly their target equivalents in the bilingual context. Automatic term extraction tools thus often mean to offer a jump start to the construction of termbases. They may exist in the form of stand-alone applications or a component in a suite of computer-aided translation (CAT) software. For instance, SDL MultiTerm Extract is available as an independent product while it can be used in connection with many other products in the SDL family like SDL MultiTerm (for building and managing termbases). On the other hand, some other computer-aided translation tools, like MemoQ and Déjà Vu, include term extraction as a function within an integrated translation environment which may also house other functions like translation memory and bilingual alignment.

As with most other computer-aided translation tools, term extraction tools do not always invite positive comments when they enter into the market. This is evident from user feedbacks obtained from classrooms and those posted on the internet. The situation, however, is not quite in concord with the many encouraging results reported from natural language processing studies on automatic term extraction all along.

While system performance could be objectively measured with reference to some benchmarking data, the reliability and validity of such quantitative measures are based on the assumption that a clear task definition exists. As far as term extraction is concerned, one must state what terms are and which expressions should or should not be extracted as terms for the task to be well defined. According to Sager (1990), terminology is the study of and the field of activity concerned with the collection, description, processing and presentation of terms, i.e. lexical items belonging to specialised areas of usage of one or more languages. In this context, terms refer to linguistic and symbolic expressions used for special purposes among experts within a certain domain, for precise and accurate communication of the concepts and relations specific to their area of expertise. A term is therefore distinguished from a word by its special denotation and usage within a given domain. This often sounds convincingly good at the theoretical level. In practice, however, the boundary between terms and words is often blurred. The actual object of study may vary in the eyes of people working in different disciplines like linguistics, philosophy and technology, and those who have more theoretical or applied goals, like terminologists and translators respectively (Cabré 1996). Similar approaches may be used by computational linguists for translation lexicon extraction and term extraction, with some additional filtering to remove the relatively common expressions for the latter. On the other hand, most professional translators, in addition to using published specialised dictionaries and official glossaries, often also keep and accumulate their own glossaries for handy reference. Such private bilingual lexicons may include both domain-specific terms and commonly used expressions. Translators may expect term extraction tools to help collect translation equivalents from text to facilitate their keeping of a glossary, perhaps without too much regard on distinguishing terms from words in a strict sense, or simply thinking that the tool could do that by default.

Most translators of the new generation would have come across some computer-aided translation tools in one way or another when they receive their translation training (Bowker 2015). Such first-time hands-on experience is often critical to their faith in translation technology for the rest of their translation career. Given that most translators are used to keeping their own glossaries, term extraction tools must have some other advantages to offer for translators to find them useful. As most term extraction tools will output a list of term candidates, the value of such tools to translators thus heavily depends on how clean the output is. In other words, it is critical whether the time saved from automating the term collection step outweighs the effort to be spent subsequently on cleaning up the suggested term list. Noise is inevitable, but whether it could be controlled within a tolerable level and what such a tolerable level to the users would be are important issues to consider. In this regard, system evaluation should not only be done by quantitative measures but also take user expectation into account.

The general software development cycle applies to translation technology, where the testing phase may involve white-box testing and black-box testing. This chapter takes term extraction as an example, and discusses the performance of term extraction tools from different perspectives, including those of the researchers, software developers and end users. We aim at uncovering the discrepancy in the expectation of these different parties and thus reconciling their perception of term extraction tools, to advance further development of the tools based on such mutual understanding.

In the rest of this chapter, for bilingual term extraction we are mainly concerned with English-Chinese term extraction, and term extraction tools are discussed in their generic sense without reference to any particular system, although specific software products may be mentioned for illustration. In Section 2, we take an overview of the operation flow in most existing term extraction tools for translators. In Section 3, we introduce the various stakeholders, putting ourselves in their shoes to explore their respective views on the tools. In Section 4, we discuss how standard evaluation measures applied to automatic term extraction match or mismatch the perspectives of various parties and suggest a more comprehensive evaluation with user expectations taken into account. The situation is exemplified with a pilot case study in Section 5, followed by some concluding remarks and recommendations in Section 6.

2 Automatic term extraction tools: the norms

Whether as a stand-alone application or a function available within a more general-purpose computer-aided translation system, automatic term extraction tools usually operate with the following work flow:

(1) Take a set of monolingual/bilingual text as input

The term extraction system will usually take a set of text provided by the user as input and extract terms from it. Most tools nowadays often allow a variety of file format such as. rtf,. doc,. pdf and. xml, in addition to the conventional plain text files. The extraction performance would depend on the size of the input text to a certain extent, especially if the extraction is statistically based, although the actual impact is often opaque to the user. For bilingual term extraction, users often have extra work in preparing bilingually aligned text for input. The aligned text will have to be in specific format such as Translation Memory eXchange (.tmx) format. For instance, bilingual texts in other formats like. doc will only be treated as monolingual ones by SDL MultiTerm Extract. To this end, the general users might need to make use of other tools (e.g. SDL Trados) to do the alignment and save/export the aligned sentences in the required format beforehand, which is a time-consuming step, while the more automatic alignment toolkits like GIZA++ (Och and Ney 2003) may even be deterrent to them. The extra pre-processing steps thus tend to keep users away, especially those who are less comfortable with computer-aided work.

(2) Run some algorithm over the text

To most users, this step is just a click of button. The details of the algorithm used by a particular tool are usually unknown to the general users. In other words, the system operates in a black box to them. Although many a time users might be told that a certain tool makes use of a statistical algorithm to come up with the term candidates, which is almost the norm of modern term extraction tools, the algorithms adopted in individual systems could have different degrees of sophistication, and this is often at least partially disclosed from the results they generate. The more computer-literate users are often able to get a clue from the output to reverse engineer the mechanism by which the tools work. For example, some tools relying primarily on simple n-gram frequencies without paying much attention to linguistic validity (e.g. phrasal structures) may output incomplete or ungrammatical word strings among the extraction results.

(3) Output a list of term candidates

Results generated by the algorithm would usually be in the form of a list of term candidates. Some expressions captured in the list are genuine terms, while the rest of the list will be considered to contain non-terms, more technically known as "noise". The term-to-noise ratio is therefore a primary criterion for evaluating the performance or usefulness of the term extraction tool. Some tools may allow the user to adjust this ratio, which would directly affect the number of potential terms to be returned. Research efforts on reducing the noise ratio will be further discussed in the next section. Most term extraction tools will show a list of term candidates, ranked by some score such as frequency and mutual information. Bilingual term candidates may include multiple potential translation equivalents.

(4) Allow the user to verify/edit the potential terms

Users would then be asked to verify the suggested terms and edit them as necessary. Some tools provide concordance from the original input text for users to check the actual usage and to decide whether a suggested expression qualifies as a term. Users may indicate their decision with check boxes or similar means, while in most cases they will have to go through every single suggested term to finish the task. The ease of this step would certainly depend on the number of candidate terms returned by the system as well as the noise ratio.

(5) Save/Export the validated terms

The filtered or validated terms are then saved or exported in the preferred format, including plain text (tab delimited) or. xml among others. Such export functions allow portability of the extracted terms to other computer-aided translation tools. For example, an extracted term list may be integrated into termbases managed by other applications, and the resulting termbases may in turn be put to good use in a computer-aided translation environment for subsequent translation tasks.

3 Views from different stakeholders

Three groups of people are obviously involved in the development and deployment of automatic term extraction tools: the *computational linguists* who are the researchers for designing and improving term extraction algorithms, the *software developers* who package everything into a desktop application available on the market, and the *end users* who are the translators and at the same time the consumers of translation technology. They have different objectives and expectations, and thus different perspectives for evaluating the products.

3.1 The computational linguists

At the core of a term extraction system is the algorithm it adopts. Algorithms and their effectiveness are the primary concerns of the computational linguists, i.e. the researchers behind the scene. Referring to the five steps in the work flow described earlier, (2) and (3) are most relevant for these researchers.

Their interests

Term extraction approaches are generally categorised as linguistic (e.g. Bourigault 1992), statistical (e.g. Daille and Morin 2005) or hybrid (e.g. Daille 1996; Drouin 2003). Linguistic insights are often helpful for extracting terms from one language as well as identifying translation equivalents in another language, by means of grammatical structures, compositionality, contextual distributions and others (e.g. Baldwin and Tanaka 2004; Hippisley, Cheng and Ahmad 2005; Bartels and Speelman 2014).

Bilingual term extraction is in a way similar to general translation lexicon extraction (e.g. Smadja, Hatzivassiloglou and McKeown 1996; Fung 1998), but as far as terms are concerned, such as biomedical term extraction (e.g. Krauthammer and Nenadić 2004), domain specificity is an issue. Measures of "unithood" and "termhood" would have to be considered (Kageura 1996). In computational terminology, this is often addressed by comparing the expressions extracted from a domain-specific corpus with those from a general corpus, and filtering out the general terms from the results (e.g. Resnik and Melamed 1997). Such a corpus comparison approach is often used as a means to measure "termhood" for domain-specific terms on the one hand, and to reduce the amount of noise in the output on the other (e.g. Chung 2003; Drouin 2003; Kit and Liu 2008). For bilingual term extraction, parallel corpora would be most preferred, but given the scarcity of parallel corpora, often it might have to make do with comparable corpora (e.g. Laroche and Langlais 2010). The TTC platform (Blancafort et al. 2013), for instance, provides a whole pipeline of tools for terminology mining from comparable corpora for several languages.

Their evaluation criteria

White-box testing is possible for computational linguists, who expend much effort to improve automatic term extraction performance and reduce the noise ratio, through testing their methods by varying different parameters such as corpus size, domain, associative measure, scoring threshold etc.

Apart from qualitative comparisons among term extraction systems (e.g. Cabré et al. 2001), evaluation may also rely on human judges to go through the system-generated term candidate list (e.g. Fulford 2001) or compare the term list against an existing term bank (e.g. Drouin 2003). Nowadays it is often preferred to have system performance to be objectively measured with reference to some benchmarking data, by *precision* and *recall*, as is popularly done for many other natural language processing tasks. *Precision* is the number of matched terms divided by the total number of terms extracted. *Recall* is the number of matched terms divided by the number of terms expected in the gold standard. However, the reliability and validity of such quantitative measures are based on the assumption that a clear task definition exists. As noted by Bernier-Colborne and Drouin (2014: 51):

> Whereas other natural language processing tasks have well-defined evaluation schemes and benchmarks, the question of how to evaluate TEs [term extractors] remains unresolved. Evaluations are regularly reported in work on term extraction, yet the methodology varies from one work to the next, such that comparisons are hard to establish.

Defining the gold standard for term extraction can sometimes be tricky, but efforts spent are apparently on the rise (e.g. Bernier-Colborne and Drouin 2014; Zadeh and Handschuh 2014), at least for monolingual data. As Drouin (2003: 107) admitted,

> As with any validation process that relies on humans, we cannot assert that the results obtained are free of subjectivity. We strongly believe that different terminologists will identify different terms in the same document and that the same phenomenon could be observed with one terminologist looking at the same corpus over a period of time.

They added that it would be interesting to take the human influence on validation into account, which is nevertheless beyond the scope of their chapter. The main problem has thus to do with spelling out the criteria for the selection and annotation of terms systematically, though as long as the experiments are done with the same set of data and compared with respect to the same gold standard, the two quantitative performance measures provide the standard way for us to do some objective assessment of the systems.

3.2 *The software developers*

While computational linguists tend to stay behind the scene, the software developers are actually the middlemen linking them up with the end users. They facilitate knowledge transfer from academic research to real applications on the one hand, and introduce computer-aided translation products to the work cycle of translators on the other. With regard to the work flow in Section 2, software developers are mostly responsible for steps (1), (4) and (5).

Their interests

In general, the system performance of modern translation tools has continuously improved. At the same time remarkable progress has been made with respect to user-friendly interfaces, streamlined workflow, increased functions, expanded coverage of languages and compatibility with diverse platforms. All these are what software developers have endeavoured to do to continuously upgrade their products.

Their evaluation criteria

The software developers are mostly technical people. They work on system analysis and design, write the program codes for implementation, test the system and maintain it. But if we take the software company as a whole group, including also the more business-minded marketing people, for instance, the success of a product would be indicated by the market share of the product, customer feedback, release of new versions etc.

3.3 The end users

Term extraction tools are just like any other software to an end user, who only supplies the input and obtains the output, without much knowledge of what happens inside and why certain outputs are obtained. Hence the system is really a black box to an end user. To most users, all they need to do is to input some text, run the program and verify the output.

While all the steps in operating a term extraction tool are relevant to an end user, the biggest obstacle often arises from the very first step, the prerequisite of which is to have a certain amount of preferably bilingual text ready. As Blancafort et al. (2013) pointed out, computer-assisted translation suffers from the terminology bottleneck, and bilingual terminologies generated with statistical machine translation toolkits, as well as commercial tools, require parallel corpora. Hence, not only is scarcity of domain-specific parallel corpora a major hindrance, but it is also impractical to expect a professional translator or translation student to supply a very large corpus, not even for monolingual materials, as readily as computational linguists.

Their interests

Users are thus typically concerned with various things at each step:

Input text:

- What file types does the system allow?
- How much pre-processing do I need to do?

Run program:

- Is the tool easy to use?
- Will the extraction take long?
- What happens if something goes wrong in the middle of the process?

Verify output:

- How many terms do I need to check?
- Are they what I want?
- Will there be more non-terms than terms?
- Why are certain terms missing?

Their evaluation criteria

Given the black-box testing, end users can only evaluate the functions available from the tool and the usefulness of the terms extracted according to their own subjective judgement. The remark by Drouin (2003) earlier will be even more salient here because end users come with different computer literacy, use the tool for possibly different purposes, and thus may have diverse expectations of the term extraction results. Consider some typical comments found in classrooms and on the internet:

- "There are too many candidates to validate. Too time consuming."
- "The result does not contain the terms I want."
- "The translations suggested are awful. I'd rather do it manually."
- "I can't undo an action."
- "Too many buttons to click to get it done."
- "It just stops working for no apparent reason. Frustrating."
- "Took me a long time to prepare the files. Results are just so-so."

It is apparent that users' evaluation of a term extraction tool usually has no reference to benchmarking data and it tends to consider much more. Their concerns are multifarious, including but not limited to:

System performance:

- Are the term candidates accurate and useful?
- Is the noise ratio acceptable?

Software design:

- Is the interface user-friendly enough?
- Are sufficient functionalities offered?
- Does it allow different file formats?
- Is it compatible with different operating systems?

User expectation:

- Can a general translation lexicon be obtained?
- Or only special terminology?

This last point on user expectation is particularly variable, depending to a large extent on individual backgrounds and demands of specific users. For instance, Xu and Sharoff (2014) found only mediocre performance of various term extraction tools working on comparable corpora, but as far as user perception was concerned, student interpreters still considered the low precision tolerable. Obviously there is no perfect consensus, especially among different groups of people. As Vivaldi and Rodríguez (2007: 244) remarked, "there is low agreement between terminologists and domain experts on what term candidates should be treated as terms". Estopà (2001) also reported a great difference in the type and number of terms manually selected by terminologists, domain experts, translators and information scientists. Hence one important thing that any gold standard for term extraction would need to consider is the diverse expectations from different parties.

4 Beyond quantitative evaluation

The standard quantitative evaluation by *precision* and *recall* thus cannot account for the broad concerns of users. In particular, these measures assume a relatively objective gold standard, but individual users may start off with different expectations of the system results. These different expectations may arise from individual users' own objectives or their incomplete knowledge of the ability and limitations of the tools, and may also be a natural consequence of the often blurred distinction between terms and other frequent expressions.

A better understanding of this confusion between terms and non-terms, both by human and by machine, is therefore necessary to bring the researchers and the end users closer. As shown in Figure 6.1, standard evaluative measures compare the items returned by the system with those in the gold standard and focus on the amount of matched items. The unmatched items, however, often receive little attention. Are the remaining system outputs, which are not expected by the gold standard, all non-terms or invalid expressions? Is there anything useful among the noise? For the expected items which are not extracted by the system, are they too infrequent to be identified or are there any intrinsic limitations of the extraction algorithm which prevent them from being identified from the text? Are they all reasonable and realistic to expect? In the next section, we present a

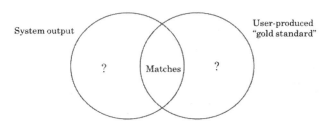

Figure 6.1 Evaluation of term extraction results

pilot case study, running SDL MultiTerm Extract on a small corpus of financial text, to get a glimpse of the matched and unmatched expressions and see what they might suggest.

5 A pilot case study

5.1 Data

Bilingual texts were taken from the section on Risk Report of the Hongkong and Shanghai Banking Corporation Limited Annual Report and Accounts 2013 from their official website.[1] Only the textual part was kept. Tables and figures were excluded. The bilingual text was sentence aligned. The text was divided into three parts, for cross-validation, and the data size is shown in Table 6.1.

5.2 System setting and "Gold standard"

SDL MultiTerm Extract was used as a sample tool in this pilot study. Most default system settings were adopted. The minimum term length and the maximum term length were set to 1 word and 4 words respectively. No maximum number of extracted terms was specified. The silence/noise ratio was set at the mid-point. The system was asked to search for translation equivalents, with maximum number of translations set at 5 and minimum translation frequency set at 2. The default English stop word list and an additional Chinese stop word list were used.

The "gold standard" was prepared by a research student in the Department of Translation, The Chinese University of Hong Kong, who was asked to go through the bilingual text manually and identify all terms deemed relevant for a financial glossary. Subjectivity was inevitable in this process, but given the student's background knowledge, experience and common sense in translation, her views could be reasonably considered representative of the average user of such translation technology tools.

5.3 Results

Table 6.2 shows the "precision" and "recall" of the term extraction results compared to the "gold standard" (put in quotes because this is not a standard evaluation but only refers to the expectation of one particular potential user of the tool).

Table 6.1 Data size for automatic term extraction

	English (words)	Chinese (chars)	Aligned Pairs
Part 1	4,208	7,481	188
Part 2	4,210	7,899	201
Part 3	4,174	7,332	194
Total	12,592	22,712	583

110 *Olivia Kwong Oi Yee*

Table 6.2 "Precision" and "Recall" for SDL MultiTerm Extract

	"Precision"	"Recall"
Part 1 (with single words)	0.115	0.095
Part 1 (no single words)	0.179	0.082
Part 2 (with single words)	0.153	0.120
Part 2 (no single words)	0.233	0.116
Part 3 (with single words)	0.094	0.070
Part 3 (no single words)	0.164	0.075
All parts (with single words)	0.114	0.253
All parts (no single words)	0.152	0.238

Table 6.3 Matched terms

Available-for-sale	Liquidity coverage ratio
Balance sheet	Liquidity risk
Banking ordinance	Loan commitments
Cash flow	Market risk
Core deposit	Net stable funding ratio
Credit rating	Non-economic assumptions
Credit risk	Non-linked insurance
Credit support annex	Obligor
Delinquency	Operational risk
EL	Retail accounts
Financial investments	Retirement funds
Group management board	Risk appetite
Held-to-maturity	Risk management committee
Hong Kong Monetary Authority	Stock borrowing
Impairment allowance	Stress scenario
Inherent liquidity risk categorisation	Stressed coverage ratio
Insurance risk	Trading assets
Internal control	Trading portfolios
Investment contract	Unencumbered asset
Liquidity behaviouralisation	Value at risk

The matched items[2] are shown in Table 6.3. The figures should not be taken as a serious indication of the performance of the system. On the one hand, only a small amount of text was used as the corpus. On the other hand, results for the individual parts were also based on the whole "gold standard", where some of the terms may not appear in individual parts. Rather, the figures allow some comparison with respect to several general considerations in term extraction.

The recall is apparently highest when all parts are considered together. This is because the "gold standard" was based on all text, and at the same time, when more text is considered, the frequency of some terms would be higher than

Evaluating term extraction tools 111

in individual parts, making them more readily identified by the system. Nevertheless, the precision is unlikely to follow the same trend, especially in view of the Zipfian distribution applicable to corpora of different sizes. Hence, this implies that when more text is used, more useful terms will be extracted, but at the same time the user will have to spend more time filtering out the invalid candidates.

5.4 "Noise" vs "expected"

As mentioned in Section 4, an analysis of unmatched items might also suggest something about the system performance, not only as quantitatively measured but also as subjectively perceived by the user. The following are some examples found among what is conventionally considered "noise", that is, results returned by the system which are not expected in the "gold standard", roughly grouped into different categories:

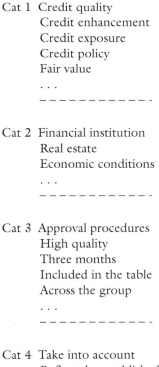

Cat 1 Credit quality
       Credit enhancement
       Credit exposure
       Credit policy
       Fair value
       . . .
       - - - - - - - - - - -

Cat 2 Financial institution
       Real estate
       Economic conditions
       . . .
       - - - - - - - - - - -

Cat 3 Approval procedures
       High quality
       Three months
       Included in the table
       Across the group
       . . .
       - - - - - - - - - - -

Cat 4 Take into account
       Reflect the established investment
       's ability

Apparently not all of these unmatched items can be properly called "noise". Many of them are grammatical linguistic expressions (noun phrases, verb phrases, prepositional phrases etc.) and some are obviously genuine financial terms. The examples in Cat 1 contain some core terms (e.g. fair value) in banking and finance, especially in the context of risk management. They also invite the question of what actually counts as a term, and in this case, given the productivity of the core concept "credit", should all noun phrases with "credit" modifying some other more common words (e.g. policy, quality) be included in a glossary? It may be worthwhile to include them for completeness, but human translators might find them trivial since knowing the equivalent of "credit" and that of "policy" will immediately make the translation of "credit policy" straightforward.

The examples in Cat 2 also contain financial terms, but perhaps more often used in broader contexts and many of them would have also entered daily life. Cat 3 contains frequently used fixed expressions in annual reports of banks and other commercial enterprises, but they do not carry particular sense in the financial domain. They may do well as translation memory segments, but obviously not entirely appropriate as part of a terminology or even a translation lexicon. Examples in Cat 4 are even less distinguishable from common usages that one could find in general English text and are perhaps the only cases that could confidently be called "noise" and should practically be treated as such.

What about the rationality of the user's expectations? The following are some examples found among the "gold standard", which were expected by the user but somehow failed to be extracted by the tool:

Cat A Contractual *cash inflows*
        Delinquency period
        Large *credit exposure*
        Liquidity and funding limit
        Contingent *liquidity risk*
        Risk management meeting
        Risk management framework
        Risk management policies
        . . .
        — — — — — — — — — — — -

Cat B Macro-economic events
        Mortgage prepayments
        Business strategy
        Structural long-term funding
        Interest rate sensitivities
        Trading assets and liabilities (asset and liability)
        . . .
        — — — — — — — — — — -

Cat C Inter alia
        . . .

We could also try to group the unmatched but expected items into various categories by their relevance. Cat C is definitely out of the question. Translators might look up general bilingual dictionaries for the translation of such expressions but they should be the least expected for a domain-specific glossary. Examples in Cat B are expressions mostly found in financial texts, but given the small corpus size, many of these terms may have only appeared once or twice and are thus too infrequent to be caught by the statistical measures of the system. The notorious difference between human and machine, and between qualitative and quantitative approaches, is that the former tends to pay attention to the details including infrequent and idiosyncratic phenomena, while the latter emphasises frequent and regular patterns ignoring the minority outliers.

Expressions in Cat A should be of more interest to us. The problem exemplified by this group of examples is closely tied to the one exhibited by the Cat 1 "noise" discussed previously, which involves the precise definition of a term and the linguistic unit to be appropriately considered. The italicised parts in the Cat A examples (e.g. cash inflows, liquidity risk) are actually among the terms extracted by the system and they also match with the "gold standard". In other words, the user has identified both "cash inflows" and "contractual cash inflows", and similarly both "liquidity risk" and "contingent liquidity risk", as relevant terms. Obviously the shorter forms corresponding to the broader concepts will have a higher frequency than the modified forms representing concepts at a sub-class level. In this regard, the user's expectation is not unreasonable if we consider terms as expressions representing the concepts and their relations within a domain-specific conceptual system. At the same time, one might have to re-consider the corresponding linguistic and statistical criteria in automatic term extraction to accommodate a more comprehensive set of concepts and their expressions.

5.5 Discussion

In view of the objectives, interests and concerns of the researchers, software developers and end users, we could attempt to reconcile the discrepancy in their evaluation and perception of automatic term extraction tools from two regards. One has to do with more fundamental issues and theoretical assumptions, and the other may have more to do with technical limitations in practice.

Fundamental issues

The issue of "term vs word" regularly recurs. Although both the computational linguists and the end users might be aware of the theoretical distinction between them, in terms of language for special purposes and language for general purposes, in practice the line is not always easy to draw. Computational linguists rely on corpus comparison to measure termhood, while end users rely on their subjective domain knowledge for the judgement. Nevertheless, neither is seriously incorporated in existing term extraction software. Most tools on the market do not work with a large reference corpus, but simply apply the statistical association measures on the text provided by the user. The noise ratio is therefore controlled mainly by some frequency or collocation scoring threshold, without actual filtering of the general expressions from the domain-specific ones.

The legitimacy of "gold standard" in system performance evaluation is another issue. In the research context, benchmarking datasets could be made, although the so-called gold standard is subjectively grounded on human decisions. This could be rectified to a certain extent by giving clear and well-defined guidelines for human annotators, and considering the decisions from two or more human annotators as the gold standard. At least the researcher could have some control over the evaluative datasets and apply them consistently in different experiments and comparisons. In real application, however, the gold standard is no longer standard because end users come with different expectations and their evaluation of system performance would depend on their individual expectation and perception. From the user's perspective, "precision" would be relatively more important as it directly affects the verification effort required.

Technical limitations

It sounds normal and natural for software users to adjust their mode of working within the constraints of a given tool. Microsoft Office, for instance, with a whole suite of applications like Word, Excel, Access, PowerPoint and others, has gradually and successfully penetrated into the work of people from different walks of life. These people certainly include translators. Why, then, do translators seem to more readily accept the constraints imposed by a general word processor but obviously more reluctant to adapt their work habit to go along with a computer-aided translation tool? This may be attributed to the technical requirements and thus the sense of helplessness experienced by users.

The requirement to provide a corpus or some text as a pre-requisite for term extraction may not be difficult to fulfil, but the corpus size is not a trivial matter. In research, computational linguists often have access to very large corpora for training and testing the systems, and the performance is reported based on sizeable data. The amount of text provided by end users, however, is rarely comparable to that usually used in research. This would not only mean a smaller number of terms to be extracted, but also the number of occurrences for some important terms may not even reach the threshold to be extracted. The data size issue is one of the reasons for the discrepancy between reported performance and perceived performance.

In addition to the data size, the pre-processing of text is another deterrent factor. Despite the encouraging results reported in bilingual term extraction research, in practice the effectiveness of bilingual term extraction, especially when Chinese text is involved, is always disappointing. On the one hand, bilingual alignment will have already created extra work for the end user, although these days one could make use of computer-aided tools to produce bilingually aligned text instead of doing it all manually. On the other hand, one cannot expect the average end users to have the facilities for word segmentation and part-of-speech tagging before feeding the text into the system. These pre-processing tasks would be more preferably in-built and reliably done within the tool itself. Unfortunately, most existing tools do not seem to have such functions. Hence, while software developers have spent much effort in enhancing the tools with respect to file formats, platform compatibility, user interface, and other needs of most end users, and relieved them from the many unfamiliar and apparently complicated intermediate processes, there is certainly more to be done to bridge the gap between research and application. It is the actual outcome which is of the greatest concern to translators, and it will be a waste not to integrate the many relatively mature natural language processing techniques into translation technology, which could enhance user experience and improve system performance.

6 Concluding remarks

The usefulness and evaluation of term extraction tools have thus been considered from the perspectives of various involved parties, or stakeholders, in the foregoing discussion. Obviously these different groups of people start off with different objectives and expectations, which consequently affect their perception and evaluation of the performance of automatic term extraction tools. We suggest that a fair assessment of these tools needs holistic consideration, taking into account the system performance, user expectation, software design issues and other relevant factors. In other words, a more user-oriented, or more specifically translator-oriented, perspective for the development and evaluation of automatic term extraction systems would be beneficial, so that they can much better fulfil their computer-aided roles in translation technology. As Agirre et al. (2000: 296) stated, "tools for translation cannot be satisfactorily designed without the cooperation of human translators". Hence, in addition to simple comparisons based on objective and quantitative measurements like precision and recall, evaluation must go more deeply into the qualitative side, so as to identify weaknesses in the extraction algorithms on the one hand, and to spot any unrealistic or mismatched expectation of the users on the other. A thorough understanding of the sources of such apparent discrepancy would be critical for researchers to develop more effective methods to suit users' needs, for software developers to take more effective and practical approaches in knowledge transfer, and for users to better appreciate the ability and limitations of the tools. This kind of mutual understanding and advancement is essential to pushing back the frontiers of not only term extraction tools specifically but also translation software development in general.

Notes

1 https://www.hsbc.com.hk (Regulatory disclosures)
2 Given the relatively poor results for extracting Chinese terms in SDL MultiTerm Extract, only the results for English term extraction are reported here.

References

Agirre, Eneko, Xabier Arregi, Xabier Artola, Arantza Díaz de Illarraza, Kepa Sarasola, and Aitor Soroa (2000) "A methodology for building translator-oriented dictionary systems", *Machine Translation* 15: 295–310.

Baldwin, Timothy and Takaaki Tanaka (2004) "Translation by machine of complex nominals: Getting it right", in *Proceedings of the Second ACL Workshop on Multiword Expressions: Integrating Processing*, Barcelona, Spain, 24–31.

Bartels, Ann and Dirk Speelman (2014) "Clustering for semantic purposes: Exploration of semantic similarity in a technical corpus", *Terminology* 20(2): 279–303.

Bernier-Colborne, Gabriel and Patrick Drouin (2014) "Creating a test corpus for term extractors through term annotation", *Terminology* 20(1): 50–73.

Blancafort, Helena, Francis Bouvier, Béatrice Daille, Ulrich Heid, and Anita Ramm (2013) "TTC Web Platform: From corpus compilation to bilingual terminologies for MT and CAT tools", in *Proceedings of TRALOGY II*, Paris.

Bourigault, Didier (1992) "Surface grammatical analysis for the extraction of terminological noun phrases", in *Proceedings of the Fourteenth International Conference on Computational Linguistics (COLING '92)*, Nantes, France, 977–981.

Bowker, Lynne (2002) *Computer-Aided Translation Technology*, Ottawa: University of Ottawa Press.

Bowker, Lynne (2015) "Computer-aided translation: Translator training", in Chan Sin-wai (ed.), *The Routledge Encyclopedia of Translation Technology*, London and New York: Routledge, 88–104.

Cabré Castellví, M. Teresa (1996) "Terminology today", in Harold Somers (ed.) *Terminology, LSP and Translation: Studies in Language Engineering in Honour of Juan C. Sager*, Amsterdam and Philadelphia: John Benjamins Publishing Company, 15–35.

Cabré Castellví, M. Teresa, Rosa Estopà Bagot, and Jordi Vivaldi Palatresi (2001) "Automatic term detection: A review of current systems", in Didier Bourigault, Christian Jacquemin, and Marie-Claude L'Homme (eds.) *Recent Advances in Computational Terminology*, Amsterdam and Philadelphia: John Benjamins Publishing Company, 53–87.

Chung, Teresa Mihwa (2003) "A corpus comparison approach for terminology extraction", *Terminology* 9(2): 221–246.

Daille, Béatrice (1996) "Study and implementation of combined techniques for automatic extraction of terminology", in Judith L. Klavans and Philip Resnik (eds.) *The Balancing Act: Combining Symbolic and Statistical Approaches to Language*, Cambridge, MA: MIT Press, 49–66.

Daille, Béatrice and Emmanuel Morin (2005) "French-English terminology extraction from comparable corpora", in Robert Dale, Wong Kam-Fai, Jian Su, and Kwong Oi Yee (eds.), *Natural Language Processing – IJCNLP 2005*, Lecture Notes in Artificial Intelligence, Berlin: Springer Verlag, 3651: 707–718.

Drouin, Patrick (2003) "Term extraction using non-technical corpora as a point of leverage", *Terminology* 9(1): 99–115.

Estopà, Rosa (2001) "Les unités de signification spécialisées: élargissant l'objet du travail en terminologie [Units of specialised meaning: Broadening the scope of terminology work]", *Terminology* 7(2): 217–237.

Fulford, Heather (2001) "Exploring terms and their linguistic environment in text: A domain-independent approach to automated term extraction", *Terminology* 7(2): 259–279.

Fung, Pascale (1998) "A statistical view on bilingual lexicon extraction: From parallel corpora to non-parallel corpora", *Lecture Notes in Artificial Intelligence* 1529 (Springer): 1–17.
Hippisley, Andrew R., David Cheng, and Khurshid Ahmad (2005) "The head-modifier principle and multilingual term extraction", *Natural Language Engineering* 11(2): 129–157.
Kageura, Kyo (1996) "Methods of automatic term recognition – A review", *Terminology* 3(2): 259–289.
Kit, Chunyu and Xiaoyue Liu (2008) "Measuring mono-word termhood by rank difference via corpus comparison", *Terminology* 14(2): 204–229.
Krauthammer, Michael and Goran Nenadić (2004) "Methodological review: Term identification in the biomedical literature", *Journal of Biomedical Informatics* 37(6): 512–526.
Laroche, Audrey and Philippe Langlais (2010) "Revisiting context-based projection methods for term-translation spotting in comparable corpora", in *Proceedings of the 23rd International Conference on Computational Linguistics (COLING 2010)*, Beijing, China, 617–625.
Och, Franz Josef and Hermann Ney (2003) "A systematic comparison of various statistical alignment models", *Computational Linguistics* 29(1): 19–51.
Resnik, Philip and I. Dan Melamed (1997) "Semi-automatic acquisition of domain-specific translation lexicons", in *Proceedings of the Fifth Conference on Applied Natural Language Processing*, Washington, DC, 340–347.
Sager, Juan C. (1990) *A Practical Course in Terminology Processing*, Amsterdam and Philadelphia: John Benjamins Publishing Company.
Smadja, Frank, Vasileios Hatzivassiloglou, and Kathleen McKeown (1996) "Translating collocations for bilingual lexicons: A statistical approach", *Computational Linguistics* 22(1): 1–38.
Vivaldi, Jorge and Horacio Rodríguez (2007) "Evaluation of terms and term extraction systems: A practical approach", *Terminology* 13(2): 225–248.
Xu, Ran and Serge Sharoff (2014) "Evaluating term extraction methods for interpreters", in *Proceedings of the 4th International Workshop on Computational Terminology*, Dublin, Ireland, 86–93.
Zadeh, Behrang, Q. and Siegfried Handschuh (2014) "The ACL RD-TEC: A dataset for benchmarking terminology extraction and classification in computational linguistics", in *Proceedings of the 4th International Workshop on Computational Terminology*, Dublin, Ireland, 52–63.

7 Terminology resources in support of global communication

Kara Warburton

Terminology and its potential as a language resource

Terminology assets or resources in electronic database form, called terminology databases or termbases, are managed with specially designed software called terminology management systems (TMS). These systems have evolved over time, allowing terminology resources to now be developed with increasingly sophisticated structure and content. Improvements in terminology management systems have opened opportunities for terminology resources to be used by a wider range of end users, and leveraged in a diverse range of natural language processing (NLP) applications that are essential for global communications.

But this is not an entirely new development; it has just intensified due to advances in technology. There is indeed ample evidence in the literature that terminological resources can be useful for purposes beyond translation, such as controlled authoring, indexing, product and content classification, keyword extraction, search engine optimisation, and construction of ontologies (Knops and Thurmair 1993; Sager 1990; Meyer 1993; Galinski 1994; Ibekwe-SanJuan, Condamines and Cabré Castellvi 2007; Buchan 1993; Cabré 1999; Strehlow 2001; Jacquemin 2001; Nazarenko and El Mekki 2007; Greenwald 1994; Wettengel and Van de Weyer 2001; Ahmad 2001; Warburton and Karsch 2012). It has, for instance, been demonstrated that terminology resources can enhance the performance of term extraction tools (Warburton 2013), a case of a terminology resource helping a terminology application. Many of these potential uses of terminology have their place in production-oriented organisational settings. Indeed, companies and organisations are becoming increasingly active in the field of terminology management, by establishing termbases and adopting practices that support their needs in producing, translating, and managing content

Terminology resources

There is no universally-recognised definition of what a *term* is, much less a *terminology resource*. According to Technical Committee 37 of the International Organization for Standardization, the standards body in this field, a term is "a verbal designation of a general concept in a specific subject field."[1] This is not a particularly helpful definition, but nevertheless, there is a consensus among scholars and practitioners alike that the key feature that distinguishes terms from words and expressions of the so-called general lexicon is that they denote concepts in a "subject field." Subject fields are fields of "special knowledge" (ISO TC37) such as law, medicine, accounting, and so forth.

Accordingly, a terminology resource would be a collection of terms that are confined to one or more subject fields. However, the boundary between special language and general language is not clear cut (Schubert 2011: 28; Myking 2007: 84), and in practice terminology resources differ widely in content as well as in structure to fit their intended purpose. Terminology resources developed by translation companies to support their translators range from simple two-column spreadsheets or text files containing terms in two languages, to slightly more sophisticated glossaries integrated into computer-assisted translation (CAT) tools. Terminology resources used by writers are often found in a style guide in the form of a list of preferred terms, words to avoid, and so forth. Nowadays, special software is available to assist writers, called controlled authoring (CA) tools, which can enforce the style rules and terminology preferences. Terminology resources developed by the linguistic services of governments tend to provide more information than the aforementioned ones but have a language-planning mission, while those developed for large non-governmental organisations, such as the United Nations, are proportionally large and comprehensive. Finally, terminology resources developed in academia explore the boundaries of structure and content for research purposes. In almost any terminology resource, one can find some words and expressions from general language in addition to terms strictly speaking.

Aside from the fact that they are presumed to contain "terms" as opposed to general language words, a principle that is not always enforced as just explained, terminology resources have some defining features that distinguish them from resources of the purely "lexical" type, or at least, they should. One of these is concept orientation; the content is structured on concepts not on words (this principle will be further described later). Another is their electronic format; they are rarely designed for the published medium. In this chapter, our discussion focusses on terminology resources as they are used to enhance content production processes such as writing and translation, with some comments on other potential uses for commercial purposes such as search optimisation.

Repurposability

The repurposability of a terminology resource is a key theme of this chapter. A terminology resource that can support a multitude of users and uses, both present and future, is deemed to be *multipurpose* and *repurposable*. It must be able to seamlessly integrate into various computing environments and software applications. This process is referred to as *interchange*, and is the reason why standards such as 16642 and 30042, described later, are considered vitally important. In today's environment of rapidly changing technology and shifting organisational structures (due to mergers, acquisitions, supply chain, partner network, trade agreements etc.) any organisation or enterprise operating globally cannot afford to build a terminology resource that is not repurposable.

Authoring and translation

We maintain that terminology resources can be used for a multitude of purposes. In this section, we briefly describe two of the main ones: authoring and translation. We will emphasise their automated forms: computer-assisted translation and controlled authoring.

Computer-assisted translation refers to translation carried out by a translator with the assistance of specially designed software applications. These applications are called computer-aided translation tools and they typically comprise a suite of functions including translation memory (TM), a translation editing interface, a terminology repository, and sometimes automated workflows and project management functions. The terminology repository comprises a terminology management system (TMS) and a database for storing terminology data that is either imported or manually added.

The use of computer-aided translation tools increases productivity of translators and reduces translation costs. The translation memory stores equivalent sentence pairs in the source language (SL) and target language (TL). During a new translation project, if a sentence in the source text matches or closely matches a sentence in the memory, then the existing translation is shown to the translator so that he or she does not have to retranslate it from scratch. If a term in the sentence matches a term in the computer-aided translation termbase, the existing translation from the termbase is shown to the translator as well.

Controlled authoring (CA) is "the process of applying a set of predefined style, grammar, punctuation rules and approved terminology to content (documentation or software) during its development" (Ó Broin 2009). Controlled authoring is increasingly recognised as a means to improve content quality and overall communications in an organisation. Content that is consistent and easy to understand is more effective at achieving its objectives, i.e. increase sales in the case of marketing material or improve product usability in the case of product information. It is also easier and less costly to translate. Global organisations can therefore realise significant benefits by implementing controlled authoring (Warburton 2014b).

Both computer-aided translation and controlled authoring, being different applications of terminology resources, require different types of data, which are referred to as *data categories* by terminologists, and even different types of terms. A repurposable terminology resource would need to be comprehensive, i.e. it would need to include the superset of all the data categories and types of terms required for all uses.

Terminological resources used in controlled authoring need a greater focus on synonyms than those developed for computer-aided translation. For example, if there are several "names" in use for some widget manufactured by a company, technical writers need to know which one the company prefers them to use.

A terminology resource designed for controlled authoring would need to include all the possible names of the widget in a single record or entry, each one accompanied by a usage indicator and possibly a usage note. This structure is called a synset (set of synonyms), and is made possible thanks to the principle of concept orientation, which will be described later. Figure 7.1 shows an example of an English synset.

Terminology resources used for controlled authoring also require more expressions from the so-called general language or general lexicon than translation-oriented resources. Writers need to be directed towards using quite common words very carefully. For instance, the adverb *almost* may be preferred to *nearly* in some contexts due to the potential spacial interpretation of the latter. Finally, controlled authoring-oriented resources tend to include many more non-nouns than computer-aided translation-oriented ones. For a more detailed description of the properties of controlled authoring-oriented terminology resources, see Warburton 2014b.

The aforementioned features of controlled authoring-oriented resources are not needed for computer-aided translation. Translators do not need to be told how to translate words from the general lexicon. Rarely do they need assistance with non-nouns. And they have little interest in synonyms in the source language (SL). They are presented with a text and asked to translate it. If they are unsure how to translate a term, they look it up to find a translation, and they want to find one quickly. For this they need minimal information: SL terms and their target

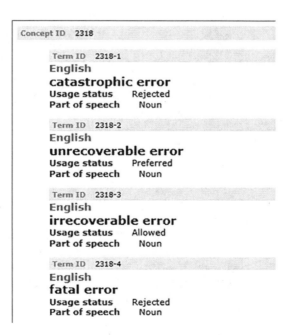

Figure 7.1 A synset for controlled authoring in TermWeb

language (TL) equivalents. In cases of uncertainty or multiple possible translations, their decision can be facilitated with a few additional data categories such as part of speech, context, and definition. On the other hand, translators need terms in the terminology resource that authors would not need, such as many more multi-word terms. Indeed, any term that can be translated in multiple ways is a strong candidate for inclusion in the termbase, and many of these would never be looked up by a company writer.

One thing that controlled authoring- and computer-aided translation-oriented termbases have in common is that both need to optimally reflect terminology that is actually in use in the company or organisation. Indeed, "terminological resources must reflect terms in active use in order to enable productive reuse" (Warburton 2014a: 266). This may seem obvious yet some, possibly many, termbases fall short of this goal, at least according to our previous research which examined the "gap" between the termbase and the corpus of four companies (Warburton 2014a). The size of the gap between a termbase and the corpus it is meant to represent is the sum of two measurements: (1) the number of terms in the termbase that do not occur, or occur very infrequently, in the corpus, and (2) the number of terms that occur frequently in the corpus but are missing in the termbase. The former are referred to as under-optimised terms; their usefulness in the termbase is questionable as they are unlikely to be sought after by writers, translators, and other users of the termbase. The latter are called un-documented terms; they represent lost opportunity to serve users with terms that they actually need. The study found that the under-optimised terms amounted to 35, 63, 73, and 76 percent of the total terms in the termbases in the four companies respectively. Even though a portion of these gaps could be explained by various factors unrelated to terminology process issues, they remain alarmingly large, and some term selection problems are undoubtedly at play. The scope of un-documented terms is more difficult to measure, as it requires a rigorous term extraction and subsequent vetting procedure to obtain a gold standard of corpus-based terminology in the company.

The study also found that the most "productive" terms in the termbase, i.e. the ones that are most frequently required by users, are bigrams and trigrams (terms that are comprised of two or three words). Terms much longer than that tend to fall into the under-optimised category, while unigrams (single-word terms) have a tendency towards polysemy which, if not represented properly in the termbase, produces usability issues for those entries.

Any sizable gap between the termbase and the corpus is a concern for terminologists; it can weaken the business value of the entire terminology management programme the strength of which is critical to funding approvals. For this reason, corpus evidence should be a key consideration when terminologists select terms for the termbase. However, although readily available, corpus analysis tools, such as concordancers and term extractors, are rarely used by terminologists and even less so by other people who often contribute terms to termbases, such as writers and translators. The increased use of such tools would improve the content of termbases (Warburton 2014a).

Since computer-assisted translation has a longer history than controlled authoring, there are more computer-aided translation tools available on the market than controlled authoring tools, and consequently, more computer-aided translation-based terminology management systems than controlled authoring-based ones. Few terminology management systems, though, can bridge the two use cases and serve both controlled authoring and computer-assisted translation. Following the standards, best practices, and principles in the next sections will not guarantee that a termbase will be repurposable, but it can help to avoid certain pitfalls that most certainly would conflict with this goal.

Standards and best practices

A repurposable terminology resource must be structured and managed according to the latest standards and best practices. Several of the most widely-known are described in the following paragraphs.

> ISO 16642, *Terminological markup framework (TMF)*, specifies a framework for representing data recorded in termbases based on some fundamental principles such as concept orientation and term autonomy. This framework includes a metamodel and methods for describing specific terminological markup languages (TMLs) expressed in XML.
>
> ISO 30042, *TermBase eXchange (TBX)*, defines an XML-based framework for representing structured terminological data that is compliant with ISO 16642. Terminological data that can be represented in a TBX-compliant format are easier to exchange between users, systems, and applications.
>
> *TBX-Basic* is a TBX-compliant markup language for terminology data that was defined as a best practice by TerminOrgs, a thinktank of terminologists working in large organisations (www.terminorgs.net/). Other useful resources are available from TerminOrgs.
>
> ISO 26162, *Design, implementation and maintenance of terminology management systems (TMS)*, provides information about the rationale for using a TMS, types of users and users' needs, steps in designing and implementing a TMS as well as the tasks of organising and managing a termbase. It also provides guidelines for selecting and using data categories for managing terminology.
>
> The *Data Category Registry (DCR)* (www.datcatinfo.net) is an online database of data categories[2] that are found in various linguistic resources. It contains a dedicated section for terminology resources.

There is an organisation dedicated to developing guidelines and best practices for terminologists working in large organisations: TerminOrgs.[3]

Fundamental principles

All terminology standards and best practices recognise some fundamental principles, three of which are briefly described here: concept orientation, term autonomy, and data elementarity.

Concept orientation is the principle whereby an individual record or *entry* in a termbase describes one and only one concept. This principle distinguishes terminology from lexicology, where an entry describes all the meanings of a word. Termbases are usually multilingual; each language term in an entry is equivalent in meaning to the others. However, because entries are meaning-based, they can also contain multiple terms in a given language. Synonyms, abbreviations, and spelling variants of a term must all be placed in the same entry. One can say that terminology resources are structured more like a thesaurus or knowledge-base than a conventional dictionary. We will come back to this point later. Concept orientation is a principle for terminology resources that is undisputed in the literature. Knops and Thurmair (1993: 96) recognise the practical advantage of concept orientation, which resonates with the goal of repurposability: "A technical advantage of this representation is its reusability."

Term autonomy is the principle whereby each term in an entry can be documented or described with the same types of information. If the database has different fields for different types of terms, such as a field for abbreviations, this is an indication that term autonomy may be lacking and that the database is poorly designed. For example, in the model below, there is no part of speech or definition field available for the abbreviation.

Term:

    Part-of-speech:
    Definition:
    Abbreviation:

All that is needed to fix this problem is to add a Term type field to replace Abbreviation, as follows:

Term:

    Part-of-speech:
    Definition:
    Term type:

where the **Term type** field allows all the necessary values for different types of terms, such as *abbreviation, acronym, full form, spelling variant*, and so forth.

Data elementarity means that there can only be one type of information in a database record or field. Separate fields are required for different types of information. For example, if you want to document the source of definitions, you need a dedicated field for that information; you should not merely append the source to the definition itself. A frequent violation of this principle is when two terms are included in one term field, such as an acronym and its expanded form:

| Term | automatic document feeder (ADF) |

Instead, this should be represented as follows, with of course additional data categories provided for each term:

Term	automatic document feeder
... additional data categories	
Term	ADF
... additional data categories	

Terminology resources as knowledge systems

To meet the increasingly diverse end-uses referred to earlier, and optimise repurposability, we maintain that terminology resources need to evolve from simple, flat files containing basic information such as term equivalents in several languages, to complex highly-structured termbases infused with hierarchical semantic relations, in effect, into systems of knowledge or knowledge bases.

Provided that it is properly structured, terminology data *is indeed* a knowledge asset in a most discreet and repurposable form. Extending translation-oriented termbases into knowledge-rich repositories is a long-overdue notion. Yet for far too long, terminology management systems designed for computer-aided translation tools, which have dominated the landscape of terminology tools, and even those more recently developed for controlled authoring, have not bought into this concept. The functionality necessary to produce a hierarchically structured knowledge-base is missing from these systems.

Although still not widely practiced, the concept of structuring terminology data in the form of a knowledge-base is not new. Over two decades ago, scholars predicted that applications beyond translation would benefit from *richly structured* terminological resources (Knops and Thurmair 1993; Juan Sager 1990; Ingrid Meyer 1993). Models, methods, and formalisms for knowledge-bases have been the focus of much research and development ever since. In 1994, Ingrid Meyer and Douglas Skuce coined the term *terminological knowledge-base (TKB)*, and developed CODE, a TKB management tool. Relations between terminology and knowledge engineering are well established in research circles.

When speaking of a database that structures linguistic representations of knowledge, the term *terminological knowledge-base* would be more precise than *knowledge-base*. A knowledge-base is a technology that stores complex structured and unstructured information for use by a computer system. As such, a knowledge-base can encompass various kinds of data including non-linguistic representations such as formulae and numbers. In a company, a knowledge-base could for example include various assets such as manuals, procedures, policies, best practices, reusable designs, and code.

What is the difference between a conventional termbase and a terminological knowledge-base? We must first acknowledge that many of the existing termbases developed for controlled authoring or computer-aided translation are quite limited in terms of their structure and range of data categories. The notion that they are termbases at all could easily be challenged. Contrary to popular belief, a list of terms in a computer file does not constitute a termbase.

Consider the use of spreadsheets. Spreadsheets have the singular advantage of being readily available and familiar to most people. Other than that, they are totally unsuitable for managing terminology (Wetzel 2008) and yet, they are still today a popular medium for storing, accessing, and exchanging terminologies, particularly among translators. Spreadsheets store information in cells that are arranged in rows and columns. Even if you use a proper terminology management system, chances are that Excel or CSV is one of the main import and export formats. This fact alone reveals that the data in the system, no matter how detailed and structured it might appear, is still essentially "flat."

Furthermore, terminology resources in spreadsheets are frequently not even concept-oriented. Concept orientation is difficult to represent in spreadsheets; it requires all terms denoting a concept, and all fields describing them, be represented in one row. This can lead to very long rows with many empty cells. To avoid rows becoming unduly long, translators using spreadsheets often enter only one translation for a given source language term, even if multiple exist. Or, they use multiple rows to represent additional source language or target language terms, even if they represent the same concept as a previously entered pair. Since termbases in computer-aided translation tools often contain data that was originally in spreadsheets, they often replicate the problems that are found in spreadsheets. This is a serious problem for any organisation wishing to use its termbase for purposes beyond translation.

It is easy to understand why terminology management systems that were developed for translators or writers tend to neglect the more sophisticated features of a knowledge system. As stated earlier, translators rarely need to know detailed linguistic or semantic properties of terms. Their needs are basic: what is the translation of this term? A tabular arrangement, or a simple computer-aided translation glossary, containing source language terms and target language terms meets this need. Companies purchase controlled authoring software to help content producers adhere to their style guides. Terminology management systems for controlled authoring focus on structures that facilitate the ranking of synonyms according to preference and provide usage information. These terminology management systems can be very effective in supporting their target users. But they lack features for developing a terminological knowledge-base or even, for that matter, any terminology resource that is multi-purpose.

Examples of terminological knowledge-bases

Our discussion so far could lead to the assumption that existing termbases are simplistic and flat. While that is certainly true for many of them, there are some notable exceptions. The first terminological knowledge-bases were developed in research settings; for example Ecolexicon, from the University of Granada,[4] and DiCoInfo, from the University of Montreal.[5] HowNet,[6] a Chinese/English

```
water


52 ENVIRONMENT
MT  5211 natural environment
BT1 aquatic environment
    BT2 physical environment
NT1 bathing water
NT1 drinking water
NT1 freshwater
NT1 groundwater
NT1 ice
NT1 percolation water
NT1 saltwater
NT1 stagnant water
NT1 surface water
RT  hydraulic energy [6626]
    hydraulic works [6831]
    hydrology [3606]
    irrigation [5621]
    use of water [5206]
    water pollution [5216]
```

Figure 7.2 Terms related to "water", from Eurovoc

terminological knowledge-base developed over the past 10 years, comprises more than 70,000 inter-related concepts. AGROVOC[7] is a multilingual thesaurus of over 32,000 concepts developed by the United Nations Food and Agriculture Organization (FAO). EuroVoc[8] is a multilingual ontology-based thesaurus covering 7,000 concepts for EU institutions (see Figure 7.2). SNOMED-CT[9] is a comprehensive systematically organised collection of over 300,000 medical concepts and over 1.3 million links in five languages. It enables safe and effective communication and reuse of meaningful health information in over 50 countries. In the private sector, both Microsoft and IBM developed termbases that include hierarchical concept relations. IBM has long been repurposing its termbase in various applications beyond translation, thanks to a solid data model. Other global companies are no doubt contemplating the same.

Search optimisation

Approaching terminology management from the perspective of a knowledge base opens opportunities to manage other types of data beyond "terms." Indeed, research has shown that many of the content expressions that *need* to be managed in a termbase to support global communications in production environments do not fit the classical notion of a term (Warburton 2014a). Unfortunately, this means that they are often overlooked by terminologists. This represents a lost opportunity to manage enterprise assets that could quite effectively be served by theories and methodologies proven in the field of terminology science. These "assets" include product catalogs, enterprise taxonomies, product properties, and search keywords. We will discuss search and keywords as an example.

In general, terminological knowledge-bases facilitate global communication, content management, and access to information by increasing semantic interoperability. Increased semantic interoperability makes information easier to manage and to find. For example, documentary searches can be made more effective by using standardised vocabularies to index documents. Search queries can be extended from beyond word forms to actual concepts by having search engines crawl through glossaries of linked synonyms, or synsets. A hierarchical series of concepts can become traversable nodes in a faceted search. And search results can be improved by adding the right keywords to web sites.

A search keyword is the word or words entered into the search field of the search engine (SE) by a user looking for information on the Internet. Having a match between the keywords entered by the user and the words on a website will help to raise that website's ranking by the SE. It is therefore in a company's interest to align words on its web site with those that are popular as search keywords for this type of content. A collection of keywords that are effective in retrieving a web page covering a given topic can be viewed as a kind of synset. Even if not totally synonymous, organising and managing keywords that are effective for a particular search objective in a synset structure, and making those synsets available to content producers and translators, helps to guarantee that the right keywords appear on web pages. Keywords are indeed another form of terminology.

But like terminology resources developed for controlled authoring and computer-aided translation, those developed for search engine optimisation (SEO) have their own unique properties. (For a full analysis, see Warburton and Karsch 2012). Among the unique data categories required is a keyword effectiveness index (KEI), sometimes even for different search engines. A workflow needs to be developed that effectively pushes the keywords to the content producers and translators at the right moment. This means that the keyword termbases may need to be incorporated into controlled authoring and computer-aided translation tools in a way that does not conflict with "ordinary" terminology. Finally, the placement of the keyword on the web page can also have an effect on SEO; this information may also need to be tracked in the keyword database.

Properties of an enterprise-scale TMS

In spite of their orientation towards one specific use case, application-specific terminology tools are known to be marketed as enterprise-level solutions, and this is where the trouble starts. Enterprise-level terminology management is knowledge management, or at least, it should be. Companies need to produce multi-purpose linguistic resources. Application-specific terminology tools are inadequate for developing and managing terminology as a knowledge resource at an enterprise or organisational scale; they limit the return-on-investment of termbases by constraining their repurposing potential.

In this section we describe some of the most essential features of a TMS that can develop multi-purpose terminology resources required by global companies and organisations.[10]

A full-featured terminology management system that can be used to develop a repurposable termbase supports the inclusion of information that cannot be represented in tabular formats such as spreadsheets. A good example is links, or relations, between parts of the data, such as to relate two or more concept entries or terms. Other hierarchical structures such as multi-level subject field taxonomies and subsetting categories, as well as conditional dependency relationships, are equally difficult if not impossible to represent as flat, linear information. For pragmatic reasons, tabular formats are also fixed with respect to cardinality, such as the number of terms and associated metadata that a concept entry can contain. Of course you can add columns as needed, but as mentioned earlier this can lead to huge, cumbersome spreadsheets that are difficult to navigate and manage.

Because, as stated earlier, belonging to a subject field is an inherent property of terms, it is a recognised best practice to include a data category for subject fields in termbases. In most terminology management systems, the subject field data category is treated like any other limited value (picklist) data field. This means that the field is restricted to a flat list of values. Given the complex nature of subject fields for human knowledge, this is quite limiting and certainly inadequate for a terminological knowledge base. A multi-level picklist field is needed to represent a subject field taxonomy, i.e. a hierarchically structured set of increasingly narrow subject fields. Figure 7.3 shows a prototype of a subject field taxonomy that was developed for the World Bank, showing one section expanded.

Concept relations are an inherent component of terminological knowledge systems; they are essentially what differentiates a knowledge system from a basic termbase. Yet few terminology management systems represent concept relations well. A concept relation is a relation between two terminological (concept)

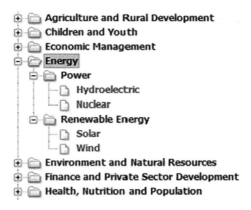

Figure 7.3 A multi-level subject field taxonomy in TermWeb

entries in the termbase. In addition to the standard generic relation (type of, "is-a") that links a broader concept and a narrower one, the terminology management system should support other types such as meronymic (or partitive), associative, cause/effect, agent/patient, and so forth. It should allow the user to define custom relation types. Further, the relation should be "bidirectional." That means that if you relate term A to term B, then the inverse relation should automatically be established from term B to term A. Relation bidirectionality is shown in Figures 7.4 and 7.5, where a generic relation has been established from "forest" to "cloud forest", and the entry for "cloud forest" has a relation back to "forest" that was set automatically.

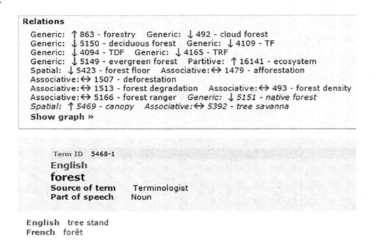

Figure 7.4 Relations between "forest" and other concepts in TermWeb

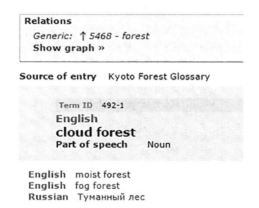

Figure 7.5 Automatic inverse relation between "cloud forest" and "forest" in TermWeb

Figure 7.6 Terminological entry with a picture in TermWeb

A picture says a thousand words, and in some industries, such as manufacturing, being able to represent a concept with a picture is essential. Many products and parts need to be consistently named. Sometimes a video would even be useful in an entry, such as to demonstrate a procedure. Figure 7.6 shows an example of an entry containing a graphic. This entry is in its first phase and does not yet contain any translations.

Terminology work involves different people playing different roles. A terminological resource will grow more quickly if a crowd-sourcing approach is adopted whereby anyone in the organisation can submit a term, a definition, a translation, and so forth. This should be encouraged. However, it would not be wise to allow anyone to make changes to the terminological entries. The terminologist and possibly several other experienced linguists should be the gatekeepers, and approve or reject changes and new contributions. Translators should be able to modify terms and associated information in their working languages only. Some users should be given read-only access while having the opportunity to provide comments or feedback. All this requires different levels of access along with workflows to channel the work to the appropriate individuals. Access controls can even be implemented at the field level, for instance, to allow only certain people to write definitions. Workflow functions that automate handoffs from one person to the next raise the productivity of everyone involved.

Figure 7.7 shows a simple workflow: when an entry is created, the process status is automatically set to "unprocessed." At the end of the day, an e-mail is automatically sent to the terminologist. The e-mail contains a link to all newly-created entries so that he or she can review and approve them.

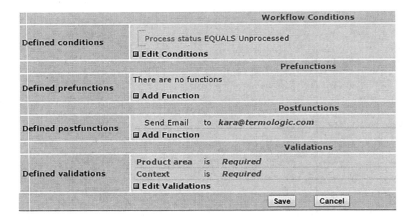

Figure 7.7 Setting up an automated workflow in TermWeb

Figure 7.8 shows a compilation of workflows that might be suitable for managing terminology in a large organisation.[11] Note the use of term extraction tools as a way to collect term candidates on a large scale.

Finally, one needs to ensure that the underlying technology for storing terminology is robust, such as that provided by a relational database management system. The tabular format described earlier should not be confused with the tables in a relational database. Modelled appropriately with a sufficient number of inter-related tables, a relational database is a powerful architecture for developing a terminological knowledge-base. IBM's termbase, built on DB2 (a relational database management system) contains many features of a full-fledged knowledge-base. On the other hand, a terminology management system that uses a relational database containing only one table – and some do – is no better than a spreadsheet. The data model has to be appropriately designed according to the ISO standards mentioned previously.

An example of an enterprise-scale terminology management system

The terminological entries we have shown as examples were created in a terminology management system called TermWeb. This terminology management system is developed by Interverbum Technology,[12] a language technology company based in Sweden. TermWeb is a standalone application: it is not part of either a controlled authoring or a computer-aided translation tool. Entirely web-based, TermWeb is the first platform-independent terminology management system with an open-architecture allowing integration with any existing enterprise application. But what is also novel is its support of bi-directional hierarchical concept relations of various kinds (generic, meronymic, associative), multi-level

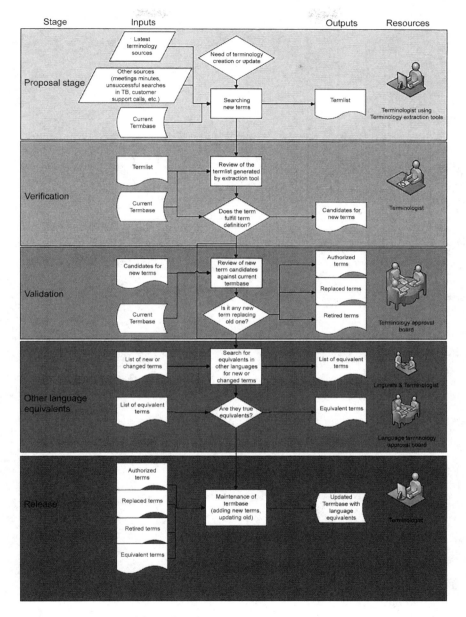

Figure 7.8 Sample workflows for a large organisation

subject-field taxonomies, granular subsetting mechanisms, a comprehensive array of unique identifiers that allows efficient management of synonyms and homonyms, and visual rendering of concept systems (sometimes called concept maps). An example of a concept map is shown in Figure 7.9. It also supports graphics,

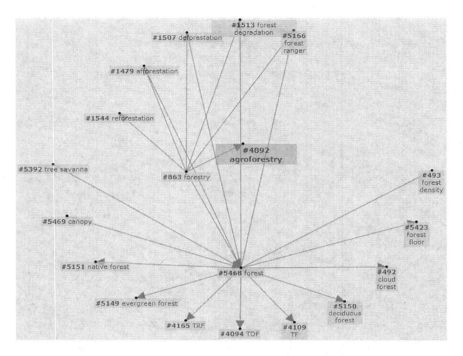

Figure 7.9 A concept map in TermWeb

and features customisable workflows. These features make TermWeb suitable for developing multipurpose terminological resources.

Conclusion

In an enterprise environment, it is essential to adopt terminology practices and data models that are capable of addressing various use cases and potential applications beyond the most conventional. With respect to suitable technologies, application-specific terminology management systems, such as those that are embedded in controlled authoring and computer-assisted translation tools, may not meet all requirements. Terminologists working in production environments should be open-minded: ready and willing to adapt conventional practices and theories to pragmatic requirements where necessary. They need to embrace innovation, such as by incorporating corpus-analysis tools into their workbench, and by exploring advances in natural language processing. Finally, they need to have the vision to anticipate and even invent new applications of terminology data that could benefit their organisation.

Notes

1. iso.i-term.dk/login.php and www.iso.org/obp/ui/.
2. A data category is a type of information one might find in a language resource. In a termbase, typical examples are: term, definition, part of speech, usage note.
3. www.terminorgs.net.
4. ecolexicon.ugr.es/en/index.htm.
5. olst.ling.umontreal.ca/cgi-bin/dicoinfo/search.cgi.
6. www.keenage.com.
7. aims.fao.org/standards/agrovoc.
8. eurovoc.europa.eu/drupal/.
9. www.ihtsdo.org/snomed-ct.
10. It is beyond the scope of this chapter to describe all the required features.
11. Courtesy of TerminOrgs.
12. www.interverbumtech.com/.

References

Ahmad, Khurshid (2001) "The role of specialist terminology in artificial intelligence and knowledge acquisition", in Sue Ellen Wright and Gerhard Budin (eds.) *Handbook of Terminology Management*, Vol. 2, Amsterdam and Philadelphia: John Benjamins Publishing Company, 809–844.

Buchan, Ronald (1993) "Quality indexing with computer-aided lexicography", in Helmi B. Sonneveld and Kurt L. Loening (eds.) *Terminology: Applications in Interdisciplinary Communication*, Amsterdam and Philadelphia: John Benjamins Publishing Company, 69–78.

Cabré, Maria Teresa (1999) *Terminology – Theory, Methods and Applications*, Amsterdam and Philadelphia: John Benjamins Publishing Company.

Galinski, Christian (1994) "Exchange of standardized terminologies within the framework of the standardized terminology exchange network", in Sue Ellen Wright and Richard Alan Strehlow (eds.) *Standardizing and Harmonizing Terminology: Theory and Practice*, Philadelphia: American Society for Testing and Materials, 141–149.

Greenwald, Susan (1994) "A construction industry terminology database developed for use with a periodicals index", in Sue Ellen Wright and Richard Alan Strehlow (eds.) *Standardizing and Harmonizing Terminology: Theory and Practice*, Philadelphia: American Society for Testing and Materials, 115–125.

Ibekwe-SanJuan, Fidelia, Anne Condamines, and Maria Teresa Cabré Castellvi (2007) *Application-Driven Terminology Engineering*, Amsterdam and Philadelphia: John Benjamins Publishing Company.

Jacquemin, Christian (2001) *Spotting and Discovering Terms Through Natural Language Processing*, Cambridge, MA: MIT Press.

Knops, Eugenia and Gregor Thurmair (1993) "Design of a multifunctional Lexicon", in Helmi B. Sonneveld and Kurt L. Loening (eds.) *Terminology: Applications in Interdisciplinary Communication*, Amsterdam and Philadelphia: John Benjamins Publishing Company, 87–109.

Meyer, Ingrid (1993) "Concept management for terminology: A knowledge engineering approach", in Sue Ellen Wright and Richard Alan Strehlow (eds.) *Standardizing Terminology for Better Communication: Practice, Applied Theory, and Results*, Philadelphia: American Society for Testing and Materials, 140–151.

Myking, Johan (2007) "No fixed boundaries", in Bassey Edem Antia (ed.) *Indeterminacy in Terminology and LSP*, Amsterdam and Philadelphia: John Benjamins Publishing Company, 73–91.

Nazarenko, Adeline and Touria Ait El Mekki (2007) "Building back-of-the-book indexes", in Fidelia Ibekwe-San Juan, Anne Condamines, and M. Teresa Cabré Castellvi (eds.) *Application-Driven Terminology Engineering*, Amsterdam and Philadelphia: John Benjamins Publishing Company, 179–202.

Ó Broin, Ultan (2009) "Controlled authoring to improve localization", *Multilingual* 20(7): 12.

Sager, Juan (1990) *A Practical Course in Terminology Processing*, Amsterdam and Philadelphia: John Benjamins Publishing Company.

Schubert, Klaus (2011) "Specialized communication studies: An expanding discipline", in Margrethe Petersen and Jan Engberg (eds.) *Current Trends in LSP Research: Aims and Methods*, Bern: Peter Lang, 19–58.

Strehlow, Richard Alan (2001) "Terminology and indexing", in Sue Ellen Wright and Gerhard Budin (eds.) *Handbook of Terminology Management*, Vol. 2, Amsterdam and Philadelphia: John Benjamins Publishing Company, 419–425.

Strehlow, Richard Alan (2001) "The role of terminology in retrieving information", in Sue Ellen Wright and Gerhard Budin (eds.) *Handbook of Terminology Management*, Vol. 2, Amsterdam and Philadelphia: John Benjamins Publishing Company, 426–444.

Warburton, Kara (2013) "Processing terminology for the translation pipeline", *Terminology* 19(1): 93–111.

Warburton, Kara (2014a) "Narrowing the gap between termbases and corpora in commercial environments", PhD dissertation, City University of Hong Kong, available from www.termologic.com/resource-area.

Warburton, Kara (2014b) "Developing lexical resources for controlled authoring purposes", paper presented at the Controlled Natural Language Workshop (W2), LREC, Reykjavik, available from www.lrec-conf.org/proceedings/lrec2014/index.html.

Warburton, Kara and Barbara Inge Karsch (2012) "Optimizing global content in Internet search", technical report presented to the University of Vienna, available from www.researchgate.net/publication/275100883_Global_search_optimization_-_Managing_multilingual_search_keywords.

Wettengel, Tanguy and Aidan Van de Weyer (2001) "Terminology in technical writing", in Sue Ellen Wright and Gerhard Budin (eds.) *Handbook of Terminology Management*, Vol. 2, Amsterdam and Philadelphia: John Benjamins Publishing Company, 445–466.

Wetzel, Michael (2008) "Structured termbases – Why spreadsheets soon fail", available from the author: michael@cmwetzel.de.

8 Corpora and CAT-based CN-EN translation of Chinese culture

Xu Bin

The strategy of "going global" of Chinese culture and Chinese-English translating practice

Since the new century, with the rising of its comprehensive national strength, China began to focus on the development of its soft power and began to pay more attention to enhancing the influence of Chinese culture in the world. In 2010, the National Social Science Foundation of China (NSFC) set up a new category of programs called "Translation Projects of Chinese Academic Works on Chinese Culture Studies." This can be seen as a measure to carry out a major national strategy aimed to enhance the influence of Chinese culture, making it "going global." The main purpose of setting up translation projects of Chinese academic works is to provide funds for the translation and publication of Chinese cultural research in other languages, enhance the spreading and understanding of contemporary research results in Chinese philosophy, social sciences, and traditional Chinese culture, and thus enhance the international influence of Chinese culture on the whole. Yang Muzhi noted that this undertaking "is required by the cultural exchanges between China and the outside world; it is necessary if we want to make the world know China better;" it is also required by the development of China's "soft power" (2007). However, this endeavor has been hindered by the bottlenecks in the efficiency and quality in translation.

Being an important part in the typography of Chinese culture translation, the translation of academic works on Chinese culture has achieved some results, and related studies have also started. In contrast, the studies on the broader topic of "Chinese culture translation" initiated earlier has made more progress. In his "Review on the study of Chinese cultural translation", Wu Yaowu and Meng (2014) point out that the development of Chinese culture translation can be divided into three stages: (1) the start-up period (1980–2002); (2) the expansion period (2003–09); and (3) the peak period (after 2010). In these three stages, the studies focus mainly on comprehensive discussions and evaluations of translation works, introduction to translators and translation strategies (mainly generalized strategies rather than specific translation skills), and theoretical analysis. Searching in China Integrated Knowledge Resources Database (CNKI) with the key words including *translation*, *culture*, *technology*, and *corpus/corpora* reveal that the findings of most retrieved papers are in accordance with this conclusion, and also reveal that these studies fail to link the translation practice of Chinese culture with modern translation technologies (terminology technology, computer-aided translation [CAT], computer-based project management, etc.).

However, we should see that the vast majority of translators and researchers involved in Chinese culture translation already have mature viewpoints in translation ethics, cultural standpoints, macro translation strategies, and other issues. Therefore, in this field, the most urgent question is how to improve the efficiency and quality in translation instead of determining the general macro translation strategies. Unfortunately, this aspect has long been neglected by the academic circle.

Based on long-term research on the application of corpora technology and computer-aided translation in translation, the author of this chapter believes that the use of modern translation technology, particularly the use of digitalized project management tools, computer monolingual and multi-lingual corpora, as well as professional computer-aided translation systems, is the most direct and rapid way of enhancing the efficiency and quality of Chinese culture translation.

Parallel corpora and Chinese culture translation

Much research has proved that corpus technology has significant value for translation practice. Searching CNKI, 450 relevant papers published since 2000 in high quality academic journals can be retrieved. Many domestic and foreign researchers argue that corpus is a valuable resource in translation teaching and translation practice. It can be used to improve the translator's language proficiency and cultural awareness, and provide a working platform and reference tool for translators. By examining the understanding of the contents in different professional fields, the selection of terms and specific expressions, Bowker (1998) finds that with the aid of corpora, there is "a general trend towards improved quality translation for the categories of subject-field understanding, correct term choice, and idiomatic expression." Many domestic researchers also suggest that Chinese-English parallel corpora have a high value for translation teaching and translation practice (Wang 2004; Wang 2011). However, other researchers also noted that using parallel translation corpora as a reference may lead to "translationese" (Baker 1993; Teubert 1996: 247).

With the realization of the significance of corpora for translation practice and studies, many scholars have developed or are developing corpora in China. However, there are some flaws and misunderstandings in the application of corpora in the practice of translating Chinese culture: (1) the purposes of current corpora development are mostly for translation studies, with very little research mentioning the applicability of such corpora in the translation practice of Chinese culture; (2) in the comparatively rare studies involving the application of Chinese-English parallel corpora in translation, the direction of language pair in the texts selected is consistent with the direction of language in translation practice. That is, when the translation direction is from Chinese into English, the designers/developers of such corpora tend to choose original Chinese works which have been translated into English. Researchers fail to notice the great reference potential that "reverse" parallel corpora have for such translation practices; (3) related research fails to point out the homogeneity between parallel corpora and translation memory, and thus fail to see the value of alignment tools found in many computer-aided translation systems in creating parallel corpora; and (4) such studies fail to pay attention to the practical process of translation, and thus fail to see the potential of computer-aided translation in significantly improving productivity in translation. So far, among all the retrieved research papers on Chinese culture translation from CNKI, none has pointed out that in the translation of Chinese culture, modern translation technology (typically computer-aided translation) can be, and should be used to improve the productivity in these translation practices.

Resources in Sinology works and the development of parallel corpora

A majority of the existing works written by western sinologists focusing on Chinese history contain a large number of descriptions about special phenomena and unique items in Chinese culture. They can serve as great translation resources for translators. Generally speaking, such resources contain two types of reference elements: (1) terms related to Chinese culture; and (2) the unique ways to interpret the phenomena in Chinese culture.

In the translation of technical text, entries of terminology often have a one-to-one correspondence. But in cultural translation, the core terms in Chinese culture, with their rich contents and connotations, tend to have a more complex "one to many" relationship with their English equivalents. Through mining and reviewing the core terms of Chinese culture in Sinology works, translators can build an awareness of the importance of terminology, and also develop their ability in choosing terms.

Apart from terminology, Chinese culture translation also involves rendering some unique ways in interpreting the cultural content. These unique expressions are typically used by Chinese researchers, and they often turn out to be obstacles for translators. By studying the works on the same subject written by western sinologists, translators can improve their ability in interpreting these ideas. And with corpora technology, we can include a large amount of texts in the databases, which provide fast searching and retrieval to assist the translators.

Based on the above analysis, while developing corpora with the aim of aiding Chinese culture translation, we should take a "reverse route" – using texts about China's history, philosophy, etc. written by western sinologists and their corresponding Chinese translations as the major source of the raw material. In practice, when we make concordances in such corpora, we can "reverse" the queries, retrieving texts written by western authors with Chinese key words and using them as translation references. By doing so, we can effectively avoid translationese.

Apart from making full use of corpora as an aid, translators of Chinese culture also need to implement computer-aided translation to improve efficiency and quality – a measure that other areas in the translation industry have already adopted for several decades worldwide. Seeing the necessity of corpora and computer-aided translation in Chinese culture translation, we know the most urgent task at present is to develop more comprehensive corpora of Sinology works. When corpora on this subject reach a certain scale and contain most of the core Chinese terms, expressions, and even full texts of Chinese classics, the efficiency and quality of translation of Chinese culture can be greatly improved.

Selection of texts for Chinese culture parallel corpora

In preparing the texts of Sinology, books like *Guoji Hanxue Zhuzuo Tiyao* (*Summary of International Sinology*) by Li Xueqin, or *Beimei Hanxuejia Cidian* (*A Guidebook to Sinologists in North America*) by An Pingqiu et al. can be used as roadmaps. With the help of state-of-the-art OCR technology and alignment tools, raw materials can be input into a computer and converted to standard translation memory databases (TMX) and term bases (TBX). Such databases are the foundation for the application of Sinology corpora in Chinese culture translation under the environment of computer-aided translation.

In addition, as an expansion to the basic design, this corpus should also include the bilingual texts of core Chinese classics, such as the major works of Confucianism, Taoism, and other philosophies, and even include some other frequently quoted texts in Chinese culture, such as poetry in the Tang and Song dynasties, etc. With such an extended version of the translation memory and terminology databases of Chinese culture, translators can access most of the core terms and quotations in Chinese culture while translating. Such corpora can also serve as valuable materials for the training of high-performance and high-quality machine translation engines specialized for Chinese culture translation.

Feasibility of sinology corpora: a case analysis

In order to test the feasibility of Sinology corpora development and application, I conducted a small-scale case study. The basic design is:

(1) Collecting Sinology works and corresponding translations, converting the texts into digital formats, and aligning bilingual texts to the sentence level.
(2) Mining the terms of Chinese culture and establishing terminology databases;
(3) Analyzing terms and their usage in translation project under computer-aided translation programs.

(1) Selection of the text

In this case, I used Chapter II "The First Unification: Imperial Confucianism" of John King Fairbank's *China: A New History* (second enlarged edition printed in 2006) as the original text. Selecting this part of the book as the basis for the corpora is mainly based on two considerations. First, Fairbank has a high reputation in the field of Sinology. His personal experiences gave him an in-depth understanding of China. He is both concise and creative in explaining China-specific phenomenon to the world in English. This book is a work of academic maturity, and the terms used in the book have stood the test of time. The Chinese translation is selected from the traditional Chinese version published in 1994 in Taipei.

(2) Aligning texts for translation memories

To prepare the texts for creating the translation memory, a scanner is used to digitalize the pages into the computer. And then an OCR program is used to "recognize" the texts both in English and Chinese. An additional three hours were required to eliminate the errors in the recognition of the full text of the chapter. Then, based on a comparison of the efficiency of different computer-aided translation tools, I chose "Snowman CAT", a Chinese computer-aided translation product, as the alignment tool.

Snowman CAT's alignment function does not simply rely on punctuations to delimit and align segments. It can make use of its various dictionaries to establish anchors to improve the alignment automatically. With this rudimentary artificial intelligence feature, human intervention in alignment is minimized. In recent years, more and more alignment tools begin to implement similar intelligent features. For example, the online alignment tool provided by TMXMall (www.tmxmall.com/aligner) uses machine translation engines to help improve the alignment results.

In addition, compared with other computer-aided translation tools, the operations in Snowman CAT are more intuitive, which can help improve the efficiency in aligning. For example, when we need to split a sentence, instead of calling the function through clicking a specially devised button, we can simply put the cursor at the position to split, and then press Enter. This operation follows the same principle as when we want to split a sentence or a paragraph in most word processing software.

Such intuitive designs can improve the efficiency of alignment. Table 8.1 shows the statistics of the alignment (錯誤! 找不到參照來源。).

Table 8.1 Statistics of alignment

File name	Words		Number of characters		Sentences		Translation Units
	SL Text	Translation	SL Text	Translation	SL Text	Translation	
China: A New History 2	9878	15040	49212	15557	388	386	386

(3) Term extraction

After the alignment, candidate terms will be extracted from the aligned texts. Based on the aim of application of the project, the terms that are to be extracted include core Chinese culture words, as well as extended concepts or expressions based on the core terms, such as people's names, institutions, objective matters, book titles, popular citations from Chinese classical works, and names of some famous sinologists and so on. Since "[r]esearching the specific terms needed to complete any given translation is a time-consuming task" (Bowker 2002: 77), preparing terminology based on the corpora construction is of high significance. Here are some examples:

Core terms of Chinese culture:

天干	celestial stems
地支	earthly branches
法家	Legalist

Extended concepts or expressions:

木生火	wood producing fire
金克木 (五行的相生相克理论)	wood conquered by metal
作奸犯科	wrongdoing
作奸犯科	malefactors
抑商	downgraded merchants

Historical figures:

始皇帝	First Emperor (Shi huangdi)
商鞅	Lord Shang

Social system or institution:

官僚制度	bureaucracy
保伍组织	units of five

Objective matters:

秦俑	ceramic soldiers
驿道	post road
城池	walled capital

Titles of classics:

易经	*Yijing*

Many famous sinologists tend to have Chinese names rather than using the transliterations from their original names. Failing to recognize and convert a famous scholar's name in translating Chinese cultural works can be a major embarrassment. So a proper list of the names of the famous sinologists is a necessity.

Names of Sinologists:

史华慈	Schwartz
墨子刻	Metzger
韩德森	Henderson

Moreover, as many works on Chinese culture often quote some famous sayings from the classics, it is necessary to include those sayings in an appropriate database. Comparing the natures of term bases and translation memory, it is more advisable to store these sayings in term bases. Here are two quotations that could be found in the text in this case:

Quotations:

其身正，不令而行；其身不正，虽令不从	When a prince's personal conduct is correct, his government is effective without the issuing of orders. If his personal conduct is not correct, he may issue orders but they will not be followed
君君臣臣父父子子	jun jun chen chen fu fu zi zi (Let the ruler rule as he should and the minister be a minister as he should. Let the father act as a father should and the son act as a son should)

The final term base contains 333 entries, a total of 1199 Chinese characters, accounting for nearly 8% of the total number of characters (15,557 characters). The "terminology density" (number of characters of Chinese cultural terms and expressions divided by the total number of characters of the Chinese version) is significantly higher than normal texts of general purposes.

Application of computer-aided translation in Chinese culture translation

One of the key resources in computer-aided translation is "translation memory", which is a bilingual parallel corpus in essence. The international translation memory standard is called Translation Memory eXchange (TMX). It is an XML-based parallel corpora format.

Corpora used in translation practice normally do not have to be as complicated as that used for corpora-based translation studies. In computer-aided translation programs, only good alignment and deep mining of terms are required for automatic term search (auto-search) or concordance functions. Such parallel corpora can be built much faster and are easier to maintain. In particular, as mentioned before, a number of computer-aided translation tools also include state-of-the-art alignment modules or features, which can be used to quickly align texts and extract terms. In addition, there are also professional alignment tools that provide more efficient alignment services.

After nearly 30 years of development, computer-aided translation technology has gradually matured. Much research and numerous reports on cases of computer-aided translation application have shown that computer-aided translation can effectively improve translation productivity by means of providing better project management, streamlining translation process, improving efficiency, and ensuring quality. In the language service industry, computer-aided translation deployment has become so essential that it determines a translation agency's survival.

At present, most translators have recognized the crucial supporting role that computer-aided translation plays in technical text translation. However, as often suggested by computer-aided translation developers, and also limited by their experiences and/or intuitions, many translators and translation researchers tend to think that computer-aided translation is only suitable in translating technical texts. While for the translation of semi-creative texts or creative texts – such as Chinese culture texts, they hold the opinion that computer-aided translation is not applicable. For example, Quah (2008: 193) argues that "most translation memory tools have been developed mainly with the translation of technical texts in mind, and consequently translation tools such as translation memory are unlikely to be as useful for semi-creative and highly creative texts." Lynne Bowker (2002: 112) points out that "[n]ot all the texts are equally suitable for inclusion in a TM," and then says "[t]ypically, technical, scientific, and legal texts tend to contain repetition, whereas literature and advertising texts tend to contain less repetition and are therefore typically less suitable for inclusion in a TM." Austermuehl (2006:139) also points out that technical texts are more suitable for translating with computer-aided translation tools. Though these researchers have not argued explicitly that computer-aided translation are not suitable for translating texts of cultural studies, most translators tend to categorize such terms as semi-creative or creative ones, and hence consider them not suitable for computer-aided translation tools.

Based on years of translation practice with computer-aided translation, I have found that translation memory systems are able to bring benefits to the translation of non-technical texts. In the book *Computer-aided Translation: A New Horizon for Translating Research and Practice*, I suggest that computer-aided translation can be used in translating non-technical texts, because it can (1) provide more a convenient and faster translation texts input environment; (2) provide a more ergonomic translation environment; and (3) provide a more friendly translation quality control environment (Xu 2010). The paper "Non-technical text translation practice based on computer-aided translation and machine translation" (Xu and Guo 2015) introduces an empirical study and systematic analysis on the applicability of computer-aided translation in translating creative texts, and further argues that a new translation model of combining machine translation, computer-aided translation, and post-editing (MT-CAT-PE) should be taken seriously by translators and translation researchers in this field. As to the translation of Chinese culture, whether the MT-CAT-PE model can aid the translators has not been verified. However, based on translation projects on other subjects which have successfully implemented this model (Xu and Hongmei 2015), we can make a reasonable deduction that a machine translation engine trained with sufficient parallel texts of Chinese culture will be highly probable in providing more support for Chinese culture translation.

At present, the vast majority of the texts to be translated for introducing and spreading Chinese culture has a considerable degree of creativity, and should be considered as non-technical texts. Though they are not literary texts, they contain many creative elements, thus making them belong to the semi-creative or creative genre. As mentioned in this chapter before, almost no research on the translation of this type of texts has ever mentioned the necessity of applying computer-aided translation technology. Nonetheless, in *Non-technical text translation practice based on CAT and MT*, I argue that the translation of Chinese culture should pay special attention to the application of computer-aided translation tools. Based on the analysis in the previous section, we find that the texts of Chinese culture have a high "terminology density", so popular features of computer-aided translation tools such as auto-search, auto-assemble (named differently in different tools, which generally means to insert corresponding terms found in the term bases into the editing text box for the segment to be translated) can make the translation of such texts much more convenient. Especially, if such functions are combined with the proposed Sinology parallel corpora, which can provide high quality and highly-related term bases and translation memories for the translation of Chinese cultural texts, the translation practice will receive much assistance.

(1) Terminology search

Many computer-aided translation tools provide functions like auto-search, which can give prompts of translation candidates for stored terms. Furthermore, translators can retrieve more information of the usage of a specific term and related examples through the function of concordance, which is normally not included in the auto-search function, but should be invoked by the user, as it searches the translation memory as well as the linked corpus more thoroughly and hence requires more computing resources. For example, when we meet the Chinese word *chengchi* (城池), by concordance, we can find the following examples in the mini-corpora:

Example 1:

> By the so-called Spring-and-Autumn period (722–481 BC) there were about 170 such states, each centered in its <u>walled capital.</u>
> 到了春秋时代（西元前七二二～四八一），诸侯国多达一百七十余个，各国都有自己的城(chéng)池(chí)。

The translation information provided by a typical bilingual dictionary is a kind of interpretation, rather than concise translation. For example, in *Modern Chinese Dictionary* (English-Chinese bilingual edition), the term *chengchi* is explained as "city wall and moat; city." Such interpretive expressions are normally inappropriate to be used in the translation without modification. By contrast, if we make a concordance search of the word *chengchi*, the corpora return "walled capital" as the corresponding term with context. Such an expression is apparently more accurate in describing the cities in the Spring and Autumn Period (770–476 BC).

Lionbridge (2009) estimates that 15% of the total cost of translation and localization projects is caused by rework or reprocessing; and the main reason for rework is inconsistency in terminology. Based on the development of Sinology parallel corpora, with deep mining of Chinese cultural terms, and under the environment of computer-aided translation tools, the translation of Chinese culture can achieve high terminology consistency, which in turn significantly reduces the chance of rework, and improves the productivity of Chinese culture translation.

(2) Translation example retrieval and translation assistance

Apart from automatic terminology search and prompting, translators can also benefit from the concordance search provided by several popular computer-aided translation tools. Such searching function provides both equivalent term translations as well as the context.

Example 2:

> The Liu clan of Earlier Han provided 13 emperors and in Later Han 14 emperors, the Li clan of the Tang dynasty 23 emperors, the Zhu clan of the Ming dynasty 17 emperors, and the Aisin Gioro lineage of the Manchus 9 emperors.
> 西汉刘氏共传位十三代皇帝，东汉共十四位。　唐代李氏延续二十三位皇帝，明代朱氏十七位，清代爱新觉罗氏则有九位。

The above example is acquired through the query of *shi* (氏). In this example, a translator can learn not only the method of translating *shi* into English, but also learn the expressions of different dynasties, as well as the special Aisin Gioro

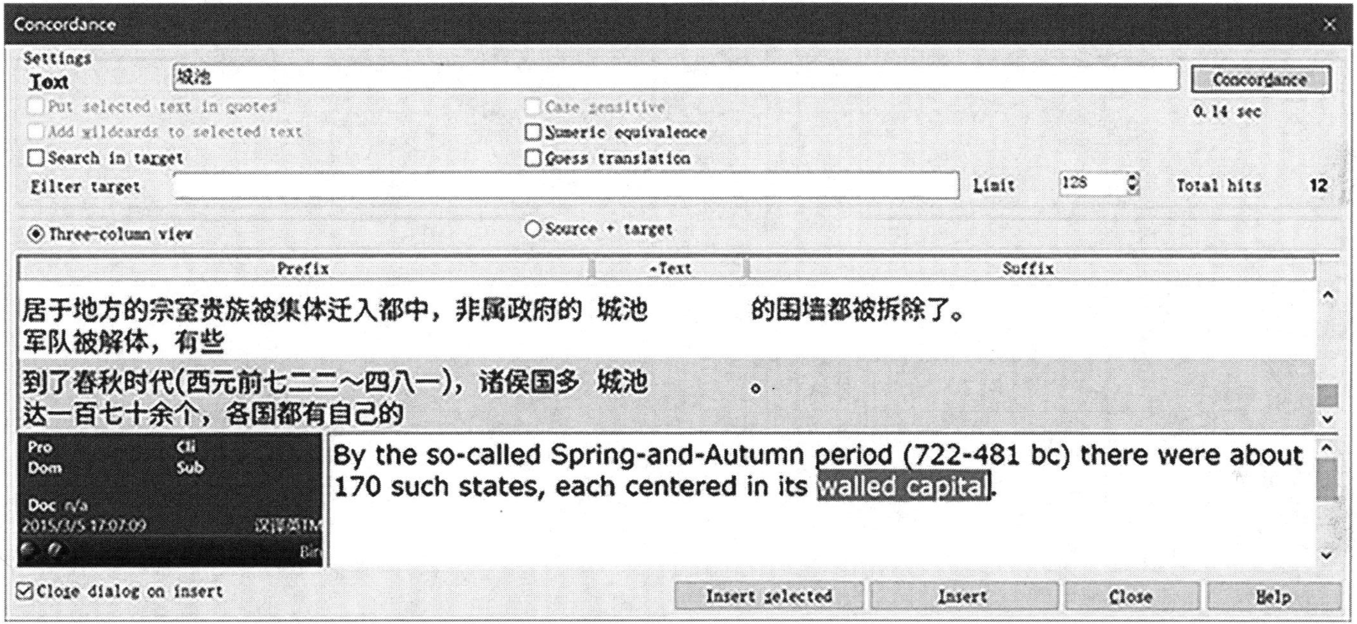

Figure 8.1 The concordance results of "chengchi"

lineage of the Manchus. More importantly, a western sinologist is normally more flexible in expression of Chinese culture (here, clan and lineage are used interchangeably); the concise structure in the sentence is also a good example for good style in writing.

Example 3:

> In the Zhou period as in the Shang, <u>veneration</u> of the ancestors through <u>sacrifices</u>, both animal and human, made use of the highest achievements of art – <u>the bronze ritual vessels</u> – and maintained the ruler's <u>legitimacy</u> by his <u>liturgical activities</u>.
> 周代与商代情形一样，经由献祭 – 不拘是献人或牲畜 – 完成的祖先崇拜仪式，使用了艺术最高成就的青铜礼器，也藉祭拜活动维持统治者的合法性

The above example is the result of searching *ji* (祭). *Modern Chinese Dictionary* (English bilingual edition) gives two meanings for this word: (1) to perform a memorial service, and (2) to offer a sacrifice to someone. Translators, however, normally cannot use the explained meanings in translation. Much consideration and proper modification will be made. The dilemma is especially acute for Chinese-English translators, as there are no Chinese-English learners' dictionaries with descriptions of language usage like that offered by *Oxford Advanced Learners' Dictionary*.

So, common bilingual dictionaries often prove to be incomplete as they severely lack usage information for translators. The meanings they provide are essentially explanations rather than translations, which can only work as some kind of hints or directions for translators, rather than strict translations. In contrast, parallel corpora that reach a certain scale can often provide more authentic examples, which are more inspiring for translation work.

Many experienced translators have recognized that "existing translations contain more solutions to more translation problems than any other available resource." (Isabelle, cited in Hunt 2003) The fact that corpora are gaining more and more attention in the field of translation research is a manifestation of this perception. Based on the analysis of Chinese culture translation, the inter-relations between corpora, translation, and computer-aided translation applications, I believe: parallel corpora of Sinology texts can assist Chinese culture translation greatly by providing more authentic references. On the basis of corpus development, after converting such corpora into translation memories, and by extracting the core terms and expressions from the TMs, all the resulted resources can be used in most standard computer-aided translation programs, and hence promote the productivity of Chinese culture translation, solving the current bottlenecks of translation efficiency and quality.

Of course, we need to notice that though there are many language pearls in Sinology works, some terms need to be scrutinized, as they may reflect different cultural standpoints than those of the Chinese people.

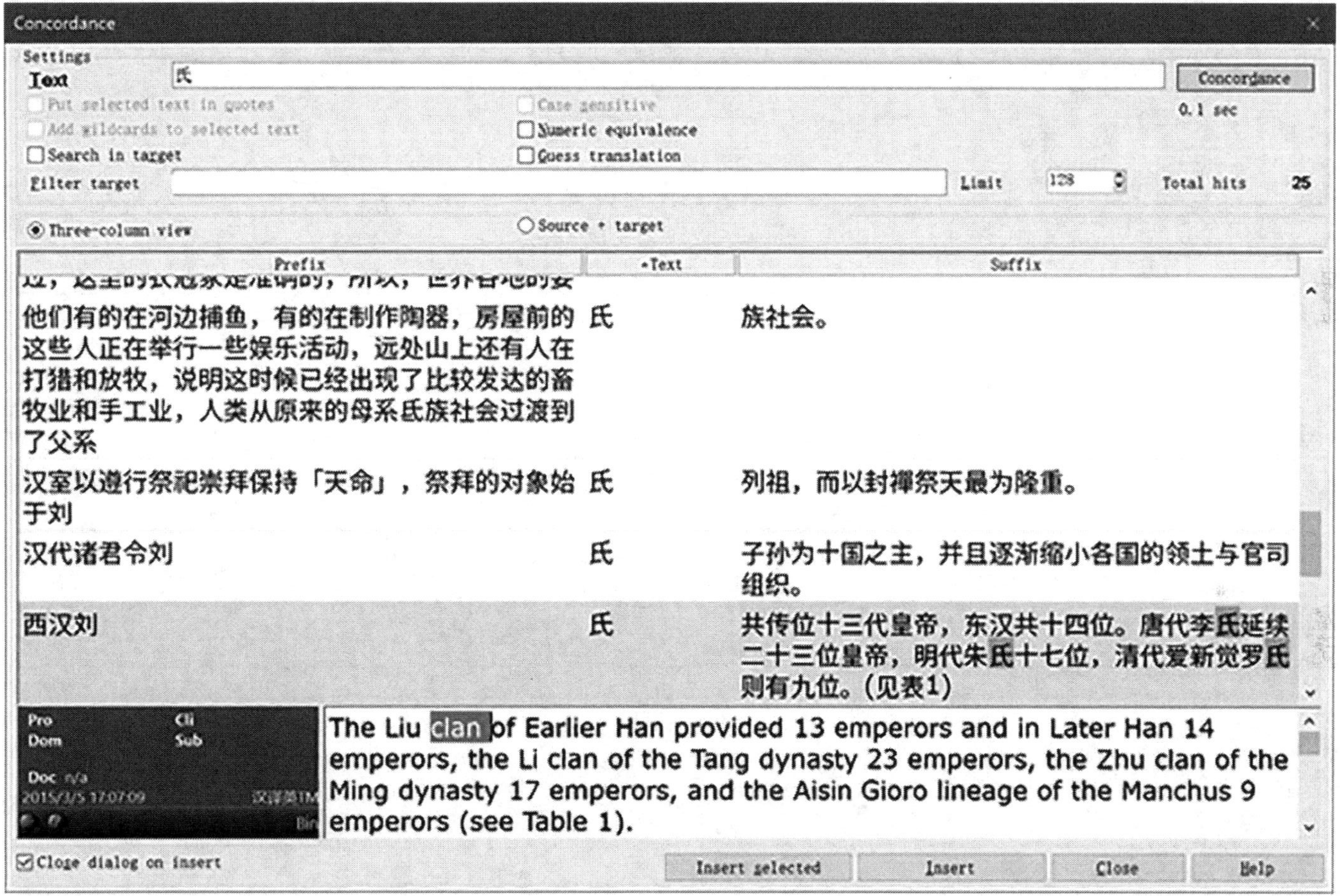

Figure 8.2 The concordance results of “shi”

Conclusion

Based on the analysis of this chapter, we know that for a long time, the relevant teaching and research on Chinese-English translation have ignored the following three points: (1) excellent Sinology works and their translations are the kind of texts that Chinese-English translators in China should give priority to in learning and studying; (2) with the application of computer-aided translation technology, translators of Chinese culture can effectively mine and recycle what has been already translated and has been accepted by translators – and readers in general; and (3) application of computer-aided translation program can help streamline project management in translation, making the whole process more controllable, and improving productivity in translation.

The combination of Sinology parallel corpora development, deep mining of core terms, and the application of computer-aided translation technology forms an overall solution to the translation of Chinese culture, which can effectively assist translators and researchers in this field.

Specifically, this corpora and MT-CAT-PE solution to the translation of Chinese culture can achieve the following four effects:

(1) Improving quality control of Chinese culture translation

Using computer-aided translation technology in translation can help improve translation efficiency and quality. If properly used in the translation projects of Chinese culture, translators can make use of the quality assurance functions to effectively reduce errors (like term inconsistency, etc.) and monitor the quality of the translation.

(2) Streamlining project management of Chinese culture translation

At present, as no research paper has ever mentioned the use of computer-aided translation in Chinese culture translation, we can safely deduce that most such translation projects are carried out using traditional collaboration methods. As a result, translators in a team do not have efficient methods to share and update terminology and translated units. So the accumulated resources and experiences by any individual translator can hardly be disseminated and shared effectively. With the deployment of network computer-aided translation platforms, and with the accumulation of core translation resources (term bases and translation memories) of Chinese culture, large-scale multi-translator collaboration can be achieved. In that case, project management goals like terminology consistency, team collaboration, team proofreading, etc., can be achieved.

(3) Developing a computer-aided translation-enabled Chinese culture translating model and accumulating resources

Translating under any computer-aided translation environment, knowledge created by human translators can be automatically stored as new translation memory and term base contents. Such data can also be used for the training of machine translation engines. In turn, the study of the feasibility of applying the post-editing method in the translation of Chinese culture (i.e., processing the source language texts with machine translation engines and editing them by human translators) can be carried out in the future.

(4) Providing the knowledge base for translator training

Resources like translation memories and term bases can be effectively reused in future projects. In addition, as the resulted translation memories can be converted to bilingual corpora, they provide valuable material for the training of translators specialized in Chinese culture translation.

References

Austermuehl, Frank (2006) *Electronic Tools for Translators* (1st ed.), Beijing: Foreign Language Education and Research Press.
Baker, Mona (1993) "Corpus linguistics and translation studies: Implications and applications", in Mona Baker, Gill Francis, and Elena Tognini-Bonelli (eds.) *Text and Technology: In Honour of John Sinclair*, Amsterdam and Philadelphia: John Benjamins Publishing Company, 233-250.
Bowker, Lynne (1998) "Using specialized monolingual native-language corpora as a translation resource: A pilot study", *Translators' Journal* 43(4): 631–651.
Bowker, Lynne (2002) *Computer-Aided Translation Technology: A Practical Introduction*, Ottawa: University of Ottawa Press.
Hunt, Timothy (2003) "Translation technology failures and future", *Globalization Insider* XII (1.4), available from www.translationdirectory.com/article440.htm.
Lionbridge (2009) "Building stronger brands around the world: A guide to effective global marketing, 2009 [OL]", available from www.slideshare.net/Lionbridge/building-strongerbrands-around-the-world, 2013–08–12.
Quah, C. K. (2008) *Translation and Technology* (1st ed.), Shanghai: Shanghai Foreign Language Education Press.
Teubert, Wolfgang (1996) "Comparable or parallel corpora?" available from http://dx.doi.org/10.1093/ijl/9.3.238.
Wang, Kefei 王克非 (2004) 〈双语平行语料库在翻译教学上的用途〉("The use of parallel corpora in translator training"), 《外语电化教学》(*Computer-Assisted Foreign Language Education*) (6).
Wang, Lifei 王立非 (2011) 〈高校《机辅商务翻译》课程建设及教学系统的研发〉("Development of the course 'Computer-aided Business Translation' and the teaching system"), 《中国翻译》(*Chinese Translators Journal*) 2: 34–37.
Wu, Yaowu 吴耀武 and Hua Meng 花萌 (2014) 〈中国文化对外翻译国内研究综述(1980–2013) – 基于国内学术期刊的数据分析〉("A survey of Chinese culture translation (1980–2013), based on an analysis of the data from academic journals in mainland China"), 《外语教学》(*Foreign Language Education*) 6: 104–109.
Xu, Bin 徐彬 (2010) 《翻译新视野 – 计算机辅助翻译研究》(*Computer-Aided Translation: A New Horizon for Translating Research and Practice*) (1st ed.), 济南 Jinan: 山东教育出版社 Shandong Education Press.

Xu, Bin 徐彬 and Guo Hongmei 郭红梅 (2015) 〈基于计算机技术的非技术文本翻译实践〉 ("Non-technical text translation practice based on computer-aided translation and machine translation"), 《中国翻译》 (*Chinese Translators Journal*) 1: 81–86.

Yang, Muzhi 杨牧之 (2007) 〈国家"软实力"与世界文化的交流 – 《大中华文库》编辑出版启示〉 ("Soft power and culture exchange in the world – Enlightenment of the publication of *Library of Chinese Classics*"), 《中国编辑》 (*Chinese Editors*) 2(12): 22–27.

9 Issues of language structure in machine translation between English and Kiswahili

Sarah Ndanu M. Ngesu

1 Introduction

The choice of translations from English into Kiswahili has been motivated by the effort made to make Kiswahili language keep up with global trends of developments (Shivachi 2001; Shitemi 2011; Bakari 2012; Kanana 2013; Khamis 2015; Momanyi 2014; Mutembei 2014,). In the twenty-first century, Kiswahili language has gained prominence. It has evolved as a national and official language in both Kenya and Tanzania, the lingua franca of the East African community and it has been one of the languages of the African Union (AU) since the year 2000. Ndiritu et al. (2016) argue that Kiswahili is spoken in 12 countries in Africa. In addition, Kiswahili is used in over 100 Universities in the diaspora. This scenario gives the language in discussion great impetus for its use in Africa and this cannot be ignored.

However, machine translation between English and Kiswahili poses great challenge due to the structural differences. Ordudary (2007) observed that languages are not nomenclatures and concepts of one language may differ radically from those of another. This is simply because each language articulates or organizes the world differently and languages do not simply name categories, instead they articulate their own. One of the problems of translation also is the disparity among languages. The bigger the gap between the source language and target language, the more difficult the transfer of the message from source language text to the target language will be. According to Neubert (2000) languages and ideas expressed by languages are created mainly in accordance with expressional needs of the surrounding culture. The motivation of this study was based on the fact that when translating different discourses, it is essential to be aware of the context in which the discourse takes place and the structural differences of the language pair. In addition, there are certain challenges that face machine translators when dealing with texts of unique language pairs and they are thought to exist in the machine translation from English into Kiswahili. The study of these texts is helpful in proposing better strategies to improve the practice of machine translation.

2 Background

Translation by computer is generally referred to as Machine Translation (MT). Machine translation is the use of computer software to translate text or speech from one natural language into another (Munday 2016; Hardmeier 2014). Machine translation does not simply involve substituting words in one language for those of another but deals with the application of complex linguistic knowledge. This complexity is quite a challenge to human beings and more challenging to computers (Herman et al. 2015).

Somers (2003) argues that the largest area of growth for translation demand is now undoubtedly based on use of the internet. This is the need of the occasional use for software to translate web pages, e-mails and other internet resources and texts, either off-line or on-line, and the demand for on-line internet-based translation services for companies. Gikambi (2015) notes that "there has been increased use of computers in the twenty-first century in different disciplines including translation that has improved the livelihood of people". For instance, a lot of material mostly written in English is being translated online into Kiswahili.

Baker (2014) as cited in Malangwa (2010: 1) contends that:

> If languages were simply nomenclature for a set of universal concepts, it would be easy to translate from one language to another; one would simply replace the source language (SL) word for a concept with the target language (TL) word. But this is not the case especially when translating between languages that are different in structure and in the levels of scientific and technical developments as in the case of Kiswahili and English.

Machine translation is quite important to users who prefer to browse and surf in their own language. According to Malmkjær (2003), Costa-Jussa and Fonollosa (2015) and Hadla (2017), the growing need for translation has gone hand in hand with the emergence of translation studies as an academic discipline in its own right. Within this discipline, there has been a development from a more traditional view of translation as a product of texts to more dynamic or optimistic approaches. Furthermore, machine translation has been useful primarily as an aid for human translators.

Machine Translations to some degree can encode at least some linguistic ability and sophistication. However, Green, Heer and Manning (2013) argue that there are complex structures of a language that can be difficult for computers, and these need human post editing. It has been the aim of translation scholars, therefore, to transform theoretical insights into guidelines for practical applications and /or into methodologies, techniques and principles that will improve the process of machine translation. With the development of computer technology, we cherish the hope that machine translation will be able to translate textual information from English to Kiswahili with great precision.

The increased use of the internet has attracted many scholars and researchers to improve on the process of machine translation. Initially, this process involved non-numerical use of computers but with time attempts to use computers to translate natural languages grew to the now well-established field of computational linguistics (CL). This is the use of the computer in any activity involving language (both written and spoken), and like many other fields it also has its theoretical, methodological and practical aspects. Change in technology is always faster than change in our behaviour as supply in technology is often ahead of consumer demand. In a very short period of time the World Wide Web has grown into a standard communication medium (Gambier and Gottlieb 2001).

Davis (2004) argues that the common trend observed in translation from the nineteenth century is that most of the translations are done from English into other languages of the world. English acts as the medium to other languages. The issue of mistranslation in machine translation, the extent of equivalence in translation between an original text and a translation depends on various factors. Some of these factors are linguistic, for example, how closely related are the language pairs involved or how far apart, as suggested by House (1981).

3 Objectives of the investigation

The investigation was guided by the following objectives:

(i)   To determine some of the mismatches in the source text (ST) and target text (TT).
(ii) To identify some of the structural differences between English and Kiswahili that affect meaning.
(iii) To discuss the effectiveness of machine translation in relation to consumer satisfaction.

4 Structural differences between English and Kiswahili

Languages differ in form and therefore quite naturally the forms must be altered if one is to maintain the content. As Nida (1964) and Nida and Taber (1982) argue, the extent to which the forms must be changed depend upon the linguistic and cultural distance between languages. For example, Kiswahili is a highly agglutinative language where the bound nominal and verbal morphemes are strung together in a sensational construction as illustrated as follows:

Nitamtembelea – I will visit him/her.

4.1 Morphology

The rules that account for the changes that occur when forming words differ from language to language, for example, one way in which English accounts for plurals is by the addition of the morpheme "s" to root e.g.

Cat	-	Cats
Dog	-	Dogs
Car	-	Cars
Chair	-	Chairs
Root	-	Roots

Kiswahili on the other hand accounts for most plurals by changing the nominal prefix for example:

Umoja (Singular)	Gloss		Wingi (plural)	Gloss
Mtu	Person	Wa + tu	Watu	People
Mwalimu	Teacher	Wa + alimu	Walimu	Teachers
Kisu	Knife	Vi + su	–Visu	Knives
Mrembo	Beauty	Wa + rembo	Warembo	Beauties
Kiongozi	Leader	Vi + ongozi	Viongozi	Leaders

In these examples, "**m**" and "**ki**" mark the singular morpheme while "**wa**" and "**vi**" mark the plural.

Mostly, in English, one can clearly distinguish the roots (free morphemes) from affixes (bound morphemes) but in Kiswahili, which is a highly agglutinative language like most of the Bantu languages, affixes are attached to roots so that there are several morphemes in a word.

For example:

A	Li	M	Pig	A
pronoun	Tense marker	Object	Stem	Suffix

Alimpiga
A – li – m – pig – a
Gloss: He/she beat him/her

Ni	Ta	Wa	Pik	Ia
Pronoun marker	Future tense	Object	Stem	Suffix

Nitawapikia
Ni – ta – wa – pik – i – a
Gloss: I will cook for them

4.2 Tenses

English is accustomed to three basic tenses: past, present and future with several tenses of relative time e.g. future perfect; in Kiswahili there is a tense maker.

4.3 Syntax

(i) Word and phrase order

Both English and Kiswahili have a dominant word order which is subject-verb-object (SVO).
For example:

English

The	lectures	Went	To	Mombasa
Article	S	V	P	O

Kiswahili

Wahadhiri	Walienda	Mombasa
S lecturers	V Went	O Mombasa

Gloss:
Lecturers went Mombasa

However, Kiswahili language syntactically is a head-initial language unlike in English where adjectives precede the noun. In other cases, English permits attributives both before and after a head word.
For example:

English
A good student will always finish his/her work on time.
Kiswahili
Mwanafunzi mwema huikamilisha kazi yake kwa wakati unaofaa.
Gloss: Student good finish his/her work in time expected.

In this example "good" which is an adjective precedes the noun "student" but in Kiswahili "mwanafunzi" which is the noun precedes 'mwema' the adjective.

(ii) Agreement

Kiswahili has an agreement system. This is the system that governs and maintains subject verb agreement in a sentence structure. Kiswahili like other Bantu languages requires that noun modifiers and verbs carry pronominal prefixes which match the noun. The agreement pattern is quite important in writing and more so in translation because it helps the reader to identify the noun referred back to in cases where there is more than one reference in the structure as suggested by

Wangia (2003). If this concordial agreement is violated, it may create ambiguities in comprehending the intended meaning. The English language does not have noun classes which poses a challenge when translating from English into Kiswahili. The noun in Kiswahili has to agree in number with its modifiers: demonstratives, possessives, pronouns, numerals, qualifiers and adjectives.

For example:

Wananchi wa Kenya wote wanatakiwa kuwa wazalendo.
Gloss: *Citizens of Kenya all are expected to be patriotic.*
Vyuo vyote vya nchi hii vinapaswa kudumisha taaluma bora.
Gloss: *All universities in this country are supposed to maintain excellent education.*

Quantifiers in Kiswahili have a concordial prefix marker attached which differs from English.

For example:

Kiswahili	Gloss	English
Matunda yote	Fruits all	all fruits
Wanafunzi wote	Students all	all students
Nyumba zote	Houses all	all houses
Viti vyote	chairs all	all chairs

(iii) Definitive and indefinitive articles

The lexicon of Kiswahili does not contain categories of definite and indefinite articles like in the English language. The use of articles in English poses a challenge to Machine Translation which is not flexible in choosing the correct word order; the indefinite articles used in English are "a" and "an".

For example:

English	Kiswahili	Gloss
An egg	Yai	Egg
A girl	Msichana	Girl
A church	Kanisa	Church
An elephant	Ndovu/Tembo	Elephant

Definite article in English is "**the**" as shown here:

English	Kiswahili	Gloss
The teacher	Mwalimu	Teacher
The exam	Mtihani	Exam

(iv) Kiswahili has more demonstratives than English

This has an implication in translation; meaning will be lost or will not be precise.

Kiswahili	Gloss	English
Mahali hapa	Place here	this place
Mahali hapo	Place there	that place
Mahali kule	Place that	that place
Mahali huko	Place that	that place
Mahali humo	Place that	that place

In Kiswahili "mahali humo" has a specific meaning that implies inside but when rendered into English this meaning is not captured.

(v) Adjectives

A common feature of Bantu languages, as in the case of Kiswahili, is the fact that the adjectives inflect for plurality depending on the number of the noun they modify. However, in English we have plurals realized in different ways.

For example, this (singular) becomes these (plural), and that (singular) becomes those (plural).

For example:

English	Kiswahili	Gloss
This house	Nyumba hii	House this
These houses	Nyumba hizi	House these
Those houses	Nyumba hizo	House those
That promise	Ahadi hiyo	Promise that
That child	Mtoto huyo	Child that
That chair	Kiti hicho	Chair that

The differences presented in this section – for example class agreement system, word order, the use of indefinite/definite articles in English which are dropped in Kiswahili, markers of gender etc. – pose intricate challenges to translation and specifically to machine translation.

5 Research methodology

This is primarily a machine translation research that is relying on critical analysis of the machine-translated text in comparison to human-translated text. The text used in this chapter has been purposefully sampled and read so as to provide a background understanding. In this type of sampling, as explained by Kothari (2016), the text was selected deliberately by the researcher as a representation of machine translation from English to Kiswahili.

Food, Agriculture & Decent Work
ILO & FAO working together

Decent Employment for the Rural Poor

Of the developing world's 5.5 billion people, 3 billion live in rural areas, nearly half of humanity. Agriculture is a source of livelihoods for an estimated 86 percent of rural people. Of these rural inhabitants an estimated 2.5 billion are in households involved in agriculture. Agriculture provides jobs for 1.3 billion smallholders and landless workers. Rural employment is a critical means for poverty and hunger reduction, as labour is often the only asset that poor people own. The main problem with employment in rural areas, however, is that many jobs do not ensure decent levels of income and sustainable livelihoods. Rural workers are at the heart of the food production system but are disadvantaged in many respects. They are among the most socially vulnerable, the least organized into trade unions, and the least likely to have gender equality in opportunities and pay, and access to effective forms of social security and protection. Many of them are employed under poor health, safety and environmental conditions.

©FAO/Guilio Napolitano

Chakula, Kilimo na Kazi Hestima
ILO & FAO kufanya kazi kwa pamoja

Heshima Ajira kwa maskini wa vijijini

Ya watu wa nchi zinazoendelea bilioni 5.5, bilioni 3 kuishi katika maeneo ya vijijini, karibu nusu ya binadamu. Kilimo ni chanzo cha maisha kwa asilimia inayokadiriwa kuwa asilimia 86 ya watu vijijini. Ya wakazi hao wa vijijini bilioni 2.5 katika makazi ino ya kaya kushiriki katika kilimo. Kilimo hutoa ajira kwa wakulima wadogo bilioni 1.3 na wafanyakazi wasiokuwa na ardhi. Ajira vijijini ni njia muhimu kwa umaskini na kupunguza njaa, kama kazi ni mara nyingi tu kwamba mali ya watu maskini wenyewe. Tatizo kubwa kwa ajira katika maeneo ya vijijini, hata hivyo, ni kwamba wengi hawana ajira kuhakikisha viwango vya heshima ya mapato na maisha endelevu. Wafanyakazi wa vijijini ni katika moyo wa mfumo wa uzalishaji wa chakula lakini ni maskini katika mambo mengi. Wao ni miongoni mwa jamii katika mazingira magumu, angalau kupangwa katika vyama vya wafanyakaao, na uwezekano mdogo wa kuwa na usawa wa kijinsia katika fursa na kulipa, na upatikanaji wa aina bora ya usalama ya kijamii na ulinzi. Wengi wao ni ajira chini ya hali mbaya ya afya, usalama na mazingira.

©FAO / Guilo Napolitano

Issues of language structure   161

Data in this chapter was elicited from one sampled text that was translated by computer (Google Translators Toolkit and Google Translate). The same text was translated by one human translator. The human translator was selected purposively because of his experience in translation. He is a Kiswahili professor with many years of practicing in translation. He has translated a number of books from English into Kiswahili.

It is hoped that the results of the study will provide a new perspective not only to the study of issues of language structure in machine translation of texts from English into Kiswahili, but also to the study of language-pair deficiency in machine translation involving all African languages with the aim of improving on these translation products through the suggestions which will be given in this chapter.

6 Presentation of data on machine and human translated text

The aim of online translation is to break the language barrier between people so that they can communicate with each other, read news, blogs, foreign websites and learn the cultures of other countries. However, structural differences between language pairs are a great challenge to a computer. Grammatical rules can be memorized or programmed but without real knowledge of a language, either a computer or a human will not be able to select between alternative meanings.

Data presented in this section was elicited from a source language text and its machine-translated version. This was then compared to the human-translated text. A corpus of text with mistranslations was identified.

Source language text

Food, Agriculture and Decent Work

ILO and FAO working together

Decent Employment for the Rural Poor

Of the developing world's 5.5 billion people, 3 billion live in rural areas, nearly half of humanity. Agriculture is a source of livelihoods for an estimated 86 percent of rural people. Of these rural inhabitants an estimated 2.5 billion are in households involved in agriculture. Agriculture provides jobs for 1.3 billion smallholders and landless workers. Rural employment is a critical means for poverty and hunger reduction, as labor is often the only asset that poor people own. The main problem with employment in rural areas, however, is that many jobs do not ensure decent levels of income and sustainable livelihoods. Rural workers are at the heart of the food production system but are disadvantaged in many respects. They are among the most socially vulnerable, the least organized into trade unions, and the least likely to have gender equality in opportunities and pay, and access to effective forms of social security and protection. Many of them are employed under poor health, safety and environmental conditions.

Rural women grow and prepare most of the food consumed in the home. They raise small livestock, collect water and fuel and care for the children, the sick and the elderly.

©FAO/Giulio Napolitano

Ensuring productive and decent work for rural workers is crucial if they are to escape from poverty and providing the means to produce or purchase adequate and nutritious food. However efforts to reduce poverty and hunger by raising on- and off-farm incomes and diversifying livelihoods can be hindered by emerging forms of employment relationships based on more flexible and casual forms of agricultural work. Dramatic changes are taking place in agricultural systems worldwide. The expansion of value chains associated with agribusiness and agro-industry, the difficulty of self-employed small farmers to earn a living wage, and labor shortages in some regions together with underemployment in others, are transforming rural labor systems. Achieving fairer conditions of employment means providing opportunities for productive work that delivers a fair income, workplace security and social protection for workers and their families, better prospects for social integration and personal development, equality of opportunities and treatment for all women and men, freedom for people to express their concerns, to organize and participate in the decisions that affect their lives. For more information on how decent and productive employment contributes to the MDGs, please click here.

The International Labour Organization (ILO) Declaration on Fundamental Principles and Rights at Work is an expression of commitment by governments to encourage fair conditions of employment, including: i) freedom of association and the right to collective bargaining; ii) the elimination of forced and compulsory labour; iii) the abolition of child labour; iv) the elimination of discrimination in the workplace. The ILO has merged these four areas into the over-arching concept of "decent work". Decent work involves opportunities for work that is productive and delivers a fair income; security in the workplace and social protection for families; better prospects for personal development and social integration; freedom for people to express their concerns, organize and participate in the decisions that affect their lives; and equality of opportunity and treatment for all women and men.

Policy coherence

At the international policy level there is increasing recognition of the importance of the linkages between rural employment, poverty reduction and food security. The report of the UN Secretary-General for the High-level segment

> (HLS) 2006 of the substantive session of the Economic and Social Council (ECOSOC) focuses on the theme: "Creating an environment at the national and international levels conducive to generating full and productive employment and decent work for all, and its impact on sustainable development".
>
> An increased focus on rural employment as a key component of rural development is critical for the achievement of the Millennium Development Goals (MDGs), particularly Goal 1, and of other commitments such as those of the 1996 World Food Summit, the World Food Summit: five years later and the World Summit on Sustainable Development (WSSD).
>
> ## Mainstreaming Employment and Decent Work
>
> The World Summit of the United Nations General Assembly (2005), the High Level Segment of the UN ECOSOC (2006) and the Chief Executives Board for Coordination (CEB) of the UN system (2007) agreed to mainstream the goals of full and productive employment and decent work in their policies, programmes and activities as a means to achieving the internationally agreed development goals.
>
> More specifically, the United Nations System CEB, at its April 2007 session, fully endorsed the Toolkit for Mainstreaming Employment and Decent Work prepared by the ILO in collaboration with FAO and others. Since then the Economic and Social Council (ECOSOC) adopted a Resolution on 17 July 2007, which calls upon all United Nations Funds, Programmes, Agencies, Functional and Regional Commissions and International Financial Institutions to collaborate in using, adapting and evaluating the application of the Toolkit.

Machine translation text

Heshima Ajira kwa maskini wa vijijini

Ya watu wa nchi zinazoendelea bilioni 5.5, bilioni 3 kuishi katika maeneo ya vijijini, karibu nusu ya binadamu. Kilimo ni chanzo cha maisha kwa asilimia inayokadiriwa kuwa asilimia 86 ya watu vijijini. Ya wakazi hao wa vijijini bilioni 2.5 katika makadirio ya kaya kushiriki katika kilimo. Kilimo hutoa ajira kwa wakulima wadogo bilioni 1.3 na wafanyakazi wasiokuwa na ardhi. Ajira vijijini ni njia muhimu kwa umaskini na kupunguza njaa, kama kazi ni mara nyingi tu kwamba mali ya watu maskini wenyewe. Tatizo kubwa kwa ajira katika maeneo ya vijijini, hata hivyo, ni kwamba wengi hawana ajira kuhakikisha viwango vya heshima ya mapato na maisha endelevu. Wafanyakazi wa vijijini ni katika moyo wa mfumo wa uzalishaji wa chakula lakini ni maskini katika mambo mengi. Wao ni miongoni mwa jamii katika mazingira magumu, angalau kupangwa katika vyama vya wafanyakazi, na uwezekano mdogo wa kuwa na usawa wa kijinsia katika fursa na kulipa, na upatikanaji wa aina bora ya usalama ya kijamii na ulinzi. Wengi wao ni ajira chini ya hali mbaya ya afya, usalama na mazingira. **Wanawake wa vijijini kukua na kujiandaa zaidi ya chakula zinazotumiwa katika nyumbani. Wao kuongeza mifugo wadogo, kukusanya maji na mafuta na huduma kwa watoto, wagonjwa na wazee.**

© FAO/Giulio Napolitano

Kuhakikisha uzalishaji na heshima ya kazi kwa wafanyakazi wa vijijini ni muhimu kama ni kutoroka kutoka umaskini na kutoa maana ya kuzalisha au kununua kutosha na chakula bora. Hata hivyo juhudi za kupunguza umaskini na njaa kwa kuongeza on-na mapato ya mbali-shamba na maisha ya mseto inaweza kuzuia kuibuka kwa aina ya mahusiano ya ajira kwa kuzingatia aina ya zaidi rahisi na ya kawaida ya kazi ya kilimo. Mabadiliko makubwa yanafanyika katika mifumo ya kilimo duniani kote. upanuzi wa minyororo thamani ya kuhusishwa na biashara ya kilimo na sekta ya kilimo, ugumu wa wakulima wadogo kujiajiri kwa kupata mshahara hai, na uhaba wa kazi katika baadhi ya mikoa pamoja na ajira isiyo toshelevu kwa wengine, ni kubadilisha mfumo wa ajira kijijini. Kufikia hali ya usawa wa ajira ina maana kutoa fursa kwa ajili ya kazi za uzalishaji kwamba alitangaza mapato ya haki, usalama mahali pa kazi na ulinzi wa kijamii kwa wafanyakazi na familia zao, ni bora zaidi matarajio ya ushirikiano wa kijamii na maendeleo binafsi, usawa wa fursa na matibabu kwa ajili ya wanawake na wanaume, uhuru kwa watu kueleza matatizo yao, kupanga na kushiriki katika maamuzi yanayohusu maisha yao. Kwa habari zaidi juu ya jinsi ya uzalishaji bora na ajira unachangia MDGs, tafadhali <u>bonyeza hapa</u>.

<u>Shirika la Kazi Duniani (ILO) Azimio juu ya Kanuni za Msingi na Haki Kazini</u> ni kujieleza na ahadi za serikali za kuhamasisha hali ya haki ya ajira, ikiwa ni pamoja na: i) uhuru wa kujumuika na haki ya kujadiliana kwa pamoja; ii) ukomeshaji wa kulazimishwa na lazima kazi; iii) ya kukomesha ajira ya watoto; iv) ukomeshaji wa ubaguzi katika sehemu za kazi. ILO zimeunganishwa maeneo haya nne katika dhana ya juu-arching ya "<u>kazi bora</u>". Kazi nzuri inahusisha fursa kwa kazi ambayo ni uzalishaji na mapato alitangaza haki, usalama katika maeneo ya kazi na ulinzi wa kijamii kwa ajili ya familia; bora matarajio ya maendeleo binafsi na ushirikiano wa kijamii; uhuru kwa watu wa kueleza matatizo yao, kupanga na kushiriki katika maamuzi yanayohusu maisha yao, na usawa wa fursa na matibabu kwa ajili ya wanawake na wanaume.

Sera ya mshikamano

Katika ngazi ya sera za kimataifa huko ni kuongeza kutambua umuhimu wa uhusiano kati ya vijijini kupunguza ajira, umaskini na usalama wa chakula. Ripoti ya <u>Katibu Mkuu wa Umoja wa Mataifa kwa ajili ya sehemu ya ngazi ya juu (HLS)</u> 2006 ya kikao makubwa ya <u>Baraza la Uchumi na Jamii (ECOSOC)</u> inalenga katika mada: "Kujenga mazingira katika ngazi ya kitaifa na kimataifa mazuri ya kuzalisha kamili na uzalishaji wa ajira na heshima ya kazi kwa ajili ya wote, na madhara yake katika maendeleo endelevu. "

kuzidi kulenga katika ajira vijijini kama sehemu muhimu ya maendeleo vijijini ni muhimu kwa ajili ya mafanikio ya <u>Malengo ya Maendeleo ya Milenia (MDGs)</u>, hasa Lengo la 1, na ahadi nyingine kama vile wale wa <u>1996 Mkutano wa Dunia wa Chakula, Chakula Mkutano wa Dunia: miaka mitano baadaye na Mkutano wa Dunia</u> wa <u>Maendeleo Endelevu (WSSD)</u>.

Kuingiza masuala ya Ajira na Kazi Heshima

<u>Mkutano wa Dunia wa Baraza Kuu la Umoja wa Mataifa</u> (2005), <u>High Level sehemu ya Umoja wa Mataifa ECOSOC</u> (2006) na <u>watendaji wakuu wa Bodi ya Kuratibu (CEB)</u> ya mfumo wa Umoja wa Mataifa (2007) walikubali tawala kamili na malengo ya uzalishaji ajira na kazi nzuri katika sera zao, mipango na shughuli kama njia ya kufikia malengo ya maendeleo zilizokubalika kimataifa.

Zaidi hasa, Umoja wa Mataifa System CEB, katika kikao chake cha Aprili 2007, kikamilifu utowaji <u>Toolkit kwa Kuingiza Ajira na Kazi Heshima</u> tayari na ILO kwa kushirikiana na FAO na wengine. Tangu wakati huo Baraza la Uchumi na Jamii (ECOSOC) lilipitisha Azimio tarehe 17 Julai mwaka 2007, ambayo inatoa wito kwa wote wa Umoja wa Mataifa ya Fedha, Mipango, Wakala, Kazi na Tume ya Kimataifa ya Mkoa na taasisi za fedha za kushirikiana katika kutumia, kurekebisha na kutathmini matumizi ya Toolkit.

Toolkit imeundwa kuwa "Lens" kuwa mashirika wanaweza kuangalia kwa njia ya kuona ni jinsi gani sera, mikakati, mipango na shughuli ni interlinked pamoja na ajira na matokeo mazuri ya kazi na jinsi gani wanaweza kuboresha matokeo haya. Ni chombo cha uhamasishaji na uchunguzi orodha ya maswali ambayo shirika wanaweza kuuliza yenyewe kwa kujitegemea kutathmini na kuongeza ajira na matokeo mazuri ya kazi ya mikakati yake, sera, mipango na shughuli.

Human translation text

KAZI NZURI KWA WATU MASKINI WANAOISHI MASHAMBANI

Kati ya idadi nzima ya watu katika nchi zinazoendelea duniani ya bilioni 5.5, bilioni 3, takribani nusu ya idadi hiyo, huishi sehemu za mashambani. Kilimo ndicho njia ya kujikimu kwa asilimia 86 ya watu wa mashambani. **Watu wapatao bilioni 2.5 waishio mashambani, huishi katika jamii zinazotegemea kilimo**. Kilimo hutoa ajira kwa wakulima wadogo wadogo na wafanyikazi wasiokuwa na ardhi yao wapatao bilioni 1.3. Ajira katika sehemu za mashambani ni mbinu muhimu ya kupunguza umaskini na njaa kwa sababu nguvu za kufanya kazi ndilo pato la pekee walilo nalo watu maskini. Tatizo kubwa kuhusu ajira ya mashambani, hata hivyo, ni kwamba **kazi nyingi** zinazopatikana haziwahakikishii wenyewe viwango vizuri mapato wala uwezo wa kujikumu kimaisha. Wafanyikazi wa sehemu za mashambani **ndio nguzo ya uzalishaji chakula lakini** wanakabiliwa na vizingiti vingi tofauti. Wao ni kati ya wale wasiokuwa na uwezo kijamii, wasiokuwa weza kuunda vyama vya kutetea masilahi yao ya kikazi, wanaokosa kabisa usawa wa kijinsia katika nafasi za kazi na pia katika malipo, wala hawana nafasi za kupata huduma kama vile vyama vya kutetea masilahi yao ya kijamii au kuwalinda kisheria. **Wengi wao hufanya kazi** katika hali duni kiafya, usalama na hata uasafi wa mazingira.

Wanawake waishio mashambani hukuza na kutayarisha sehemu kubwa ya chakula kinachotumika nyumbani. Wao hufuga mifugo wachache, huteka maji na kutafuta kuni na pia huwatunza watoto, wagonjwa na pia wazee.

Kuhakikisha wafanyikazi wa mashambani wanapata kazi nzuri ni jambo muhimu ili kuwawezesha **kuepuka umaskini** na kupata uwezo wa kukuza au **kununua yakula vya kutosha na vyenye lishe bora.** Lakini, juhudi za kupunguza umaskini na njaa kwa kuongeza mara kwa mara mapato kutokana an kilimo na **kuongeza ajira za aina tofauti** zinaweza kuzuiwa kutokana na kuzuka kwa aina mpya za **ajira zinazotokana** na **kazi za vibarua** katika sekta ya kilimo. Kuna mabadiliko makubwa katika sekta ya kilimo kote ulimwenguni. **Kupanuliwa kwa msururu wa kuboresha bidhaa** unaohusishwa na biashara pamoja na viwanda vya kilimo, matatizo ya wakulima wadogo wanaojiajiri wenyewe kujipatia pato la kujikimu kimaisha, uhaba wa wafanyikazi **katika sehemu zingine** pamoja na ukosefu wa ajira katika sehemu fulani, **yote yamebadilisha mifumo** ya utendakazi katika sehemu za mashambani.Ili kufikia hali nzuri ya ajira, kuna haja ya kukuza nafasi za kufanya kazi yenye kuleta faida na mapato ya kuridhisha, mazingira salama ya kufanyia kazi, ulizi wa kijamii kwa wafanyikazi na familia zao, uwezekano mzuri wa kutangamana kijamii na kujiendeleza kibinafsi, **nafasi sawa na kutendewa usawa kwa wanawake na wanaume**, uhuru wa watu **kuelezea matakwa yao**, kupanga na kushiriki katika maamuzi yanayowahusu kimaisha.

Azimio la Shirika la Wafanyikazi Duniani (SWD), "Azimio juu ya Maongozi ya Kimsingi na Haki kwenye Mahali pa Kazi ni maelezo ya kujitolea kwa serikali kuhimiza masharti nafuu ya ajira, yakiwa ni pamoja na (i) uhuru wa kujiunga pamoja na haki ya kufanya maafikiano ya pamoja na waajiri; (ii) **kuondolewa kabisa kwa ajira ya kulazimishwa na kushurutishwa.** (iii) **kupigwa marufuku kwa ajira ya watoto,** (iv) **kuondolewa kwa ubaguzi kazini**,) **Shirika la SWD/ ILO limejumuisha** maudhui haya manne katika dhana kuu yaani "**kazi nzuri au ajira nzuri**." Ajira nzuri inahusu nafasi za kazi ambayo **huzalisha faida** na inaleta pato zuri; usalama katika mahali pa kazi na kulindwa kijamii kwa familia; uwezekano mzuri wa kujiendelza kibinafsi na kutangamana kijamii;wa watu kuelezea matakwa yao, kupanga na kushiriki katika **maamuzi yanayoathiri maisha yao**; usawa katika nafasi za kazi na kutendewa sawa kwa wanawake na wanaume wote.

Muumano wa Sera

Katika kiwango cha sera ya kimataifa, umuhimu wa uhusiano wa karibu kati ya ajira ya mashambani, upunguzaji wa umaskini na utoshelevu wa chakula umetambuliwa wazi.Ripoti ya Katibu Mkuu wa Umoja wa Mataifa Kiwango cha Juu (KCJ) 2006 **iliyotokana na kikao kikuu** *cha Halmashauri ya Uchumi na Masuala ya Kijamii, (HUJ/ECOSOC) inazingatia kauli-mbinu: "Kubuni mazingira katika* **viwango vya kitaifa na kimataifa yatakayowezesha** *kubuni nafasi* *za kutosha za ajira yenye natija na pia kazi bora kwa wote na taathira yake juu ya maendeleo endelevu."*

Uzingatiaji *wa ajira ya mashambani kama kipengele muhimu katika juhudi za kutimiza Malengo ya Maendeleo ya Milenia (MMM), hasa lengo la 1 pamoja na* **shabaha zingine** *kama zile za* **Kongamano kuhusu Chakula Ulimwenguni la mwaka wa 1996,** *na pia miaka mitano baadaye na Kongamano la Ulimwengu kuhusu Maendeleo Endelevu (KUME).*

7 Key findings

The data is presented in the form of linguistic categories: namely morphology, syntax and semantics. The words that are listed in English are elicited from source text and those in Kiswahili from machine translation and human translation. Using personal intuition and linguistic background, the researcher compared the choice of equivalents in machine translation and human translation. All the italicized words and phrases in the table which follows constitute mistranslations that occurred during machine translation. Issues of language structure between English and Kiswahili account for the mistranslations.

8 Data analysis and discussion

In this section, there is an analysis of the data presented in text 1. Data collected was in the form of sentences, clauses, phrases and words. There were structural differences related to morphology in the two languages under study. Machine translation reveals the use of tense and plurals which end up conveying a different meaning from that of the source text.

8.1 *The morphology category*

The data reveals that there is violation of the use of Kiswahili language on tense. See examples:

> Source text: Of these rural inhabitants an estimated 2.5 billion are in households involved in agriculture.
> Machine Translation: *Ya wakazi hao wa vijijini billion 2.5 katika makadirio ya kaya kushiriki katika kilimo.*
> Human translation: *Watu wapatao bilioni 2.5 waishio mashambani, huishi katika jamii zinazotegemea kilimo.*

In the above example, the machine translation: the reader cannot identify the tense marker. The tense marker in the source text is present perfect tense but in the target text the tense is not marked. This results in lack of clarity and loss of meaning. The human translator was able to capture the tense effect as it was rendered in the ST. Tense relates to the time of the action, event or state of affairs

Table 9.1 Comparison of machine translated text and human translation text

	Source language text	Machine Translation text	Gloss	Human translation text	Gloss
Morphology (i)Tense	Are in households	Kushiriki katika kilimo	Involved in Agriculture	Huishi katika jamii	Live in community
	Are employed	Wao ni ajira	They are work	Hufanya kazi	Are working
	Are transforming systems	Ni kubadilisha mfumo	Is to change system	yamebadilisha mifumo	Are transforming systems
	Are intended to help	Ni nia ya kusaidia	Aim of helping	yamenuiwa kuhakikisha	Are intended to make sure
	FAO is currently undertaking	FAO kwa sasa ni ahadi yake	FAO for now is its own promise	FAO kwa sasa inatathmini	FAO for now is evaluating
(ii)Plurals	Livelihoods	Maisha	Live	Njia ya kujikimu	The way of survival
	Households	Katika makadirio ya kaya	To the estimate of households	Jamii	Households
	Jobs	Ajira	Work	Kazi nyingi	Jobs many
	Casual forms	Aina ya zaidi rahisi	A type of more simple	Kazi za vibarua	Works of casual
	Commitments	Ahadi nyingine	Another promise	Shabaha	Commitments/ objectives
Syntax Concordial agreement	Of the substantive session of the economic and social council (ECOSOC)	Ya kikao **makubwa ya** baraza la uchumi na jamii (ECOSOC)	For a big session of council on economy and society	Iliyotokana na kikao **kikuu cha** Halmashauri ya uchimi na masuala **ya** kijamii (ECOSOC)	That came as a result of

	at the national and international levels conducive to	Katika ngazi ya kitaifa na kimataifa mazuri ya	At the level of national and international good for	Katika viwango vya kitaifa na kimataifa vitakavyowezesha.	At the national and international levels which enable
	Internationally agreed development goals	Malengo ya maendeleo zilizokubalika kimataifa	Objectives developments which are agreed internationally	Malengo yaliyoafikiwa kimataifa kuhusu shabaha za maendeleo	Objectives that were agreed internationally concerning development goals
	An organization may	Shirika wanaweza	Organization they can	Shirika litaweza	Organization will
	The food consumed	Chakula zinazotumiwa	Food which are consumed	Chakula kinachotumika	Food that is consumed
Word order	To purchase adequate and nutritious food	Kununua kutosha na chakula bora	To buy enough and good food	Kununua vyakula vya kutosha na vyenye lishe bora	To purchase adequate and nutritious food
	The world food summit	Chakula mkutano wa dunia	Food meeting of world	Kongamano kuhusu chakula ulimwenguni	The world food summit
	More specifically	Zaidi hasa	More especially	Hasa	Especially Specifically
	The abolition of child labour	Ya kukomesha ajira ya watoto	For ending child labour	Kupigwa marufuku kwa ajira ya watoto	The abolishing of child labour
	The elimination of forced and compulsory labour	Ukomeshaji wa kulazimishwa na lazima kazi	Elimination for being forced and forced work	Kuondolewa kabisa Kwa ajira ya kulazimishwa na kushurutishwa	Total eradication Of forced and conditioned employment
	How it could better deliver	Jinsi gani inaweza bora kutoa	How it could better give	Jinsi lingeweza kupata matokeo bora	How it could achieve good results
	Most of the food	Zaidi ya chakula	More for food	Sehemu kubwa ya chakula	Most of the food

(*Continued*)

Table 9.1 (Continued)

	Source language text	Machine Translation text	Gloss	Human translation text	Gloss
Definite and indefinite articles	The developing world's 5.5 billion people	Ya watu wa nchi zinazoendelea billion 5.5	Of people in developing countries 5.5 billion	Kati ya idadi nzima ya watu katika nchi zinazoendelea, billion 5.5	Among the entire population in developing world
	An estimated 2.5 billion are in household	Ya watu bao wa vijijini bilioni 2.5	Of those people living in rural areas 2.5 billion	Watu wapatao billion 2.5 waishio mashambani	Population of about 2.5 billion living in rural
	The ILO has	Katika makadirio ILO zimeunganishwa	On estimate ILO are joined	Shirika la ILO limejumuisha	The ... labour organization has included
	An increased focus	Kuzidi kulenga	Surpass aim	Uzingatiaji	The commitment
	The United Nations system CEB	Umoja wa mataifa system CEB	United Nations system	Mfumo wa Umoja wa mataifa	The UN system
	It is an awareness raising tool	Ni chombo cha uhamasishaji	Is an instrument for sensitization	Ni kifaa cha kuelimisha	It is all education instrument/tool
Semantics (i) mismatches	Employment relationship	Mahusiano ya ajira	Relationship for employment	Ajira zinazotokana na	Jobs that originate from
	Decent work	Kazi beshima	Work respect	Kazi bora	Productive work
	Fully endorsed	Kikamilifu utowaji	Fully given	Kiliidhinisha	It approved
	Some regions	Baadhi ya mikoa	Some of provinces	Sehemu zingine	Other parts/areas
	Diversifying livelihoods	Maisha ya mseto	Mixed livelihoods	Kuongeza ajira za aina tofauti	To increase various forms of employment

Literal translation	Generating full and productive	Kuzalisha kamili na uzalishaji	To generate full and productive	Kuzalisha kwa wingi	To generate much
	Agreed to mainstream	Walikubali tawala	They accepted rule	Walikubaliana kushirikisha	They agreed to involve
	All United Nations Fund	Wote wa Umoja wa mataifa ya fedha	All of United Nations for money	Mashirika yote ya ufadhili wa umoja wa mataifa	All non donor agencies
	FAO is currently undertaking	FAO kwa sasa ni ahadi yake	FAO now is its promise	Shirika la FAO kwa sasa linatathmini	FAO is now evaluating
	Many of them are employed	Wengi wao ni ajira	Most of them are employment	Wengi wao hufanya kazi	Most of them do work
	Delivers a fair income	Alitangaza haki	He/she announced right	Huzalisha faida	Delivers profit
	Mainstreaming employment and decent work	Kuingiza masuala ya ajira na kazi heshima	To introduce issues of employment and work respect	Kushirikisha ajira na kazi bora	Involves employment and productive work
	Raise small livestock	Kuongeza mifugo wadogo	To add small livestock	Hufuga mifugo wachache	Keep few livestock
	Care for the children	Huduma kwa watoto	Service to children	Kuwatunza watoto	To care for children
	At the heart of the food production system	Katika moyo wa mfumo wa uzalishaji chakula	At the heart of system for producing food	Ndio nguzo ya uzalishaji chakula	It is the backbone of food production
	If they are to escape from	Kama ni kutoroka kutoka	If is to escape to get out	Ili kuwawezesha kuepuka	So as to help the escape
	Grow and prepare	Kukua na kujiandaa	To grow and prepare	Hukuza na kutayarisha	Produces and prepares
	Expansion of value chains	Upanuzi wa minyororo thamani	Expansion of chains value	Kupanuliwa kwa msururu	Expansion of the line of
	Collect water and fuel	Kukusanya maji na mafuta	To collect water and fuel	Kuteka maji na kutafuta kuni	To fetch water and look for firewood

(*Continued*)

Table 9.1 (Continued)

	Source language text	Machine Translation text	Gloss	Human translation text	Gloss
Ambiguity	Agreed to	Walikubali	They agreed	Walikubaliana	They agreed
	Such as those of the 1996	Na nyingine kama vile **wale** wa 1996	And another one like **those** of 1996	Kama zile za	Like those of
	Which calls upon all United Nations Funds	Ambayo inatoa wito kwa wote wa umoja wa mataifa ya fedha	Which calls upon all those of United Nations for money	Ambalo lilitoa mwito kwa mashirika yote ya ufadhili wa . . .	Which made an appeal to/for donor all organization which
	Delivers a fair income	Mapato alitangaza haki	Income announced right	Huzalisha faida	Generate profit
	Treatment for all women and men	Matibabu kwa ajili ya wanawake na wanaume	Treatment for the sake of women and men	Kutendewa sawa kwa wanawake na wanaume wote	Equal treatment of all Women and men
	The elimination of discrimination in the place of work	Ukomeshaji wa ubaguzi takika sehemu za kazi	Elimination of discrimination at sections of work	Kuondolewa kwa ubaguzi kazini	Removal of discrimination at work place
	Policy coherence	Sera ya mshikamano	Policy for cohension	Muumano wa sera	Policy cohesion

referred to in the sentence to the time of utterance as suggested by Lyons (1968). This relationship between "the rural inhabitants and their involvement in Agriculture" in relation to time is not presented by machine translation.

In other cases, mistranslation was caused by incorrect use of plurals. Rules that account for the changes when forming words differ from language to language. For example, English accounts for plurals by adding the morpheme(s) to root. Kiswahili on the other hand accounts for most plurals by changing the nominal prefix. Machine Translation applied English rules into Kiswahili translation which led to mistranslation as the intended meaning was not rendered into TT.

The example below illustrates inappropriate use of the plurals.

>Source Text: *jobs*.
>Machine Translation: *Ajira*.
>Gloss: *Employment*.
>Human Translation: *Kazi nyingi*.
>Gloss: *Many jobs*.
>Source Text: *Commitments*.
>Machine Translation: *Ahadi nyingi*.
>Gloss: *Many promise*.
>Human Translation: *Shabaha nyingi*.
>Gloss: *Many commitments*.
>Source Text: *Courses*.
>Machine Translation: *Kozi*.
>Gloss: *Course*.
>Human Translation: *Mafunzo*.
>Gloss: *lessons*.

The machine translation failed to capture the intended meaning. For example "*jobs*" in ST gives an idea of many not one "*Ajira*" as rendered by machine translation.

The human translator was able to capture the intended meaning by using an adjective to account for plural "*kazi nyingi*".

The use of "*kozi*" in machine translation for "*courses*" is also a mistranslation since the idea of many that was expressed in the source text is rendered as one. This idea was captured in human translation, by the use of "*mafunzo*" for "*lessons*".

8.2 The syntax category

Nida and Taber (1982) note that languages have distinctive characters (form) and therefore the forms must be changed in order to preserve the content.

Kiswahili has an agreement system. The noun dominates the other words in a sentence such that they are brought into concordial agreement. In our data, machine translation seemed to violate this rule thus creating a problem of mistranslation.

For example:

> Source text: Internationally agreed development goals
> Machine Translation: Malengo ya maendeleo zilizokubalika kimataifa
> Human translation: Malengo yaliyoafikiwa kimataifa kuhusu shabaha za maendeleo

In the above example, although the meaning is comprehensible, the structure of languages should be respected for the sake of producing a well-formed translation in the target language. Kiswahili readers will find this translation unnatural to Kiswahili structure. The human translator was able to adhere to the rules of agreement in Kiswahili.

The following examples illustrate violation of Kiswahili class agreement systems.

> Source Text: Of the substantive session of the . . .
> Machine Translation: Ya kikao makubwa ya . . .
> Gloss: Of the big session of. . . .
> Human Translation: Iliyotokana na kikao kikuu cha . . .
> Gloss: That came as a result of substantive session of . . .
> Source Text: An organization may . . .
> Machine Translation: shirika wanaweza . . .
> Gloss: Organization they may . . .
> Human Translation: Shirika litaweza . . .
> Gloss: Organization may . . .
> Source Text: The food consumed.
> Machine Translation: Chakula zinazotumiwa
> Gloss: Food that are consumed
> Human Translation: Chakula kinachotumika.
> Gloss: Food that is consumed

In these examples machine translation violates the system of paired classes in Kiswahili whereby the class to which the head noun belongs must be reflected throughout the entire sentence.

Machine translation reveals a mix up of concordial agreement in sentence structure. For example, "**kikao**" (session) belongs to class 7/8 (**ki-vi**), but machine translation gives it a concord system of class 5/6 (**li-ya/ji-ma**). The word "**shirika**" (organization) belongs to class 5/6 (**li-ya/ji-ma**), but machine translation gives it an affix that reflects concord system of class 1/2 (**a-wa/mu-wa**).

Another example is "**chakula**" (food) which belongs to class 7/8 (**ki-vi**), but the affix that machine translation attaches to this noun reflects a grammatical system of class 13/14 (**i-zi**) or 17/18 (**u-zi**). Nurse and Philippson (2006) note that Bantu scholars tend to generally agree that the noun class prefixes exhibit predictable semantic reference. Therefore, violation of class system in Kiswahili leads to mistranslation of the intended meaning.

This violation is caused by the structural differences between English and Kiswahili. Machine translation is not flexible on the Kiswahili agreement system that is not systematic.

8.3 Violation of word order

While English permits attributes to come both before and after a head word, Kiswahili requires that attributes come after the word they modify. Kiswahili is a head initial language. In machine translation, each word in the source text has been substituted by another.

For example:

>Source text: To purchase adequate and nutritious food
>Machine Translation: Kununua kutosha na chakula bora
>Human Translation: Kununua vyakula vya kutosha na vyenye lishe bora.

The mistranslation that is manifested in machine translation is mainly due to the different structures of the source language and target language. There is no flexibility in the machine translation due to the literal nature of the translation. The focus of machine translation is on the source text structure and it tends to retain the source language structure features.

A human translator requires not only vocabulary and grammar but also knowledge gathered from past experiences. This is evident in the above examples. Instead of just translating **"nutritious food"** as **"chakula bora"** he translates **"lishe bora"**.

8.4 The semantics category

Words cover areas of meaning and different languages have different semantic areas of corresponding words that make it complex for machine translation to make a choice of the right word.

The examples below explain this scenario:

Mismatches:

>Source Text: Some regions
>Machine Text: Baadhi ya mikoa
>Gloss: Some provinces
>Human Translation Text: Sehemu zingine
>Gloss: Some regions
>Source Text: Many of them are employed
>Machine Text: Wengi wao ni ajira
>Gloss: Many of them are employment
>Human Translation Text: Wengi wao hufanya kazi
>Gloss: Many of them are employed/ working

> Source Text: Delivers a fair income
> Machine Text: Alitangaza haki
> Gloss: He/she announced right/s
> Human Translation Text: Huzalisha faida
> Gloss: Delivers/generates income/profit

The examples reveal a high degree of mistranslation or violation of meaning. The main rationale behind any translation is to render as much as possible the meaning as intended by the source text writer into the target text. The machine-translated clauses produce associations with no sense e.g. "regions" meaning "mikoa" which in English is **"provinces"**. The human translation renders **"regions"** as **"sehemu"** which is quite appropriate.

8.5 Literal translation

A word can be considered fully comprehended when it has been adequately interpreted in its context of use.

Zaky (2000) as cited in Malangwa (2010) argues that meaning of a particular word or term is not only governed by what it signifies but also by the way it has been used in a specific context to cause a certain effect.

Machine translation is not capable of using different strategies to create that same effect as it had in the source text. It literally translates words, phrases, clauses or sentences from the source text into the target text. The following examples from text 1 show literal translation in machine translation.

> Source Text: Raise small livestock
> Machine Translation: Kuongeza mifugo wadogo
> Gloss: Add small livestock
> Human Translation: Hufuga mifugo wachache
> Gloss: Keeps few livestock
> Source Text: Care for the children
> Machine Translation: Huduma Kwa watoto
> Gloss: Service to children
> Human Translation: Kuwatunza watoto
> Gloss: To take care of the children

The machine translation, as in the examples, gives literal translation that not only leads to loss of meaning but also creates ambiguity. The above machine translation can be interpreted in different ways. Machine translation has translated the symbolic meaning literally, for example, **"kuongeza mifugo wadogo"** implies to add on the existing livestock. **"Huduma kwa watoto"** implies any service to the children but not total care for the children.

The human translator makes use of translation strategies to come up with relevant equivalents **"kutunza watoto"** which means to take care of the children and **"hufuga mifugo"** which is a collocation in Kiswahili that implies keeping livestock.

9 Questionnaire for assessment of consumer satisfaction

The questionnaire was composed of five open-ended questions and three comprehension questions, each with five subdivisions. The respondents were expected to tick the appropriate answer to questions 1–5 and written answers to questions 6–8.

9.1 Tabulation

The following table represents the summary of the questionnaire responses of the first five open-ended questions. The mean for each question was calculated by adding up the 20 scores which were then divided by 20.
   Ngesu (2011)
From the data presented in the previous table on the responses of the respondents from the questionnaires, the highest score for the question on the customer satisfaction on the machine translation scored below average.
   See the key of scores below:

5 – Excellent
4 – Outstanding
3 – Very good
2 – Good
1 – Satisfactory or poor

Table 9.2 Analysis of responses from informants for questions 1–4

INFORMANT	Q1	Q2	Q3	Q4
1	1	2	2	2
2	1	2	2	3
3	1	2	1	2
4	2	2	2	3
5	2	2	2	2
6	2	2	3	3
7	2	2	1	4
8	2	2	1	2
9	1	3	2	2
10	1	1	2	2
11	2	2	2	3
12	2	1	2	1
13	2	1	2	3
14	2	4	3	2
15	2	4	2	2
16	2	2	2	3
17	2	2	1	2
18	2	2	2	2
19	1	2	1	4
20	2	1	1	2
Average	**1.7**	**2.05**	**1.8**	**2.45**

Table 9.3 Analysis of frequency of scores (1): Customer satisfaction on machine translation between English and Kiswahili

	Q1	Q2	Q3	Q4
Score1	6	4	6	1
Score2	14	13	12	11
Score3	0	1	2	6
Score4	0	2	0	2
Score5	0	0	0	0

Table 9.4 Analysis of frequency of scores (2)

	Score1	Score2	Score3	Score4	Score5
Q1	6	14	0	0	0
Q2	4	13	1	2	0
Q3	6	12	2	0	0
Q4	1	11	6	2	0

Table 9.5 Average score per question: Responses on customer satisfaction on English to Kiswahili machine translation

Q1	Q2	Q3	Q4
1.70	2.05	1.80	2.45

In these tables we see for instance that question 1, which sought to evaluate the usefulness of machine translation from English into Kiswahili, scored an average score of 1.70 (see Table 9.5).

In question 2, the respondents were asked to indicate how far the Kiswahili version done by machine translation can be used as an adequate substitute of those who do not understand English. The response of the respondents to this question scored an average score of 2.05. This gives an indication that respondents recognize that machine translation from English to Kiswahili can be useful to those who do not understand English.

The rating of the Kiswahili version translated by machine in comparison to the original text was 1.80 (question 3). In this question, there were no respondents that rated it outstanding (4) – a clear indication that the Kiswahili version of machine translation according to the respondents was not a fair translation of the original text.

Table 9.2 shows that question 4 had the highest score of 2.45. In this question the respondents were required to rate the adequacy of the Kiswahili lexicon in expressing concepts from English language. Their responses show that Kiswahili has an adequate lexicon to express concepts from the English language. The mistranslation in machine translation is mainly due to structural differences.

There were three comprehension questions. The respondents were asked to give 5 points for each question. The following responses were given. On question 6 the respondents were asked to state the major challenges of machine translation from English into Kiswahili. The responses to this question were: machine translation translates word for word, a violation of Kiswahili structure.

In question 7 the respondents were asked to suggest ways in which such challenges that they had suggested in question 6 could be resolved. Most of the responses gave the following possible solutions:

(i) To improve on machine translation such that it can translate meaning according to the context. Translation needs to be sensitive to total context.
(ii) The corpus should include the structure of each language in the data base.
(iii) To feed the machine with a wider corpus of Kiswahili words and terminologies.
(iv) To have various online Kiswahili dictionaries for various disciplines as they are in hard copies.
(v) To upload more Kiswahili books in the internet.
(vi) To encourage many Kiswahili scholars to write online articles on different registers.

In spite of the obvious limitations of the output of machine translation, the respondents appreciate the role of machine translation. The respondents were asked to explain the major advantages of using machine translation from English into Kiswahili. The following responses were given:

(i) It is faster than human translation (humans can translate 2,000–3,000 words a day, while Systran's software can translate 3,700 words a minute).
(ii) It is cheaper.
(iii) It gives equivalents of terminologies.
(iv) It can translate texts from any field.
(v) It has a wide content coverage.
(vi) It gives accurate translations in limited domains of discourse and limited vocabulary.
(vii) It's a remarkable effort to make information universally accessible through translation.

9.2 Analysis of frequency of responses of the first open-ended questions

For question 1 from English into Kiswahili, six respondents rated it satisfactory or poor, 14 respondents rated it good and none gave a rating of very good (3), outstanding (4) or excellent (5).

For question 2 in which the respondents were to evaluate how far can the Kiswahili version done by machine translation be used as a substitute for those who do not understand English, the responses were as follows:

Four respondents rate it satisfactory,13 respondents said it was good, 1 respondent said it was very good, 2 respondents felt it was outstanding.

The comparison of the Kiswahili version translated by machine to the original text was captured in question 3 and the responses were shown as follows: 12 respondents rated it good, 2 respondents said it was very good and none of the respondents gave it a rating of satisfactory, outstanding or excellent.

Question 4 was the only question that had respondents giving a fairly good representation of high scores (scores 3 and 4)

The respondents were asked to rate the adequacy of the Kiswahili lexicon in expressing concepts from English language. The following were the responses of the respondents. One respondent said it was satisfactory or poor, 11 respondents felt it was good, 6 respondents rated it as very good, 2 respondents rated it outstanding, and there was no respondent that gave it score 5 (excellent).

10 Conclusion

In this chapter, an attempt has been made to analyze the issues of language structure in machine translation with the aim of coming up with a standard description and explanation that would help the programmers, terminologists, linguists and engineers of machine translation to enhance their programs in order to improve consumer satisfaction.

The analysis has revealed that:

(i) There are mistranslations in the categories of morphology, syntax and semantics in machine translation of text from English into Kiswahili.
(ii) The structural differences: word order, the use of definite and indefinite articles and class agreement between Kiswahili and English account for mistranslations.
(iii) In machine translated texts, there are cases where the meaning of words or phrases has been distorted. The machine translation could not select between alternative meanings.
(iv) There are cases where machine translation translated symbolic meaning literally and this led to mistranslation. Any translation needs to be sensitive to total context but machine translation translated word for word.
(v) As suggested by Nida and Taber (1969), language has a great role in translation which has its basis in linguistics, and therefore language structure has to be emphasized in translation. Violation of language structure affects communication.
(vi) Machine Translation is limited in the way it is programmed to use different strategies, e.g. coinage, adoption, unpacking, loan translation etc. when faced with issues of equivalence.
(vii) Human translation involves ordering and selection of different strategies in order to reader meaning as it was in the SL text.

(viii) Machine Translation is a remarkable effort to make information universally accessible through translation.
(ix) Machine Translation is useful as an aid for human translation.

11 Recommendations

The chapter has revealed that programmers and translators of machine translation involving English and Kiswahili need to undergo special training in general and on comparative linguistics as well as terminology development in order to improve on machine translation between the two languages.

The study further recommends that the abovementioned groups of people should work as a team to enhance machine translation. In addition, as the structural differences between English and Kiswahili pose great challenges to machine translation, there is a need to improve on the Kiswahili corpus as well as the online Kiswahili Dictionary.

References

Bakari, N.K. (2012) "Terminology development in the context of multilingualism: A case of translating into Kiswahili", Unpublished M.A. Thesis, University of Nairobi.
Baker, Mona (2014) "Translation as re-narration", in Juliane House (ed.) *Translation: A Multidisciplinary Approach*, Basingstoke: Palgrave Macmillan, 158–177.
Costa-Jussa, Marta R. and Jose A. Fonollosa (2015) "Latest trends in hybrid machine translation and its applications", *Computer Speech and Language* 32(1): 3–10.
Davis, B. (2004) *Taijiquan Classics: An Annotated Translation*, Berkeley, CA: North Atlantic Books.
Gambier, Yves and Henrik Gottlieb (2001) *Multimedia Translation: Concepts, Practices and Research*, Amsterdam and Philadelphia: John Benjamins Publishing Company.
Gikambi, H.P. (2015) "Teknolojia ya Lugha katika Utafiti wa Kiswahili: Kifani cha Mradi wa Salama", Master's dissertation, University of Nairobi.
Green, Spence, Jeffrey Heer, and Christopher D. Manning (2013) "The efficacy of human post-editing for language translation", in *Proceedings of the SIGCHI Conference on Human Factors in Computing Systems*, Stanford University, 29 April, 439–448.
Hadla, Laith S. and Abeer Alhasan (2017) "Chapter seven: The influence of machine translation on students of a translation department", in Wafa Abu Hatab (ed.) *Translation Across Time and Space*, Newcastle upon Tyne: Cambridge Scholars Publishing, 97–116.
Hardmeier, C. (2014) "Discourse in statistical machine translation", doctoral dissertation, Acta Universitatis Upsaliensis.
Hermann, Karl Moritz, Tomas Kocisky, Edward Grefenstette, Lasse Espeholt, Will Kay, Mustafa Suleyman, and Phil Blunsom (2015) "Teaching machines to read and comprehend", in *Advances in Neural Information Processing Systems*, 1693–1701. Google DeepMind. Oxford: University of Oxford.
House, J. (1981). *A Model for Translation Quality Assessment*, Tubingen: Narr.
Kanana Fridah, Erastus (2013) "Examining African languages as tools for national development: The case of Kiswahili", *Journal of Pan African Studies* 6(6): 41–68.

Khamis, Said A.M. (2015) "Nguvu versus power-resilience of Swahili language as shown in literature and translation", *Matatu: Journal for African Culture and Society* (46): 49.

Kothari, C.R. (2016) *Research Methodology: Methods and Techniques* (2nd ed.), New Delhi: Wiley Eastern Limited.

Lyons, John (1968) *Semantics*, Cambridge: Cambridge University Press.

Malangwa, Pendo Salu (2010) "Handling technical translation: The case of translations of computer programmes from English into Kiswahili", doctoral thesis, University of Dar es Salaam.

Malmkjær, Kirsten (2003) "Looking forward to the translation: On 'A dynamic reflection on human activities'", in Gunilla Anderson and Margaret Rogers (eds.) *Translation Today: Trends and Perspective*, Clevedon: Multilingual Matters, 76–85.

Momanyi, Clara (2014) "Language and the quest for development in Kenya: Kiswahili at cross roads", *Kenya Studies Review* 7(2): 117–123.

Munday, Jeremy (2016) *Introducing Translation Studies: Theories and Application*, London and New York: Routledge.

Mutembei, Aldin (2014) "African languages as a gateway to sustainable development, democracy and freedom: The example of Swahili", *Alternation Journal* 13: 326–351.

Ndiritu, Meshack, Noorali Jiwaji, Abdulkarim Mhandeni, and Collins Mito (2016) "Kiswahili translation on the scientific and space-related terminology", *Acta Astronautica* 128: 330–334.

Neubert, A. (2000). *Competence in Language, in Languages, and in Translation*, Amsterdam/Philadelphia: Benjamins Translation Library, 38, 3–18.

Ngesu, Sarah N. (2011) "Issues of language structure in machine translation: A case study of English and Kiswahili", master's dissertation, University of Nairobi, Kenya.

Nida, Eugene A. (1964) *Towards a Science of Translating*, Leiden: E.J. Brill.

Nida, Eugene A. and Charles R. Taber (1969/1982) *The Theory and Practice of Translation*, Leiden: E.J. Brill.

Nurse, D., & Philippson, G. (2006) *The Bantu Languages*, London and New York: Routledge.

Ordudary, M. (2007) "Translation procedures, strategies and methods", *Translation Journal* 11(3), available from www.translationdirectory.com.

Shitemi, N.L. (2011) *Mhadhara wa Uzinduzi Kubidhaisha na Kuwezesha Lugha kama Sarafu ya Kiuchumi: Kielelezo cha Taaluma za Kiswahili na Tafsiri*, Eldouret, Kenya: Moi University Press.

Shivachi, C. (2001) "Languages in contact: English and Kiswahili in open air preaching in Kenya", seminar paper presented at the Institute of Postgraduate Studies, Maseno University.

Somers, Harold (2003) *Computers and Translation*, Amsterdam and Philadelphia: John Benjamins Publishing Company.

Wangia, J.I. (2003) "Aspects of mistranslation in the 1951 Lulogooli Bible", unpublished PhD thesis, Kenyatta University.

Zaky, M.M. (2000) "Translation and meaning", *Translation Journal* 4(4), available from www.Translationdirectory.com.

10 Quality estimation of machine translation for literature

Mozhgan Ghassemiazghandi and Tengku Sepora Tengku Mahadi

Introduction

Various qualities of Machine Translation (MT) inevitably need a multitude of attempts to post-edit the output. Human evaluations of machine translation are extensive, but they take a huge amount time and hence are expensive. Therefore, quality estimation is required in order to utilize the total potential of machine translation suggestions. Machine Translation has developed within a short time since the statistical approaches became prominent two decades ago (Brown, Pietra, Pietra, and Mercer 1993). Nowadays, machine translation is used in industry in order to improve translation productivity, especially for technical texts (Plitt and Masselot 2010). The present study examines the applicability of machine translation for literature, as these two terms seems to be incompatible. Few scholars' researches have been done on the assessment of machine translation in literary text and quality estimation of machine translation in translation workflow (Hunsicker and Ceausu 2014; Toral andWay 2014). A study by Genzel, Uszkoreit, and Och investigates the ability to produce translations with meter and rhyme for phrase-based machine translation and investigates the impact of some constraints on translation quality. They concluded that the form is preserved in machine translation at the price of producing an inappropriate translation (Genzel, Uszkoreit andOch 2010). Besacier presents an experimental evaluation where a short story is translated and post-edited and then revised by non-professional translators from English to French (Besacier 2014). The author concludes that machine translation system and automatic evaluation can be practical as a low-cost alternative to translating literary works at the price of losing translation quality.

There are a few other studies related to the translation of poetry as well (Kuppan and Devi 2009; Jiang and Zhou 2008). However, the applicability of machine translation to literature has not been studied specifically in English-Persian translation.

Evaluation of machine translation is a difficult task due to different possible interpretations. There are a few proposed methods to facilitate the evaluation of machine translation systems, as the human evaluation is expensive and takes a great deal of time. Bilingual Evaluation Understudy (BLEU) is the most widely used evaluation metrics to achieve a high correlation with human judgments of quality (Papineni et al. 2002). Doddington proposed NIST metric based on the International Business Machines (IBM) work (Doddington 2002). Metric for

Evaluation of Translation with Explicit ORdering (METEOR) is another proposed method for machine translation evaluation based on a generalized concept of unigram matching between the machine-produced translation and human-produced reference translations (Banerjee and Lavie 2005). Global Autonomous Language Exploitation (GALE) proposed Translation Error Rate (TER) as an error measure based on the number of edits by a human (Olive 2005). Finding only the minimum number of edits, without generating a new reference is the measure defined as TER. Finding the minimum of edits to new targeted references is defined as human-targeted TER (or HTER). Statistical Machine Translation (SMT) has not been used for translation between English and Persian.

Background

Machine translation of literature is apparently one of the most challenging tasks to be considered in machine translation and computational linguistics. Even the most professional translators are not able to translate it accurately. Most research scholars mention its difficulties rather than focusing on a solution to the untranslatability of literature, especially poems by machine translation. Frederking and Nirenburg measured machine translation error by post-editing machine translation output based on number of keystrokes to convert the system output into a "canonical" human translation (Frederking and Nirenburg 1994). Knight and Chander tried to improve machine translation performance based on automatic post-editing algorithms (Knight and Chander 1994). Post-editing measures have been shown useful for evaluating summaries on news articles (Mani et al. 2002). Post-editing evaluation technique has also been shown effective for Natural Language Generation (NLG) and Machine Translation (MT) systems (Sripada, Reiter, and Hawizy 2004). An optimal automatic measure of accuracy is preferred for the sake of rapid feedback and reliability while developing machine translation systems. Human-based evaluation fails in the aspect of memory and time (Ghassemiazghandi and Mahadi 2014) and has mostly been replaced by purely automatic machine translation evaluations. METEOR is an evaluation measure based on the number of exact word matches between the system output and reference, which correlated perfectly with human judgments. Then, unmatched words are stemmed and matched. Additional penalties are estimated to rearrange the words between the hypothesis and reference (Banerjee and Lavie 2005). Maximum Matching String (MMS) has been proven to make a significant correlation with human judgments. The MMS evaluation method allows a string to be corresponded once and permits string reordering as well (Turian, Shen and Melamed 2003). While TER tries to reduce the number of edits between the reference and the hypothesis, the MMS method precisely favors long contiguous matches. There is a correlation between human judgments of machine translation quality; therefore, all automatic measures of machine translation quality is very low, contrary to findings of Papineni and Doddington's research (Doddington 2002; Papineni et al. 2002). This chapter represents an evaluation based on Translation Error Rate (TER) and Human-targeted Translation Error Rate (HTER), which are briefly described in the next section.

Discussion

Degree of freedom of the translation and narrowness of the domain should be considered to analyze the applicability of statistical machine translation (SMT) to translate literary text for English-Persian languages. Narrower domain and smaller degree of freedom of the translation lead to more practical SMT (Toral and Way 2014). Consequently, SMT works for technical documentation perfectly, while products are considerably worse for the complicated and unpredictable texts.

Quality estimation

An indicative grade for the translation quality is required to exploit the full potential of machine translation suggestions. The decoder of machine translation determines internal scores to obtain the best hypothesis from the translation options, but these scores cannot be assigned to estimate the quality of output. Quality estimation provides a quality indicator to inform the reader whether or not a given translation is good enough for publishing. It filters out sentences that require post-editing by professional translators as well. The applicability of machine translation to the literary text can be assessed by measuring the degree of freedom of the translations and the limitation of the domain. Hence, we analyze how literal the translations are and how specific or general that text is to measure the usefulness of machine translation for translating the literary text.

A predictive grade for machine translation quality would be very useful to provide an upfront estimation of the quality of a given translation. Accordingly, the manual post-editing effort by the professional translator is graded according to the following scheme (Figure 10.1):

- Good: It requires little to no editing. (23%)
- Usable with the minor correction: It requires editing, but it is comprehensible. (33%)
- Usable with the major correction: It requires significant editing effort to reach a publishable level. (30%)
- Unusable: It requires retranslation from scratch. (14%)

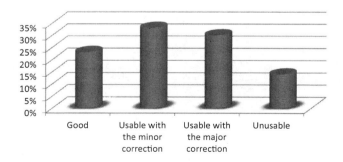

Figure 10.1 Human evaluation of differed levels of post-editing efforts

In this study, we use the results of Pars, the Persian machine translation system. First lines from the top 100 novels for the period between 1719–2002 are chosen to serve the purpose of this study, which looks at the usefulness of MT for literature. The reason for selecting these 100 novels from the seventeenth to the twenty-first century is to have a mix of writers with different styles of writing, which includes various ways of expressing the words. The writing style can be complex or simple, either formal or informal. Therefore, this will give us a better reference to evaluate the data. These sentences were chosen based on an American book review website for English-Persian language direction. These 100 lines had also been annotated with human judgments of fluency and adequacy. A professional Persian translator was assigned to post-edit each sentence.

Accordingly, a corpus of 100 sentences translated from English to Persian has been chosen to analyze the confidence grade. Such a corpus is large enough to be illustrative and small enough to be manageable, particularly for the limited purposes of this chapter. Translating these texts with machine translation and then post-editing the outputs by the professional translator created the selected data. The corpus of 100 sentences (3156 words) consists of 23 cases of the good translation, 33 cases of the usable translation with minor correction, 30 cases of the usable translation with major correction and 14 instances of the unusable translations. The sample data are created by translating these texts with machine translation and then post-editing the results. Earlier I used Persian translation systems for translation of the sources' texts, but eventually we understood that Google translator uses a much more advanced algorithm, which is the baseline for other translators as well. Hence, we used Google translator to ensure we have used the best tool to get the best result. TER and HTER methods are used for automatic evaluation of machine translation in the literary texts as well.

TER

Translation Error Rate (TER) is an error metric for machine translation that estimates the required post-editing to modify a system output into one of the references (Snover et al. 2005). TER shows the least amount possible of edits in order to change a hypothesis so that it accurately matches one of the references, normalized by the average length of the references. Since it is concerned with the minimum number of edits needed to modify the hypothesis, the number of edits to the closest reference will be measured by the TER score (Snover et al. 2005). Specifically:

$$\text{TER} = \frac{N \text{ of edits}}{\text{average N of reference words}}$$

These editions include the addition, deletion, substitution and shift. The number of edits for TER is ascertained by the professional translator who was assigned to post-edit each sentence.

Consider the below reference/hypothesis pair, where differences between the reference and hypothesis are underlined:

Reference: Many years later, as he <u>faced</u> the firing squad, <u>Colonel</u> Aureliano Buendía was to remember that <u>distant afternoon</u> when his father took him to discover ice.

Hypothesis: Many years later, as he the firing squad Aureliano Buendia was to remember that <u>afternoon distant faced</u>, <u>Colonel</u> when his father <u>when</u> discover ice

Number of words: 34

The hypothesis means the same thing as (except for untranslated noun) as the reference but TER does not count it as a proper match. First, some "shifted" position can be seen in the text. Second, we note that the phrase "Aureliano Buendía " in the reference remained untranslated in the hypothesis (this counts as two separate deletions). Finally, the word "took" appears only in the reference.

Regarding TER to this pair, the number of edits is 4 (1 Shift, 2 Deletions, and 1 Insertion), giving a TER score of 4 = 31%.

In general, the number of edits is 503; the average number of reference words is 957. Hence, the TER is 52.56.

HTER

Although there are many translation systems, still human judgment plays a significant role in the context of evaluating machine translation systems (Zaidan and Callison-Burch 2010). The TER score does not thoroughly reveal the acceptability of a hypothesis, which ignores the notions of semantic equivalence. In this study, we use Human-targeted Translation Edit Rate (HTER) for evaluating the machine translation of literary text from English to Persian. HTER requires hiring human translators to post-edit the texts. It correlates with human judgment of machine translation quality efficiently. Obtaining HTER scores for machine translation output is very difficult since this would require hiring and training human translators to post-edit the texts. HTER is a procedure for creating targeted references. HTER employs human annotators to generate another targeted reference to measure the required number of edits accurately with the same meaning as the references. An automatic system output (hypothesis) and human references are applied for the HTER method. A native speaker of English creates a new reference translation targeted for this system output by editing the hypothesis with the same meaning as the reference (Snover et al. 2005). Professional translators could give more accurate results but are much more expensive and take more time (7 to 10 minutes per sentence) to complete the task.

In this work, we evaluate the post-editing efforts from human translators, via the online Pars Translate.

HTER = (Substitutions + Insertions + Deletions + Shifts)/Reference Words.

A sample of references, hypothesis and product of human-targeted reference are demonstrated as follows:

Reference 1: The expert, who asked not to be identified, added, "This depends on the conditions of the bodies."

Reference 2: The experts who asked to remain unnamed said, "the matter is related to the state of the bodies."

Hypothesis: The expert who requested anonymity said that "the situation of the matter is linked to the dead bodies".

Targeted Reference: The expert who requested anonymity said that "the matter is linked to the condition of the dead bodies".

Here is another sample:

Reference translation	Three employees of a haulage firm have been arrested on suspicion of dumping the chemical waste. Currently it is not yet clear what the waste is that came from the plastics plant.
MT Output	Of the three officers arrested for dumping the chemical waste, a freight industry is still not clear what is the waste from a plastics factory.
HTER	Three officers of a freight industry were arrested for dumping the chemical waste, but it is still not clear what the waste is that came from a plastics factory.

Error count = 10 (2 Deletions, 6 Insertions, 2 Shifts)
Word count = 34
HTER = 29.412

We provide a subset of 3156 words translated from English into Persian, and with a single translation per source sentence by the machine translation, HTER score is: 33.73.

	No of edits	*Average no of words*	*Score*
TER	503	957	52.56
HTER	362	1073	33.73

Conclusion

The degree of applicability of machine translation to literature depends on relatedness of the language pair and the literary genre. Since English and Persian are unrelated languages, translations should be more literal and complex phenomena, and consequently more post-editing effort is required. We evaluated the translation of the first lines from the top 100 novels (3156 words) based on an American book review website for English-Persian language direction. TER score of 52.56 and HTER score of 33.73 are obtained to assist human translation by means of post-editing or interactive machine translation. We expect this score would generalize to other related language pairs as well. TER is a good indicator of human judgments of translation quality. It can be concluded that TER is highly correlated with human judgments based on the manual post-editing effort by professional translators in the translation of literature from English to Persian. It can be concluded that there is an increase of readability by 34% after human intervention for the sample data in this study. In other words, humans can predict ranking significantly better than any automatic metric systems in the literary texts. Based on the score result of TER and HTER, annotators can be trained on how to minimize the edit rate while preserving the meaning of the reference translation.

References

A, A. R., S. Kuppan and S. L. Devi (2009). "Automatic generation of Tamil lyrics for melodies", paper presented at the NAACL HLT Workshop on Computational Approaches to Linguistic Creativity, Boulder, Colorado.

Banerjee, Satanjeev and Alon Lavie (2005) "METEOR: An automatic metric for MT evaluation with improved correlation with human judgments", paper presented at the ACL 2005 Workshop on Intrinsic and Extrinsic Evaluation Measures for MT and/or Summarization.

Besacier, L. (2014). *Traduction automatisée d'une oeuvre littéraire: une étude pilote*, Marseille, France: Traitement Automatique du Language Naturel (TALN).

Brown, P. F., S. A. D. Pietra, V. J. D. Pietra and R. L. Mercer (1993) "The mathematics of statistical machine translation: Parameter estimation", *Computational Linguistics* 19(2): 263–313.

Doddington, George (2002) "Automatic evaluation of machine translation quality using N-gram co-occurrence statistics", in *Proceedings of the Second International Conference on Human Language Technology Research*, United States.

Frederking, Robert and Sergei Nirenburg (1994) "Three heads are better than one", paper presented at the Fourth Conference on Applied Natural Language Processing, ANLP-94.

Genzel, D., J. Uszkoreit and F. Och (2010) "'Poetic' statistical machine translation: Rhyme and meter", paper presented at the Empirical Methods in Natural Language Processing, Cambridge, MA.

Ghassemiazghandi, M. and T. S. T. Mahadi (2014) "Losses and gains in computer-assisted translation: Some remarks on online translation of English to Malay", paper presented at the 'Translating and the Computer 36', London, United Kingdom.

Hunsicker, S. and A. Ceausu (2014) "Machine translation quality estimation adapted to the translation workflow", paper presented at the 'Translating and the Computer 36', London, United Kingdom.

Jiang, Long and Zhou Ming (2008) "Generating Chinese couplets using a statistical MT approach", paper presented at the 22nd International Conference on Computational Linguistics, Manchester, United Kingdom.

Knight, Kevin and Ishwar Chander (1994) "Automated post-editing of documents", paper presented at the National Conference on Artificial Intelligence (AAAI).

Mani, Inderjeet, Gary Klein, David House, Lynette Hirschman, Therese Firmin, and Beth Sundheim (2002) "SUMMAC: A text summarization evaluation", *Natural Language Engineering* 43–68.

Olive, Joseph (2005) "Global Autonomous Language Exploitation (GALE)", DARPA/IPTO Proposer Information Pamphlet.

Papineni, Kishore, Salim Roukos, Todd Ward, and Zhu Wei-Jing (2002) "BLEU: A method for automatic evaluation of machine translation", paper presented at the 40th Annual Meeting of the Association of Computational Linguistics, Philadelphia, United States.

Plitt, M. and F. Masselot (2010). "A productivity test of statistical machine translation post-editing in a typical localisation context", The Prague Bulletin of Mathematical Linguistics 93, 7–16.

Ramakrishnan A, A., Kuppan, S., & Latitha Devi, S. (2009). *Automatic generation of Tamil lyrics for melodies*. Paper presented at the NAACL HLT Workshop on Computational Approaches to Linguistic Creativity, Boulder, Colorado.

Snover, Matthew, Bonnie Dorr, Richard Schwartz, John Makhoul, Linnea Micciulla, and John Makhoul (2005) "A study of translation edit rate with targeted human annotation", paper presented at the Association for Machine Translation in the Americas Conference, Cambridge.

Sripada, Somayajulu G., Ehud Reiter, and Lezan Hawizy (2004) "Evaluating an NLG system using post-editing", Technical Report AUCS/TR0402: Department of Computing Science, University of Aberdeen.

Toral, Antonio and Andy Way (2014) "Is machine translation ready for literature?", paper presented at the 'Translating and the Computer 36', London, United Kingdom.

Turian, Joseph P., Luke Shen, and I. Dan Melamed (2003) "Evaluation of machine translation and its evaluation", paper presented at the MT Summit IX.

Zaidan, Omar F. and Chris Callison-Burch (2010) "Predicting human-targeted translation edit rate via untrained human annotators", paper presented at the Human Language Technologies: The 2010 Annual Conference of the North American Chapter of the Association for Computational Linguistics, Los Angeles, CA.

Appendix

1. *Call me Ishmael.* – Herman Melville, *Moby-Dick* (1851)

    Number of Words: 3
    Level of post editing efforts: 3
    Number of edits: 2
    Average number of reference words: 8

2. *It is a truth universally acknowledged, that a single man in possession of a good fortune, must be in want of a wife.* – Jane Austen, *Pride and Prejudice* (1813)

    Number of Words: 23
    Level of post editing efforts: 2
    Number of edits: 3
    Average number of reference words: 7

3. *A screaming comes across the sky.* – Thomas Pynchon, *Gravity's Rainbow* (1973)

    Number of Words: 6
    Level of post editing efforts: 1
    Number of edits: 0
    Average number of reference words: 8

4. *Many years later, as he faced the firing squad, Colonel Aureliano Buendía was to remember that distant afternoon when his father took him to discover ice.* – Gabriel García Márquez, *One Hundred Years of Solitude* (1967; trans. Gregory Rabassa)

    Number of Words: 34
    Level of post editing efforts: 3
    Number of edits: 4
    Average number of reference words: 11

5. *Lolita, light of my life, fire of my loins.* – Vladimir Nabokov, *Lolita* (1955)

    Number of Words: 9
    Level of post editing efforts: 1
    Number of edits: 0
    Average number of reference words: 6

6 *Happy families are all alike; every unhappy family is unhappy in its own way.* – Leo Tolstoy, *Anna Karenina* (1877; trans. Constance Garnett)

Number of Words: 14
Level of post editing efforts: 2
Number of edits: 2
Average number of reference words: 6

7 *riverrun, past Eve and Adam's, from swerve of shore to bend of bay, brings us by a commodius vicus of recirculation back to Howth Castle and Environs.* – James Joyce, *Finnegans Wake* (1939)

Number of Words: 27
Level of post editing efforts: 3
Number of edits: 6
Average number of reference words: 13

8 *It was a bright cold day in April, and the clocks were striking thirteen.* – George Orwell, *1984* (1949)

Number of Words: 14
Level of post editing efforts: 2
Number of edits: 0
Average number of reference words: 7

9 *It was the best of times, it was the worst of times, it was the age of wisdom, it was the age of foolishness, it was the epoch of belief, it was the epoch of incredulity, it was the season of Light, it was the season of Darkness, it was the spring of hope, it was the winter of despair.* – Charles Dickens, *A Tale of Two Cities* (1859)

Number of Words: 60
Level of post editing efforts: 3
Number of edits: 1
Average number of reference words: 7

10 *I am an invisible man.* – Ralph Ellison, *Invisible Man* (1952)

Number of Words: 5
Level of post editing efforts: 1
Number of edits: 4
Average number of reference words: 6

11 *The Miss Lonelyhearts of the New York Post-Dispatch (Are you in trouble? – Do-you-need- advice? – Write-to-Miss-Lonelyhearts-and-she-will-help-you) sat at his desk and stared at a piece of white cardboard.* – Nathanael West, *Miss Lonelyhearts* (1933)

Number of Words: 38
Level of post editing efforts: 4
Number of edits: 13
Average number of reference words: 10

12   *You don't know about me without you have read a book by the name of* The Adventures of Tom Sawyer; *but that ain't no matter.* – Mark Twain, *Adventures of Huckleberry Finn* (1885)

Number of Words: 25
Level of post editing efforts: 3
Number of edits: 1
Average number of reference words: 5

13   *Someone must have slandered Josef K., for one morning, without having done anything truly wrong, he was arrested.* – Franz Kafka, *The Trial* (1925; trans. Breon Mitchell)

Number of Words: 18
Level of post editing efforts: 3
Number of edits: 1
Average number of reference words: 5

14   *You are about to begin reading Italo Calvino's new novel, If on a winter's night a traveler.* – Italo Calvino, *If on a Winter's Night a Traveler* (1979; trans. William Weaver)

Number of Words: 26
Level of post editing efforts: 2
Number of edits: 4
Average number of reference words: 11

15   *The sun shone, having no alternative, on the nothing new.* – Samuel Beckett, *Murphy* (1938)

Number of Words: 10
Level of post editing efforts: 1
Number of edits: 6
Average number of reference words: 7

16   *If you really want to hear about it, the first thing you'll probably want to know is where I was born, and what my lousy childhood was like, and how my parents were occupied and all before they had me, and all that David Copperfield kind of crap, but I don't feel like going into it, if you want to know the truth.* – J. D. Salinger, *The Catcher in the Rye* (1951)

Number of Words: 63
Level of post editing efforts: 2
Number of edits: 3
Average number of reference words: 13

17   *Once upon a time and a very good time it was there was a moocow coming down along the road and this moocow that was coming down along the road met a nicens little boy named baby tuckoo.* – James Joyce, *A Portrait of the Artist as a Young Man* (1916)

Number of Words: 38
Level of post editing efforts: 4
Number of edits: 17
Average number of reference words: 19

18 *This is the saddest story I have ever heard.* – Ford Madox Ford, *The Good Soldier* (1915)

Number of Words: 9
Level of post editing efforts: 1
Number of edits: 0
Average number of reference words: 7

19 *I wish either my father or my mother, or indeed both of them, as they were in duty both equally bound to it, had minded what they were about when they begot me; had they duly considered how much depended upon what they were then doing; – that not only the production of a rational Being was concerned in it, but that possibly the happy formation and temperature of his body, perhaps his genius and the very cast of his mind; – and, for aught they knew to the contrary, even the fortunes of his whole house might take their turn from the humours and dispositions which were then uppermost: – Had they duly weighed and considered all this, and proceeded accordingly, – I am verily persuaded I should have made a quite different figure in the world, from that, in which the reader is likely to see me.* – Laurence Sterne, *Tristram Shandy* (1759–1767)

Number of Words: 145
Level of post editing efforts: 3
Number of edits: 4
Average number of reference words: 17

20 *Whether I shall turn out to be the hero of my own life, or whether that station will be held by anybody else, these pages must show.* – Charles Dickens, *David Copperfield* (1850)

Number of Words: 27
Level of post editing efforts: 2
Number of edits: 4
Average number of reference words: 12

21 *Stately, plump Buck Mulligan came from the stairhead, bearing a bowl of lather on which a mirror and a razor lay crossed.* – James Joyce, *Ulysses* (1922)

Number of Words: 22
Level of post editing efforts: 3
Number of edits: 4
Average number of reference words: 11

22 *It was a dark and stormy night; the rain fell in torrents, except at occasional intervals, when it was checked by a violent gust of wind which swept up the streets (for it is in London that our scene lies), rattling along the house-tops,*

and fiercely agitating the scanty flame of the lamps that struggled against the darkness. – Edward George Bulwer-Lytton, *Paul Clifford* (1830)

Number of Words: 59
Level of post editing efforts: 2
Number of edits: 3
Average number of reference words: 11

23 *One summer afternoon Mrs. Oedipa Maas came home from a Tupperware party whose hostess had put perhaps too much kirsch in the fondue to find that she, Oedipa, had been named executor, or she supposed executrix, of the estate of one Pierce Inverarity, a California real estate mogul who had once lost two million dollars in his spare time but still had assets numerous and tangled enough to make the job of sorting it all out more than honorary.* – Thomas Pynchon, *The Crying of Lot 49* (1966)

Number of Words: 79
Level of post editing efforts: 3
Number of edits: 5
Average number of reference words: 15

24 *It was a wrong number that started it, the telephone ringing three times in the dead of night, and the voice on the other end asking for someone he was not.* – Paul Auster, *City of Glass* (1985)

Number of Words: 31
Level of post editing efforts: 2
Number of edits: 4
Average number of reference words: 12

25 *Through the fence, between the curling flower spaces, I could see them hitting.* – William Faulkner, *The Sound and the Fury* (1929)

Number of Words: 13
Level of post editing efforts: 2
Number of edits: 2
Average number of reference words: 13

26 *124 was spiteful.* – Toni Morrison, *Beloved* (1987)

Level of post editing efforts: 1
Number of edits: 0
Average number of reference words: 5
Number of Words: 3

27 *Somewhere in la Mancha, in a place whose name I do not care to remember, a gentleman lived not long ago, one of those who has a lance and ancient shield on a shelf and keeps a skinny nag and a greyhound for racing.* – Miguel de Cervantes, *Don Quixote* (1605; trans. Edith Grossman)

Number of Words: 44
Level of post editing efforts: 2

Number of edits: 3
Average number of reference words: 11

28 *Mother died today.* – Albert Camus, *The Stranger* (1942; trans. Stuart Gilbert)

Number of Words: 3
Level of post editing efforts: 1
Number of edits: 0
Average number of reference words: 6

29 *Every summer Lin Kong returned to Goose Village to divorce his wife, Shuyu.* – Ha Jin, *Waiting!* (1999)

Number of Words: 13
Level of post editing efforts: 3
Number of edits: 5
Average number of reference words: 5

30 *The sky above the port was the color of television, tuned to a dead channel.* – William Gibson, *Neuromancer* (1984)

Number of Words: 15
Level of post editing efforts: 1
Number of edits: 0
Average number of reference words: 4

31 *I am a sick man . . . I am a spiteful man.* – Fyodor Dostoyevsky, *Notes from Underground* (1864; trans. Michael R. Katz)!

Number of Words: 10
Level of post editing efforts: 1
Number of edits: 0
Average number of reference words: 5

32 *Where now? Who now? When now?* – Samuel Beckett, *The Unnamable* (1953; trans. Patrick Bowles)

Number of Words: 6
Level of post editing efforts: 2
Number of edits: 2
Average number of reference words: 10

33 *Once an angry man dragged his father along the ground through his own orchard. "Stop!" cried the groaning old man at last, "Stop! I did not drag my father beyond this tree."* – Gertrude Stein, *The Making of Americans* (1925)

Number of Words: 32
Level of post editing efforts: 2
Number of edits: 3
Average number of reference words: 8

34 *In a sense, I am Jacob Horner.* – John Barth, *The End of the Road* (1958)

Number of Words: 7
Level of post editing efforts: 1
Number of edits: 0
Average number of reference words: 6

35 *It was like so, but wasn't.* – Richard Powers, *Galatea 2.2* (1995)

Number of Words: 6
Level of post editing efforts: 3
Number of edits: 3
Average number of reference words: 5

36 *– Money . . . in a voice that rustled.* – William Gaddis, J R (1975)

Number of Words: 6
Level of post editing efforts: 3
Number of edits: 4
Average number of reference words: 7

37 *Mrs. Dalloway said she would buy the flowers herself.* – Virginia Woolf, *Mrs. Dalloway* (1925)

Number of Words: 9
Level of post editing efforts: 1
Number of edits: 0
Average number of reference words: 5

38 *All this happened, more or less.* – Kurt Vonnegut, *Slaughterhouse-Five* (1969)

Number of Words: 6
Level of post editing efforts: 1
Number of edits: 0
Average number of reference words: 4

39 *They shoot the white girl first.* – Toni Morrison, *Paradise* (1998)

Number of Words: 6
Level of post editing efforts: 4
Number of edits: 3
Average number of reference words: 5

40 *For a long time, I went to bed early.* – Marcel Proust, *Swann's Way* (1913; trans. Lydia Davis)

Number of Words: 9
Level of post editing efforts: 2
Number of edits: 1
Average number of reference words: 5

41 *The moment one learns English, complications set in.* – Felipe Alfau, *Chromos* (1990)

Number of Words: 8
Level of post editing efforts: 4
Number of edits: 4
Average number of reference words: 9

42 *Dr. Weiss, at forty, knew that her life had been ruined by literature.* – Anita Brookner, *The Debut* (1981)

Number of Words: 13
Level of post editing efforts: 3
Number of edits: 3
Average number of reference words: 5

43 *I was the shadow of the waxwing slain/By the false azure in the windowpane;* – Vladimir Nabokov, *Pale Fire* (1962)

Number of Words: 15
Level of post editing efforts: 4
Number of edits: 8
Average number of reference words: 11

44 *Ships at a distance have every man's wish on board.* – Zora Neale Hurston, *Their Eyes Were Watching God* (1937)

Number of Words: 10
Level of post editing efforts: 4
Number of edits: 4
Average number of reference words: 7

45 *I had the story, bit by bit, from various people, and, as generally happens in such cases, each time it was a different story.* – Edith Wharton, *Ethan Frome* (1911)

Number of Words: 24
Level of post editing efforts: 2
Number of edits: 2
Average number of reference words: 9

46 *Ages ago, Alex, Allen and Alva arrived at Antibes, and Alva allowing all, allowing anyone, against Alex's admonition, against Allen's angry assertion: another African amusement . . . anyhow, as all argued, an awesome African army assembled and arduously advanced against an African anthill, assiduously annihilating ant after ant, and afterward, Alex astonishingly accuses Albert as also accepting Africa's antipodal ant annexation.* – Walter Abish, *Alphabetical Africa* (1974)

Number of Words: 59
Level of post editing efforts: 3
Number of edits: 4
Average number of reference words: 6

47 *There was a boy called Eustace Clarence Scrubb, and he almost deserved it.* – C. S. Lewis, *The Voyage of the Dawn Treader* (1952)!

Number of Words: 13
Level of post editing efforts: 4
Number of edits: 7
Average number of reference words: 8

48 *He was an old man who fished alone in a skiff in the Gulf Stream and he had gone eighty-four days now without taking a fish.* – Ernest Hemingway, *The Old Man and the Sea* (1952)

Number of Words: 27
Level of post editing efforts: 2
Number of edits: 3
Average number of reference words: 8

49 *It was the day my grandmother exploded.* – Iain M. Banks, *The Crow Road* (1992)

Number of Words: 7
Level of post editing efforts: 2
Number of edits: 1
Average number of reference words: 5

50 *I was born twice: first, as a baby girl, on a remarkably smogless Detroit day in January of 1960; and then again, as a teenage boy, in an emergency room near Petoskey, Michigan, in August of 1974.* – Jeffrey Eugenides, *Middlesex* (2002)

Number of Words: 37
Level of post editing efforts: 3
Number of edits: 9
Average number of reference words: 12

51 *Elmer Gantry was drunk.* – Sinclair Lewis, *Elmer Gantry* (1927)

Number of Words: 4
Level of post editing efforts: 1
Number of edits: 0
Average number of reference words: 3

52 *We started dying before the snow, and like the snow, we continued to fall.* – Louise Erdrich, *Tracks* (1988)

Number of Words: 14
Level of post editing efforts: 3
Number of edits: 4
Average number of reference words: 8

53 *It was a pleasure to burn.* – Ray Bradbury, *Fahrenheit 451* (1953)

Number of Words: 6
Level of post editing efforts: 1
Number of edits: 0
Average number of reference words: 4

54 *A story has no beginning or end; arbitrarily one chooses that moment of experience from which to look back or from which to look ahead.* – Graham Greene, *The End of the Affair* (1951)

> Number of Words: 25
> Level of post editing efforts: 2
> Number of edits: 2
> Average number of reference words: 5

55 *Having placed in my mouth sufficient bread for three minutes' chewing, I withdrew my powers of sensual perception and retired into the privacy of my mind, my eyes and face assuming a vacant and preoccupied expression.* – Flann O'Brien, *At Swim-Two-Birds* (1939)

> Number of Words: 36
> Level of post editing efforts: 3
> Number of edits: 5
> Average number of reference words: 8

56 *I was born in the Year 1632, in the City of York, of a good Family, tho' not of that Country, my Father being a Foreigner of Bremen, who settled first at Hull; He got a good Estate by Merchandise, and leaving off his Trade, lived afterward at York, from whence he had married my Mother, whose Relations were named Robinson, a very good Family in that Country, and from whom I was called Robinson Kreutznaer; but by the usual Corruption of Words in England, we are now called, nay we call our selves, and write our Name Crusoe, and so my Companions always call'd me.* – Daniel Defoe, *Robinson Crusoe* (1719)

> Number of Words: 106
> Level of post editing efforts: 3
> Number of edits: 35
> Average number of reference words: 47

57 *In the beginning, sometimes I left messages in the street.* – David Markson, *Wittgenstein's Mistress* (1988)

> Number of Words: 10
> Level of post editing efforts: 2
> Number of edits: 1
> Average number of reference words: 6

58 *Miss Brooke had that kind of beauty which seems to be thrown into relief by poor dress!* – George Eliot, *Middlemarch* (1872)

> Number of Words: 17
> Level of post editing efforts: 4
> Number of edits: 7
> Average number of reference words: 9

59 *It was love at first sight.* – Joseph Heller, *Catch-22* (1961)

> Number of Words: 6
> Level of post editing efforts: 1

Number of edits: 0
Average number of reference words: 5

60 *What if this young woman, who writes such bad poems, in competition with her husband, whose poems are equally bad, should stretch her remarkably long and well-made legs out before you, so that her skirt slips up to the tops of her stockings?* – Gilbert Sorrentino, *Imaginative Qualities of Actual Things* (1971)

Number of Words: 44
Level of post editing efforts: 3
Number of edits: 11
Average number of reference words: 13

61 *I have never begun a novel with more misgiving.* – W. Somerset Maugham, *The Razor's Edge!* (1944)

Number of Words: 9
Level of post editing efforts: 3
Number of edits: 2
Average number of reference words: 4

62 *Once upon a time, there was a woman who discovered she had turned into the wrong person.* – Anne Tyler, *Back When We Were Grownups* (2001)

Number of Words: 17
Level of post editing efforts: 2
Number of edits: 1
Average number of reference words: 7

63 *The human race, to which so many of my readers belong, has been playing at children's games from the beginning, and will probably do it till the end, which is a nuisance for the few people who grow up.* – G. K. Chesterton, *The Napoleon of Notting Hill* (1904)

Number of Words: 39
Level of post editing efforts: 2
Number of edits: 2
Average number of reference words: 11

64 *In my younger and more vulnerable years my father gave me some advice that I've been turning over in my mind ever since.* – F. Scott Fitzgerald, *The Great Gatsby* (1925)

Number of Words: 23
Level of post editing efforts: 2
Number of edits: 2
Average number of reference words: 8

65 *You better not never tell nobody but God.* – Alice Walker, *The Color Purple* (1982)

Number of Words: 8
Level of post editing efforts: 1

Number of edits: 0
Average number of reference words: 6

66 *"To be born again," sang Gibreel Farishta tumbling from the heavens, "first you have to die."* – Salman Rushdie, *The Satanic Verses* (1988)

Number of Words: 16
Level of post editing efforts: 4
Number of edits: 8
Average number of reference words: 9

67 *It was a queer, sultry summer, the summer they electrocuted the Rosenbergs, and I didn't know what I was doing in New York.* – Sylvia Plath, *The Bell Jar* (1963)

Number of Words: 23
Level of post editing efforts: 1
Number of edits: 1
Average number of reference words: 9

68 *Most really pretty girls have pretty ugly feet, and so does Mindy Metalman, Lenore notices, all of a sudden.* – David Foster Wallace, *The Broom of the System* (1987)

Number of Words: 19
Level of post editing efforts: 4
Number of edits: 6
Average number of reference words: 8

69 *If I am out of my mind, it's all right with me, thought Moses Herzog.* – Saul Bellow, *Herzog!* (1964)

Number of Words: 15
Level of post editing efforts: 4
Number of edits: 7
Average number of reference words: 8

70 *Francis Marion Tarwater's uncle had been dead for only half a day when the boy got too drunk to finish digging his grave and a Negro named Buford Munson, who had come to get a jug filled, had to finish it and drag the body from the breakfast table where it was still sitting and bury it in a decent and Christian way, with the sign of its Saviour at the head of the grave and enough dirt on top to keep the dogs from digging it up.* – Flannery O'Connor, *The Violent Bear it Away* (1960)

Number of Words: 88
Level of post editing efforts: 3
Number of edits: 14
Average number of reference words: 16

71 *Granted: I am an inmate of a mental hospital; my keeper is watching me, he never lets me out of his sight; there's a peephole in the door, and my keeper's eye is the shade of brown that can never see through a blue-eyed type like me.* – Günter Grass, *The Tin Drum* (1959; trans. Ralph Manheim)

Number of Words: 48
Level of post editing efforts: 2
Number of edits: 1
Average number of reference words: 14

72 *When Dick Gibson was a little boy he was not Dick Gibson.* – Stanley Elkin, *The Dick Gibson Show* (1971)

Number of Words: 12
Level of post editing efforts: 1
Number of edits: 0
Average number of reference words: 7

73 *Hiram Clegg, together with his wife Emma and four friends of the faith from Randolph Junction, were summoned by the Spirit and Mrs. Clara Collins, widow of the beloved Nazarene preacher Ely Collins, to West Condon on the weekend of the eighteenth and nineteenth of April, there to await the End of the World.* – Robert Coover, *The Origin of the Brunists* (1966)

Number of Words: 54
Level of post editing efforts: 2
Number of edits: 4
Average number of reference words: 15

74 *She waited, Kate Croy, for her father to come in, but he kept her unconscionably, and there were moments at which she showed herself, in the glass over the mantel, a face positively pale with the irritation that had brought her to the point of going away without sight of him.* – Henry James, *The Wings of the Dove* (1902)

Number of Words: 51
Level of post editing efforts: 3
Number of edits: 14
Average number of reference words: 11

75 *In the late summer of that year we lived in a house in a village that looked across the river and the plain to the mountains.* – Ernest Hemingway, *A Farewell to Arms* (1929)

Number of Words: 26
Level of post editing efforts: 1
Number of edits: 1
Average number of reference words: 8

76 *"Take my camel, dear," said my Aunt Dot, as she climbed down from this animal on her return from High Mass.* – Rose Macaulay, *The Towers of Trebizond* (1956)

Number of Words: 21
Level of post editing efforts: 2
Number of edits: 2
Average number of reference words: 9

77 *He was an inch, perhaps two, under six feet, powerfully built, and he advanced straight at you with a slight stoop of the shoulders, head forward, and a fixed from-under stare which made you think of a charging bull.* – Joseph Conrad, *Lord Jim* (1900)

Number of Words: 40
Level of post editing efforts: 3
Number of edits: 11
Average number of reference words: 12

78 *The past is a foreign country; they do things differently there.* – L. P. Hartley, *The Go-Between* (1953)

Number of Words: 11
Level of post editing efforts: 1
Number of edits: 0
Average number of reference words: 7

79 *On my naming day when I come 12 I gone front spear and kilt a wyld boar he parbly ben the las wyld pig on the Bundel Downs any how there hadnt ben none for a long time befor him nor I aint looking to see none agen.* – Russell Hoban, *Riddley Walker* (1980)

Number of Words: 48
Level of post editing efforts: 4
Number of edits: 13
Average number of reference words: 17

80 *Justice? – You get justice in the next world, in this world you have the law.* – William Gaddis, *A Frolic of His Own* (1994)

Number of Words: 15
Level of post editing efforts: 2
Number of edits: 1
Average number of reference words: 7

81 *Vaughan died yesterday in his last car-crash.* – J. G. Ballard, *Crash* (1973)

Number of Words: 8
Level of post editing efforts: 1
Number of edits: 0
Average number of reference words: 5

82 *I write this sitting in the kitchen sink.* – Dodie Smith, *I Capture the Castle* (1948)

Number of Words: 8
Level of post editing efforts: 2
Number of edits: 1
Average number of reference words: 5

83 *"When your mama was the geek, my dreamlets," Papa would say, "she made the nipping off of noggins such a crystal mystery that the hens themselves yearned*

toward her, waltzing around her, hypnotized with longing." – Katherine Dunn, *Geek Love* (1983)

Number of Words: 35
Level of post editing efforts: 3
Number of edits: 12
Average number of reference words: 13

84   *In the last years of the Seventeenth Century there was to be found among the fops and fools of the London coffee-houses one rangy, gangling flitch called Ebenezer Cooke, more ambitious than talented, and yet more talented than prudent, who, like his friends-in-folly, all of whom were supposed to be educating at Oxford or Cambridge, had found the sound of Mother English more fun to game with than her sense to labor over, and so rather than applying himself to the pains of scholarship, had learned the knack of versifying, and ground out quires of couplets after the fashion of the day, afroth with Joves and Jupiters, aclang with jarring rhymes, and string-taut with similes stretched to the snapping-point.* – John Barth, *The Sot-Weed Factor* (1960)

Number of Words: 124
Level of post editing efforts: 4
Number of edits: 37
Average number of reference words: 16

85   *When I finally caught up with Abraham Trahearne, he was drinking beer with an alcoholic bulldog named Fireball Roberts in a ramshackle joint just outside of Sonoma, California, drinking the heart right out of a fine spring afternoon.* – James Crumley, *The Last Good Kiss* (1978)

Number of Words: 38
Level of post editing efforts: 3
Number of edits: 7
Average number of reference words: 11

86   *It was just noon that Sunday morning when the sheriff reached the jail with Lucas Beauchamp though the whole town (the whole county too for that matter) had known since the night before that Lucas had killed a white man.* – William Faulkner, *Intruder in the Dust* (1948)

Number of Words: 40
Level of post editing efforts: 3
Number of edits: 7
Average number of reference words: 8

87   *I, Tiberius Claudius Drusus Nero Germanicus This-that-and-the-other (for I shall not trouble you yet with all my titles) who was once, and not so long ago either, known to my friends and relatives and associates as "Claudius the Idiot," or "That Claudius," or "Claudius the Stammerer," or "Clau- Clau-Claudius" or at best as "Poor Uncle Claudius," am now about to write this strange history of my life; starting from my earliest childhood and continuing year by year until*

I reach the fateful point of change where, some eight years ago, at the age of fifty-one, I suddenly found myself caught in what I may call the "golden predicament" from which I have never since become disentangled. – Robert Graves, *I, Claudius* (1934)

Number of Words: 122
Level of post editing efforts: 4
Number of edits: 31
Average number of reference words: 18

88 *Of all the things that drive men to sea, the most common disaster, I've come to learn, is women.* – Charles Johnson, *Middle Passage* (1990)

Number of Words: 19
Level of post editing efforts: 2
Number of edits: 2
Average number of reference words: 9

89 *I am an American, Chicago born – Chicago, that somber city – and go at things as I have taught myself, free-style, and will make the record in my own way: first to knock, first admitted; sometimes an innocent knock, sometimes a not so innocent.* – Saul Bellow, *The Adventures of Augie March* (1953)

Number of Words: 44
Level of post editing efforts: 2
Number of edits: 2
Average number of reference words: 14

90 *The towers of Zenith aspired above the morning mist; austere towers of steel and cement and limestone, sturdy as cliffs and delicate as silver rods.* – Sinclair Lewis, *Babbitt* (1922)

Number of Words: 25
Level of post editing efforts: 2
Number of edits: 1
Average number of reference words: 1

91 *I will tell you in a few words who I am: lover of the hummingbird that darts to the flower beyond the rotted sill where my feet are propped; lover of bright needlepoint and the bright stitching fingers of humorless old ladies bent to their sweet and infamous designs; lover of parasols made from the same puffy stuff as a young girl's underdrawers; still lover of that small naval boat which somehow survived the distressing years of my life between her decks or in her pilothouse; and also lover of poor dear black Sonny, my mess boy, fellow victim and confidant, and of my wife and child. But most of all, lover of my harmless and sanguine self.* – John Hawkes, *Second Skin* (1964)

Number of Words: 118
Level of post editing efforts: 3
Number of edits: 21
Average number of reference words: 21

92 *He was born with a gift of laughter and a sense that the world was mad.* – Raphael Sabatini, *Scaramouche* (1921)

Number of Words: 16
Level of post editing efforts: 1
Number of edits: 0
Average number of reference words: 8

93 *Psychics can see the color of time it's blue.* – Ronald Sukenick, *Blown Away* (1986)

Number of Words: 9
Level of post editing efforts: 3
Number of edits: 1
Average number of reference words: 5

94 *In the town, there were two mutes and they were always together.* – Carson McCullers, *The Heart is a Lonely Hunter* (1940)

Number of Words: 12
Level of post editing efforts: 2
Number of edits: 1
Average number of reference words: 8

95 *Once upon a time two or three weeks ago, a rather stubborn and determined middle-aged man decided to record for posterity, exactly as it happened, word by word and step by step, the story of another man for indeed what is great in man is that he is a bridge and not a goal, a somewhat paranoiac fellow unmarried, unattached, and quite irresponsible, who had decided to lock himself in a room a furnished room with a private bath, cooking facilities, a bed, a table, and at least one chair, in New York City, for a year 365 days to be precise, to write the story of another person – a shy young man about of 19 years old – who, after the war the Second World War, had come to America the land of opportunities from France under the sponsorship of his uncle – a journalist, fluent in five languages – who himself had come to America from Europe Poland it seems, though this was not clearly established sometime during the war after a series of rather gruesome adventures, and who, at the end of the war, wrote to the father his cousin by marriage of the young man whom he considered as a nephew, curious to know if he the father and his family had survived the German occupation, and indeed was deeply saddened to learn, in a letter from the young man – a long and touching letter written in English, not by the young man, however, who did not know a damn word of English, but by a good friend of his who had studied English in school – that his parents both his father and mother and his two sisters one older and the other younger than he had been deported they were Jewish to a German concentration camp Auschwitz probably and never returned, no doubt having been exterminated deliberately, and that, therefore, the young man who was now an orphan, a displaced person, who, during the war, had managed to escape deportation by working very hard on a farm in Southern France, would be happy and grateful to be given the opportunity to come to America that great country he had heard so much about and yet knew so little about to start a new life, possibly go to school, learn a trade, and become a good, loyal citizen.* – Raymond Federman, *Double or Nothing* (1971)

Number of Words: 390
Level of post editing efforts: 3
Number of edits: 47
Average number of reference words: 56

96 *Time is not a line but a dimension, like the dimensions of space.* – Margaret Atwood, *Cat's Eye* (1988)

Number of Words: 13
Level of post editing efforts: 2
Number of edits: 1
Average number of reference words: 5

97 *He – for there could be no doubt of his sex, though the fashion of the time did something to disguise it – was in the act of slicing at the head of a Moor which swung from the rafters.* – Virginia Woolf, *Orlando* (1928)

Number of Words: 38
Level of post editing efforts: 2
Number of edits: 2
Average number of reference words: 11

98 *High, high above the North Pole, on the first day of 1969, two professors of English Literature approached each other at a combined velocity of 1200 miles per hour.* – David Lodge, *Changing Places* (1975)

Number of Words: 29
Level of post editing efforts: 3
Number of edits: 11
Average number of reference words: 12

99 *They say when trouble comes close ranks, and so the white people did.* – Jean Rhys, *Wide Sargasso Sea* (1966)

Number of Words: 13
Level of post editing efforts: 2
Number of edits: 1
Average number of reference words: 5

100 *The cold passed reluctantly from the earth, and the retiring fogs revealed an army stretched out on the hills, resting.* – Stephen Crane, *The Red Badge of Courage* (1895)

Number of Words: 20
Level of post editing efforts: 2
Number of edits: 1
Average number of reference words: 7

11 Optimising the use of computer translation systems by examining disciplinary differences and characteristics of genres as well as various approaches applied in computer translation

Cecilia Wong Shuk Man

1 Introduction

"Xin Da Ya", or fidelity, fluency and elegance, are the traditional three main requirements or standards in translating a text as suggested by Fu Yan. Scholars have different views on the third requirement. For example, Tung (2010) suggested using "felicity" to substitute for "elegance". There are also various translations to those three words, such as, "faithfulness" to "fidelity", "expressiveness" to "fluency", and "beauty" to "elegance". No matter which principle and translation you take, it does matter in accordance with the needs and characteristics of different genres.

As is known, there are different ways to do translations, such as literal translation is done by translating explicit word meanings of the text. It is particularly good for translating texts requiring fidelity and faithfulness. Free translation is done by translating messages expressed or intentions of the writers in order to achieve specific effects, such as, emotional impact and persuasive aims. It is obvious and generally agreed that machine translation is more suitable and useful for translating texts that need literal translation with absolute consistency as computers cannot perform human interpretation that is not explicitly expressed in texts.

However, researchers recently have reported on the investigations on the many advancements made in machine translation and proved that it can extensively increase productivity of translators and the quality of the corresponding translation. Guerberof Arenas (2014) has successfully proven that machine translation can improve productivity of translators as well as quality of translation in a localization project. The time spent on post-editing machine-generated translation output is less than that used on editing fuzzy match output generated by using translation memory. Huang et al. (2014) have further introduced a method to estimate the confidence value of machine translation output in order to help improving machine translation post-editing productivity by 10% for a document specific model. Many improvements on different approaches employed in machine translation systems are also revealed. Bertoldi et al. (2014) have suggested an online framework to improve the post-editing quality for phrase-based statistical machine translation that can be implemented efficiently.

This chapter investigates how to optimise the use of machine translation systems. Sections 2.1 and 2.2 will discuss on the differences and features of genres as well as the corresponding preferred translation principles. Section 2.3 will focus on discussing the various approaches employed in machine translation systems. In the conclusion, examining the feasibility in using machine translation systems for free translation will be followed by suggesting aids or extra measures to be used or incorporated to facilitate better performance in using machine translation systems. In evaluating the translation performance, attention will be particularly paid to fidelity/faithfulness and fluency as they are generally accepted as the basic criteria in defining a good translation. Mitchell, O'Brien and Roturier (2014) have also addressed fidelity and fluency in evaluating the quality of community post-edited content. The examples used in this chapter are mainly based on English-Chinese translation.

2 Optimising use of machine translation systems

As there are different ways to translate, according to various requirements and needs of different genres, we need to achieve different standards and focus on the corresponding translations. In order to optimise the results translated by machine translation systems, we have to pay attention to the disciplinary differences of the genres as well as the effects brought by the various approaches applied in the machine translation procedures.

2.1 Examining disciplinary differences and characteristics of genres

Domain specificity is generally used to describe the different types of genres in various disciplines. It is believed that texts in each domain have their own characteristics. However, when applying the same concept in machine translation, it sometimes is too general and too broad. Domain-specific texts include texts of particular domain types such as legal, financial, communication, literary, religious and scientific texts, which may actually consist of various types of genres within the same "domain". For instance, legal documents may be comprised of judgement cases and ordinances. In which case, judgement may contain quotations, proper nouns and sometimes some colloquial expressions in the description of the court cases. The syntactic structures involved are usually "normal". While in the ordinances, texts are always expressed in an "abnormal" and unusual syntactic structure with long chunks of nominal phrases and verbal phrases. The sentences are usually lengthy. Compared with the judgements, expressions used in ordinances are absolutely fixed whereas there is still a little flexibility in the expressions of judgements. Due to their authoritative nature, the translations of ordinances have to be absolute and consistent. The linguistic features exhibited in these two types of genres within the same domain require different needs in the translation treatments. In my opinion, the term, "data relatedness" is more precise and accurate in referring to the specificity of the genres for machine translation. In the following, characteristics of different genres in different domains will be listed followed by the specific features that may be advantageous to some types of machine translation.

2.1.1 Professional domains: legal

Legal text translations require absolute consistency in terminologies and even phrasal expressions. The unique syntactic structures and expressions, such as the use of a series of embedded or relative clauses or verbal phrases in ordinances, may lead to difficulties in machine translation. For example, in the Sale of Goods Ordinance: Sale and agreement to sell, an extract from the Contract of sale and its corresponding Chinese translation are stated as follows.

> (3) Where under a contract of sale the property in the goods is transferred from the seller to the buyer, the contract is called a sale; but where the transfer of the property in the goods is to take place at a future time or subject to some condition thereafter to be fulfilled, the contract is called an agreement to sell.
> (3) 凡貨品的產權根據一份售賣合約由賣方轉讓給買方，該份合約稱為一宗售賣；但如貨品的產權將來才轉讓，或待某些須於其後符合的條件得以符合後才轉讓，則該份合約稱為一項售賣協議。
> (Department of Justice: Bilingual Laws Information System)

Machine translation systems, such as Google Translate, translate according to the statistics of the data stored in their corpus. The result is as follow.

> (3) 凡根據售賣的商品屬性是從賣方轉移給買方合同，合同被稱為銷售；但如果物業在貨物轉移是發生在未來某一時間或受某些條件之後必須履行，合同被稱為協議出讓。

If the purpose of translation is for understanding the ordinance, it is good enough to let laymen understand the meaning of the ordinance easily. However, if it is for professional translation, the authoritative nature of the ordinances requires it to be absolutely accurate with the exclusion of any possible misinterpretation of the rule. The terminologies involved have to be absolutely consistent and precise.

For instance, "contract of sale" can only be translated as "合約", not "合同". "An agreement to sell" is "售賣協議" which cannot be interpreted as "協議出讓". The use of nominal chunks, such as, "the transfer of the property in the goods" should be translated as "貨品的產權" but it can easily be mistranslated by machine translation systems as it involves the identification of noun phrases correctly with the accurate interpretation of their components. "物業在

貨物轉移" is a clause not a noun phrase. It becomes neither readable nor comprehensible in the text. The unusual sentence structure also has to be addressed in the process of translation so that the results generated by machine translation systems can guarantee an accurate translation for this kind of authoritative genre.

However, in judgements, the syntactic structures of the sentences are relatively simple. Sometimes, even colloquial expressions exist in the descriptions of different court cases. When comparing with those in ordinances, the translation of the ordinances requires absolute authoritative accuracy by its nature, machine translations have to be absolutely consistent and identical to what have to be included in the law. The main similarity between the two genres is the domain specific legal terminologies. A legal glossary for each concerned language in a translation is essential. A successful example is to use an Example-based machine translation approach to handle the translations of Hong Kong legal texts gathered from the Bilingual Law Information System (BLIS) with automatic multiple level alignments (Kit, Pan and Webster 2002).

2.1.2 Professional domains: financial

Financial text translations also require consistency in the use and interpretation of terminologies, specifically in translation of the annual financial report of listed companies. The machine translation system to be used for financial translation has to be good at translating numbers correctly, e.g. "one million ten thousand" should be translated as "一百萬零一萬" which cannot be translated as "百萬10000" as in the translation of Google Translate (translate.google.com). Some tools may perform better, such as Systranet (www.systranet.com), which translated it as "一百萬一萬", but it is still not satisfactory. However, Google Translate translated "twenty thousand" as "兩萬" which is more accurate, expressive and pragmatical than "二萬" that was translated by Worldlingo (www.worldlingo.com). When it refers to the number "two", we would translate it as "二" but when it is used with a classifier or another quantifier, it should be translated as "兩". Figures and graphs are also important to be handled accurately by the systems. Moreover, proper nouns, such as names of companies, are particularly crucial in the financial field. Since the formats of finance-related documents are usually uniform, and the expressions of financial terminologies are very regular, it is beneficial to create certain templates for financial document translations. Specific types of financial texts like stock news updates have an extra requirement that is quick refresh of data, so that the response time for the machine translation systems is relatively critical.

2.1.3 Professional domains: practical

Practical text translations serve to provide specific functions. Take the user manual as an example. It provides users with information about a specific product and gives users instructions on how to use it. The texts usually have particular syntactic characteristics. A user manual usually involves imperative sentence structure as instructions illustrating how to use a product step by step. Data in such kinds of texts are very specific in a way that the same type of products from different brands may have a different way to name the same thing in their user manuals. Thus, they will have a different translation for the same thing in different brands. Terminologies to be included in a user-defined dictionary have to be specifically identified as a brand-specific dictionary. Sometimes even sentence patterns and writing styles can also be diverse. For example, a digital camera of brand A uses imperative sentences to express the instructions like "In mode M, you choose both the aperture and the shutter speed", whereas brand B expresses it as a declarative sentence like "When the brightness changes, the aperture (F value) and shutter speed also change while maintaining the shift amount" (Chan et al. 2014). It hinders the use of a domain-specific translation memory for the translation of these genres, as the same translation unit may not be able to be reused for other brands. Therefore, the use of a brand-specific translation memory or example base with a specific glossary is suggested in order to make the translation of this kind of texts more practical and accurate.

2.1.4 Professional domains: scientific

In the scientific domain, terminologies and jargons have played a very important role in that the interpretations are always unique and fixed in a way which is different from the usual uses in general situations. A good domain-specific glossary is essential for translating terms into the correct corresponding terminology. However, this glossary is a general domain-specific one which may apply to different types of texts in the same domain for the meanings of the terminologies are usually identical in various genres. Special needs, such as the ability to handle the correct translation of a formula, may require special symbols to be encrypted in such a domain. Chemistry textbook translation is an example.

2.1.5 Professional domains: communication

Press Release is one of the typical examples in the communicative text domain. The translation data availability is very high, especially for government documents. The quality requirements for this kind of translation is quite high as even style and register need to be accurate and appropriate. In such a case, human translation quality is the aim of translation standards. Online search portals have the advantage of quick access to the released data, which may obtain a good result in generating the corresponding translation. Otherwise, sometimes it is claimed that translating this kind of texts by computer systems is hopeless, as it involves a great deal of human interpretation of the underlying message that the writers intend to convey. Moreover, much of various language manipulation and rhetorical strategies are employed in the texts according to the different cultures of the corresponding source and target languages. Advertisement can be an example which serves to illustrate why.

Advertisement, as a kind of communicative text, usually involves the use of many rhetorical writing techniques aiming at creating specific persuasive effects, such as selling a product or service and advocating ideas. The corresponding translations are extremely flexible, free and very culture-specific. Sometimes colloquial usages of the corresponding languages maybe adopted in order to create a certain mood. Besides, other means or effects such as vision and sound in a television commercial, or intonation and stress in a speech will also be used as an aid of the language alone.

Fortunately, Martinez (2004) has reported research on comparing the time and effort being spent on post-editing machine translation results and human translation of marketing brochures. The findings shed light on the feasibility of machine translation for difficult texts and reassured the value of machine translation on saving translators' or editors' time and energy concerning tasks in order to increase productivity.

However, in the same domain, electronic mail communication can also be an example. In contrast, it requires only readability and comprehensibility of the text without strict demands on the translation quality since the texts are usually short lived and used by specific limited readers only. This can be a favourable feature for machine translation.

The main disadvantage of the translations performed by search engines in translating communicative texts is the inconsistency of the translation. As the data from the World Wide Web being indexed and fed into those search engines may accordingly change the frequency of the occurrence of the same term in the corpus. When the data are updated frequently from the internet information, every time you use the same translation system to translate the same term or even same text may result in a very different translation. For example, a male name, "Andy", is translated according to the pronunciation as "安迪" by Google Translate. If there is corresponding information in the system base, "Andy Lau" will be translated as the name of a Hong Kong celebrity, "劉德華". At the same time, "Andy Liu" is also translated as "劉德華" according to the Mandarin pronunciation of the surnamewhereas "Andy Chan" is translated as "安迪．陳" as there is no such name entity example in the corpus. "Andy Wong" is translated as "王子安". It shows that the translation result is highly dependent on the content stored in the corpus base of the system for the statistical translation. It also relates to the frequency of the name entity occurrences and also how famous the person is.

2.1.6 Professional domains: literature

Free translation may be one of the requirements in literary translation. The emphasis may then be put more on elegance, rather than fidelity and fluency. In translating literary texts, such as ancient poems and modern novels or fiction, aims may be on creating emotional impacts, mood and atmosphere, and/or describing an image of the situation and for imagination. The translation of these kinds of texts may require a very high standard of interpretation of the writers' intention and the context involved which are very difficult for machine translation systems to analyse. Usually, we tend to keep the underlying message that the writers intend to convey and offset the syntactic structure of the original text in doing such a kind of translation. Some religious writings, such as Chinese Buddhist writings, are also an example of belonging to this domain as most of these works are written in archaic languages.

Free translation is more suitable for this genre. An author-specific translation memory, an example-based machine translation system or an author-specific corpus-based statistical machine translation system may help to create the authors' writing styles in the corresponding translations. A dictionary defined for the specific interpretation of archaic terms and phrases can be useful as well. Use of a rich thesaurus for finding synonyms in order to enrich the flexibility on word choices in translations can also be one of the strategies. Interestingly, current machine translation systems actually can do a good job in translating ancient Chinese poems into their literal meanings (Wong 2012). In the conclusion section, I will make use of an extract of a popular modern children's story as an example for investigating the feasibility of using machine translation systems to perform free translation.

2.2 Favourable translation principles according to genre characteristics

To sum up, in treating texts in the same domain, similarities lay on the use of those domain-specific terminologies and jargons. Therefore, what we need to have is a domain-specific dictionary that includes all the necessary terms with a domain-specific sense that substituted the original meaning specified in the system dictionary. The actual data relatedness and closeness are then more crucial in determining what strategies have to be taken in doing the corresponding computer translation.

Here I would like to summarise the characteristics of some genres that are in favour of the specific kind(s) of translation principle in Table 11.1.

2.3 Investigating the effects generated from various approaches applied in machine translation

There are two main streams of approaches in doing machine translation. They are rule-based and corpus-based approaches. A rule-based approach is to analyse the source language text into a corresponding representation and use transfer rules to transform it into a representation for generating the target language text. The rationale is similar to how humans translate using the corresponding prescribed grammatical and lexical knowledge of the involved languages stored in their mind, whereas the computer translates using the prescribed grammatical rules and lexical information of the electronic lexicon of the involved language

Table 11.1 Special features of genre and translation principles

Domain: Genre	Specific Features	Translation Principles
Legal: Judgement	Absolute consistency on terminologies	Fidelity and Fluency Literal Translation and Glossaries
Legal: Ordinance	Absolute consistency for the whole texts Abnormal syntactic structure	Fidelity and Fluency Absolute Literal Translation
Financial: Annual financial report	Fixed syntactic framework and expressions, Numeral accuracy, Name entity accuracy	Fidelity and Fluency Literal Translation and Transliteration or Glossaries for name entities
Financial: Stock news	Numeral accuracy, Name entity accuracy, Quick and prompt response	Fidelity and Fluency Literal Translation and Transliteration or Glossaries for name entities
Practical: User manual	Imperative sentence structure, Listing, Product specific, brand specific terminologies and syntax.	Fidelity and Fluency Literal Translation and Specific Glossaries
Scientific: Textbook	Domain specific terminologies, Descriptive texts	Fidelity and Fluency Literal Translation and Glossaries
Communicative: Press release	Absolute formal expressions and syntactic structure, Consistency, Information correctness	Fidelity and Fluency Literal Translation
Communicative: Advertisement	Intended purpose and target readers, Cultural differences, Writers' intention, Visual and other aids	Free Translation for intend purpose
Literary: Ancient poem	Archaic languages, Emotional impact, Picture description, Poetic pose or rhyme	Free Translation with attention paid on rhyme and pose
Literary: Religious	Archaic languages, Cultural differences, Writers' intention	Free Translation according to the writing purpose for intended target readers
Literary: Modern fiction	Emotional impact, Many descriptions, Many dialogues	Free Translation

pairs built within the systems. A corpus-based approach, on the other hand, is an empirical approach using previously translated data stored in a parallel corpus as the basis for new translation. Translation can then be done by following what one-self has done in order to preserve consistency. Systems may employ statistical information generated from the corpus data as in statistical approach or retrieve segments of the data from the corpus as new translations as in an example-based approach.

2.3.1 Rule-based approach and knowledge-based approach

Following the traditional linguistic way to do translation, rule-based approach computer translation systems are based on the built-in electronic lexicon and the corresponding rules of the source and target languages, which may include syntactic and semantic rules, prescribed in the systems by linguistic experts.

Rule-based approach translation (RBMT) systems analyse the source language text according to the corresponding rules and transfer it into a structural representation in order to map it up with its corresponding target language structure. An example is the phrase-structure tree representation. Sentences are usually being broken down into smaller linguistic units, usually words for easier manipulation in looking for the corresponding target language equivalences. Features of rule-based translation are as follows:

- It is very labour intensive in that prescribed linguistic rules have to be pre-defined and pre-set by experts.
- Rules have to be expressive enough to cover all kind of sentence structure types but should not be able to generate any ungrammatical sentence in that language.
- Generation of the target language texts has to conform to the target language grammar.
- It can take care of the differences between natural languages as long as the rules are stated in the systems.
- Errors in this kind of systems are usually predictable which may help in making the post-editing process more efficient.
- Translations are language dependent.
- With the aid of appropriate dictionary, data customisation can be achieved.

Hence, the knowledge-based approach translation (KBMT) system is built on the basis of a rule-based approach in which all the necessary components to be included in a rule-based system are essential. Additionally, a knowledge base is being incorporated in the system in order to help it to learn to think like human beings with logical common sense reasoning. Logical reasoning rules can be one of the methods to help the system draw inferences of the real world knowledge. Ontology is another way for capturing all the concepts, properties and relations among real world objects for the computer to draw the correct inferences for accurate interpretation of writers' messages. However, it is quite costly to define an ontology that captures all knowledge in the world. Therefore, it is usually limited to a certain domain. An advantage of the knowledge-based approach is that logicality can be guaranteed in the generated translation output if the knowledge base or rule built-in a system included the expression of the related field. For example, "Peter drinks the coke." Google Translate translates it as "彼得喝焦炭". Logically, "焦炭" is in a form of solid which cannot be drunk. In a successful knowledge-based machine translation system, it should be able to figure out the rule that "coke" here is a kind of drink and to translate it as "可樂" as in "Peter drinks the Coke".

2.3.2 Statistics-based approach and example-based approach

By calculating the frequency and context statistics from corpus data, statistical machine translation systems can be based on the statistical information generated from the natural text data pre-stored in the system to determine the new translation. Such an algorithm seems to have no linguistic rationale involved during the translation process but is "blindly" based on calculation using statistical models. However, the performance has been proven to be quite effective, especially for translating general texts with a rapid update. Such an approach has the following features.

- It needs a large amount of data support as the basis for learning. It is not suitable for languages with scarce resources.
- It is language independent and easy to update by incorporating corpus.
- Translations are inconsistent in a way that the outputs will change from time to time as more and more data are fed in the system. Hence, the errors generated are unpredictable, which will decrease the efficiency and productivity of translators or post-editors.

Example-based machine translation (EBMT) systems, when compared to the statistical approach, retrieve the data directly from the corpus from the associated system as the new translations. It is somehow different from the statistical approach.

- It can be used with limited example-based segments.
- Examples can be reused.
- It is more suitable for translating very closely related type of texts and texts that need absolutely identical translations.
- Translation example outputs can directly inherit the accurate syntax from the examples base even if there is no linguistic analysis done by the system.
- It may involve much more processing runtime during translation according to the amount of data stored in the corpus of the system. (Scaling may be essential.)
- As proved by Dandapat et al. (2011), EBMT can tackle translation of language with scarce resources.

2.3.3 Matchings among different approaches with suitable text types

Features and characteristics of the various approaches may help a machine translation system to do translation in a more accurate and fluent way for specific genres.

Hereafter, I have listed out the features and text types that are favourable for specific approaches.

Rule-based (RBMT)

Features:

> Simple sentence structure with general interpretation of words.
> Ambiguous text with an aid of good domain specific dictionaries.
> Languages with scarce sample resources.
> Texts that need literal translation.
> Syntactic structural differences between source and target language are limited.
> Language with linguistic resources.

Text type suitable for RBMT:

- Literary: Modern fiction translated with related glossaries, such as, authors' specific glossary in order to preserve styles of specific writers or translators for keeping consistent style in the way they translate.

Knowledge-based (KBMT)

Features:

> Logical reasoning involved.
> Text with a lot of cohesive devices to connect relations among words and maintain the context.
> Information intensive.

Text type suitable for KBMT:

- Scientific: Logical translations to provide accurate information.
- User Manual: Descriptively translates instructional information with correct figuration of the concerned components for a product.

Statistics-based (SMT)

Features:

> Flexibility in translation.
> High frequency terms and texts.

Text type suitable for SMT:

- Practical: Press Release
- Literary: Religious texts and ancient poems with author-specific glossaries as some fixed expressions were usually used by specific authors.
- Legal: Judgement with legal term and name entities glossaries.
- Financial: Stock news with domain-specific and author-specific glossaries.

Example-based (EBMT)

Features:

Segments reused in translations.
Fixed expression and absolute identical translation.
Less ambiguous texts.
Languages with scarce resources.

Text type suitable for EBMT:

- Legal: Ordinances: absolute consistency should be preserved with strict syntactic structure.
- Financial: Annual financial reports with domain-specific glossary.
- Scientific texts that need fixed expressions translations and interpretations with domain specific dictionary.
- Literary: Ancient poems with author-specific glossary and religious texts with domain-specific glossaries.

3 Conclusion

Texts that need free translation, such as literary texts, including fiction and advertisements, are believed to have no hope in using a machine translation system to translate. However, with advances in technology, the development of machine translation has proven to be able to increase translators' productivity extensively. An extract (Extract 1) of a story, "Mr Chatterbox" from the famous children's fiction, "Mr. Men and Little Miss" series is being used as an example for investigating the feasibility of using machine translation systems to perform free translation. The content of the extract and the corresponding human translation in Chinese are shown in Appendix I.

The text contains a lot of dialogues just like other stories. One of the aims of such a genre is to generate an amusing effect in the aid of picture illustrations. As most of modern fiction, it uses a plain and descriptive language to present the story in an easy-to-understand way for the intended target readers. In describing the characters' personalities and the situations which happened to them, sometimes colloquial expressions may be involved.

Table 11.2 Machine translation approaches' suitability match for different genres

Domain: Genre	Suitable translation approaches
Legal: Judgement	RBMT or SMT with legal term glossary and name entities glossary
Legal: Ordinance	EBMT with legal term glossary
Financial: Annual financial report	EBMT or Translation Memory with domain specific glossary and name entities glossary
Financial: Stock news	RBMT or SMT with domain specific glossary
Practical: User manual	Translation Memory with very specific glossaries or KBMT with specific glossaries
Scientific: Textbook	EBMT or KBMT with domain specific dictionary
Communicative: Press release	RBMT, KBMT, SMT or TM with domain-specific and author-specific glossaries
Communicative: Advertisement	RBMT or KBMT, with product-specific and author-specific glossaries
Literary: Ancient poem	EBMT or SMT with author-specific glossary
Literary: Religious	SMT, EBMT with religious glossaries (e.g. Biblical terms, Buddhist terms)
Literary: Modern fiction	RBMT or KBMT with author-specific glossary or TM

In evaluating the translation performance of machine translation systems in this chapter, attention is being paid to fidelity, then to fluency. A human translation as shown previously is being used as the benchmark for comparing the machine translation systems generated translations for evaluation. The evaluation judges the fidelity and fluency of the systems-generated translations individually according to the scale shown in Table 11.3.

The scale is based on the scale quoted in Mitchell, O'Brien and Roturier (2014), which followed the scale of LDC (2005) with adaptation to Chinese. An in-depth peer group evaluation should be applied in order to compare the performance of the concerned systems objectively in the future. This chapter focuses on investigating the feasibility in applying extra measures to improve the usability of the translation generated and to optimise the use of the systems.

3.1 Feasibility in free Translation using machine translation systems

The machine translation systems used include free online version tools: Google Translate: www.google.com and Worldlingo: www.worldlingo.com as well as the full product version of: Dr. Eye X, Kingsoft Translation Express, LogoMedia Translation, Systran and Transwhiz.

Table 11.3 Scales for fluency and fidelity (based on LDC 2005)

Fluency	Fidelity
How do you judge the fluency of this translation? It is:	How much of the meaning expressed in the gold-standard translation is also expressed in the target translation?
5 Flawless Chinese	5 All
4 Good Chinese	4 Most
3 Non-native Chinese	3 Much
2 Disfluent Chinese	2 Little
1 Incomprehensible	1 None

According to the translation results shown in Appendix II, all of the tested machine translation systems can generate the target text in accordance with the same display format as the original text. Space lines serve to show special formatting is kept. Except LogoMedia and Transwhiz, other systems failed to arrange the dialogues according to the usual order as in the target languages. Only Worldlingo is able to display the correct quotation marks as in the target language display. Some phrases repeated in several sentences may have to be omitted in the target language in order to avoid redundancy. For example, "He used to" is repeated in several sentences. However, it should be omitted in its second and third occurrences. "For the time of year" should be regarded as part of the greeting phrase. So, it can be omitted in the target language. The machine translation systems however have translated it literally.

As shown in Table 11.4, an individual evaluation on the fluency (Fl) and fidelity (Fi) of machine-generated translations is performed according to LDC's 5-point scale (Table 11.3). The resultant scores are as follows.

Among the seven tools, Dr. Eye X obtains the highest scores in both fidelity and fluency aspects. Google Translate has the lowest scores on both aspects. This result correlates to the analysis mentioned in 2.3.3 as Google Translate employs a statistical approach in machine translation, which is not an appropriate tool for translating modern fiction literary texts. Dr. Eye X is a kind of rule-based system with different types of dictionaries and corpus data including regional languages, which does help in figuring out the correct meanings that the writers intend to express and translate them precisely. Although the translation results are far from perfect, they do exhibit the feasibility in using machine translation systems on literary texts.

Table 11.6 in Appendix III shows critical translation segments that influence the translation quality of Extract 1. The best result(s) of each segment are shown in bold. The segments that correlate to more than one segments are represented in parentheses. In general, Dr. Eye X performs the best among the other tools. In order to fine-tune the result of that, measures to optimise the use of the machine translation systems are to be investigated in the following section.

Table 11.4 Evaluation scores comparison

Sentence number	Google		•Worldlingo		Dr. Eye X		Kingsoft		LogoMedia		Systran		Transwhiz	
	Fl	Fi	Fl	Fi	Fl	Fi	Fl	Fi	Fl	Fi	Fl	Fi	Fl	Fi
1	1	2	3	4	4	5	5	5	2	2	4	2	5	5
2	1	2	3	3	4	4	3	4	3	3	4	3	4	4
3	1	1	3	3	3	3	3	3	3	3	3	3	3	3
4	1	1	3	3	3	3	3	3	3	3	3	3	3	3
5	2	2	2	2	4	5	3	5	2	2	3	3	3	4
6	2	2	4	5	4	4	5	4	4	5	5	4	5	5
7	2	2	3	4	3	3	4	3	3	4	4	3	4	4
8	5	2	3	4	5	5	3	3	2	3	3	3	4	3
9	3	2	3	2	3	2	2	2	2	2	2	2	2	1
10	3	1	3	3	5	4	2	3	2	2	4	3	3	2
Sub-Total:	21	17	30	33	38	38	33	35	26	29	35	29	36	34
Total:	38		63		76		68		55		64		70	

3.1.1 Measures to optimise machine translation performance for literary genre

In section 2.3.3, the analysis suggests building an author-specific glossary for modern fiction literary text translations. More precisely, it can also be a translator-specific glossary. Our first investigation is to use a translator-specific glossary to help to improve the translation. A glossary (Table 11.7 in Appendix III) is being built for storing special expressions found in the translated ten sentences (Extract 1 in Appendix I) according to the human translation (the gold-standard translation). Then, with the application of such a glossary, the two extracts (Extracts 1 and 2 in Appendix I) from the same story are translated by Dr. Eye X – both with and without the glossary for testing. In this way, the glossary serves as the function of a translation memory or example base in an EBMT system. Figuratively, it combines corpus base and rule base approaches. The comparisons of the translations are shown in Table 11.8 in Appendix III. The evaluation result is shown in Table 11.5.

The translation result for Extract 1 has greatly improved after applying the glossary, whereas the one for Extract 2 has improved by using the correct translation for the character's name only. The segments stored in the glossary now include all words, phrases and clauses. A division to the size of the segments can be done in order to further improve the evaluation results.

Because of the cultural differences and the free translation principle, the human translations of the texts include many extra phrases and clauses to describe the personality of the character and the situations of the story in order to make them

224 *Cecilia Wong Shuk Man*

Table 11.5 Comparison of the translations of Extract 1 and Extract 2

Sentence number	Dr. Eye X Extract 1		Dr. Eye X w/ glossary Extract 1		Dr. Eye X Extract 2		Dr. Eye X w glossary Extract 2	
	Fl	Fi	Fl	Fi	Fl	Fi	Fl	Fi
1	4	5	5	5	4	3	4	3
2	4	4	4	4	3	2	3	3
3	3	3	5	5	2	4	2	5
4	3	3	5	4	1	2	1	2
5	4	5	5	5	2	2	2	2
6	4	4	5	4				
7	3	3	3	3				
8	5	5	5	3				
9	3	2	5	5				
10	5	4	5	4				
Sub-Total:	38	38	47	42	12	13	12	15
Total:	**76**		**89**		**25**		**27**	

more lively and funny. For example, some colloquial expressions are added in the translation to describe the action of non-stop talking, such as, "劈哩啪啦就說". Or to add an extra sentence to describe the postman's action as knocking at the door to refer to the action, "arrived" as in the source text. These cannot be catered to by computer translation systems. However, the testing given earlier still can prove the validity in using a story-specific glossary or example base to help improve the translation of texts in certain aspects. To extend this idea, a specific translation memory can also be helpful for improving the translation result of the systems.

3.2 Concluding remarks and future development

Machine translation seemed to be diminishing but is now "alive" as it is used in combination with computer-aided translation systems. Computer-aided translation undoubtedly does better in customisation and localisation as it, in a word, has tailor-made translations for a specific purpose, specific project, specific need, specific customers, specific language pairs and/or domains or more specifically genres. Though machine translation may not be able to generate a perfect translation for all kinds of texts, it can extensively increase translators' productivity and translation quality.

As a user, we may not be able to change the underlying backbone engine of the machine translation systems; we however, may take note of the specific features and characteristics of different genres in order to choose the best type of machine translation systems for the corresponding texts we are going to translate. Through exploring to the real data relatedness of the texts instead of domain specificity, we can get a better match for the suitable machine translation approach to be used. Through the analysis shown in this chapter, different machine translation tools have their own strengths and weaknesses in translating specific genres. As long as we understand the correlation between the disciplinary differences of the genres and the corresponding translation requirements, we can choose the suitable tools according to our own needs and make the best use of them accordingly in an effective way.

For future development, the evaluation method used in this chapter can be further developed to a more objective scale by combining a human-ranking evaluation with an automatic statistical evaluation, such as the Bleu scoring algorithm, to compare the performances of different machine translation systems on literary texts in the aspects of translation output quality and post-editing effort.

References

Bertoldi, Nicola, Patrick Simianer, Mauro Cettolo, Katharina Waschle, Marcello Federico, and Stefan Riezler (2014) "Online adaptation to post-edits for phrase-based statistical machine translation", *Machine Translation* 28(3–4): 309–339.

Chan, C.Y., W.F. Cheung, S.W. Lam, and Y.T. Lam (2014) "Examples quoted in the presentation of project assignments for the course Computer-assisted Translation", The Hong Kong Polytechnic University.

Dandapat, Sandipan, Sara Morrissey, Andy Way, and Mikel L. Forcada (2011) "Using example-based MT to support statistical MT when translating homogeneous data in a resource-poor setting", in *Proceedings of the 15th Annual Meeting of the European Association for Machine Translation*, Leuven, Belgium, pp.201–208.

Department of Justice (2015) Bilingual Laws Information System (BLIS), "Hong Kong special administrative region", available from www.legislation.gov.hk/chi/home.htm.

Guerberof Arenas, Ana (2014) "Correlations between productivity and quality when post-editing in a professional context", *Machine Translation* 28(3–4): 165–186.

Hargreaves, Roger (accessed in 2015a) *Mr Chatterbox*, Mr. Men 4 Original Story Index, Taipei: Joy Asia Corporation. Ltd.

Hargeaves, Roger (accessed in 2015b) 《多嘴先生》. 林煌虔, 張馨予 (eds.), Taipei: Joy Asia Corporation. Ltd.

Huang, Fei, Xu Jian-Ming, Abraham Ittycheriah, and Salim Roukos (2014) "Improving MT post-editing productivity with adaptive confidence estimation for document-specific translation model", *Machine Translation* 28(3–4): 263–280.

Kit, Chunyu, Pan Haihua, and Jonathan Webster (2002) "Example-based machine translation: A new paradigm", in Chan Sin-wai (ed.) *Translation and Information Technology*, Hong Kong: The Chinese University Press, 57–78.

LDC (2005) "Linguistic data annotation specification: Assessment of fluency and adequacy in translation", Revision 1:5.

Martinez, Lorena Guerra (2004) "Human translation versus machine translation and full post-editing of raw machine translation output", *International Journal of Translation* 16(2): 81–113.

Mitchell, Linda, Sharon O'Brien, and Johann Roturier (2014) "Quality evaluation in community post-editing", *Machine Translation* 28(3–4): 237–262.

Tung, Chung-Hsuan (2010) "The three requirements of translation: A reconsideration", *Intergrams* 10.2–11.1, available from http://benz.nchu.edu.tw/%7Eintergrams/intergrams/102-111/102-111-tung.pdf.

Wong, Shuk Man Cecilia (2012) "Comparing performance of different state-of-the-art translation systems using a Chinese poem", paper presented at 'New Trends in Translation Technology: The 10th Anniversary Conference of the Master of Arts in Computer-aided Translation', Hong Kong: The Chinese University of Hong Kong.

Appendix I

Extract 1 and the corresponding gold-standard translation (human translation):

Mr. Chatterbox
　Mr Chatterbox was one of those people who simply couldn't stop talking.
　He used to talk to anybody and everybody about anything and everything, going on and on and on.
　And on and on and on!
　And on and on and on!
　And, when he didn't have anybody else to talk to, he used to talk to himself.
　"Good morning, Mr Chatterbox", he used to say to himself.
　"Good morning to you", he used to reply to himself.
　"Nice day, isn't it?"
　"Yes it is for the time of year".
　And so on, and so on, and on and on!

(Hargreaves 2015a: 29)

多嘴先生
　多嘴先生是个名副其实的大嘴巴，说话是他最大的嗜好。
　他只要话匣子一打开，就很难停下来。
　不管遇到任何人，他都可以和对方天南地北地聊个没完没了。
　他就这样不停地讲呀讲！
　持续没完没了的继续讲！
　即使没有谈话的对象，多嘴先生也不会闲下来，他还是可以自己对自己说话:「早安！」
　然后再回答自己:「早啊！」
　「今天天气真好啊。」
　「是啊，是啊......」
　然后就这样自言自语个不停。

(林煌虔, 张馨予 2015b: 2–8)

Extract 2 and the corresponding gold-standard translation (human translation):

One morning the postman arrived with a letter for him.
 "Morning Mr Chatterbox", said the postman.
 "Ah, good morning to you, Postman", replied Mr Chatterbox.
 "Although, as I was saying to myself only yesterday, or was it the day before, I forget, however, it's not quite so good a morning, in my opinion, but I might be wrong, although I'm not very often, as it was the other day, Monday I think it was, or perhaps it was Tuesday, but never mind, because it is quite a good morning, don't you agree, yes of course you do, because that's what you said to me in the first place, and . . ."
 And he went on and on all morning and the poor postman was late delivering all his letters.

(Hargreaves 2015a: 30)

一天早上，邮差来到叽哩呱啦小屋门前，轻轻敲了几下。叩！叩！叩！
 多嘴先生打开大门，邮差递了一封信给他：「早安！多嘴先生，你的信！」
 多嘴先生接过信，打开话匣子劈哩啪啦就说：「早安！我昨天才自己和自己道过早安。噢，不对不对，其实是前几天。我记得前些天，可能是星期一吧？哦！不对，可能是星期二，哎呀！都无所谓啦！你刚才．．．．．．」
 他就这样不停地说了一个早上的话，可怜的邮差先生要派送的信都因此耽误了。

(林煌虔，张馨予 2015b: 10–12)

Appendix II

The machine translation systems generated translations:

1. ***Google Translate (translate.google.com) (SMT):*** 话匣子先生是这些人谁根本无法停止说话之一。

    他曾经跟任何人说话，每个人对任何事情，一切，马上就要和和。
    和和和！
    和和和！
    而且，当他没有任何人倾诉，他用自言自语。
    "早上好，先生话匣子，"他常对自己说。
    "早上好给你，"他用回复自己。
    "好天，不是吗？"
    "是的，它是一年的时间。"
    等等，等等，并在与上！

2. ***Worldlingo (www.worldlingo.com):***

    chatterbox先生是不可能简单地停止谈那些人的之一。
    他曾经与任何人和大家谈话关于任何东西和一切，继续不停和。
    并且不停和！
    并且不停和！
    并且，当他没有任何人谈话对，他曾经与他自己谈话。
    「早晨好，Chatterbox先生」，他曾经对他自己说。
    「早晨好对您」，他曾经回复他自己。
    「好天儿，是？」
    「是它是在季度。」
    等等，等等和不停！

    Product Versions:

3. ***Dr Eye X:***

    先生 唠唠叨叨的人
    唠唠叨叨的人先生是完全不能停止交谈的那些人之一。
    他过去常常与任何人和每个人谈任何事情和一切，继续，和不停。
    并且在上和不停！

并且在上和不停！
并且，当他没有其他人要交谈时，他过去常常自言自语。
"早上好，唠唠叨叨的人先生，"他过去常常对他自己说。
"对你早上好，"他过去常常对他自己说。
"天气很好，不是吗？"
"是是年的时间。"
等等，等等，并且不停！

4 Kingsoft Translation Express

喋喋不休者先生
喋喋不休者先生是只是无法停止讲话的那些人们之一。
他过去一直和关于任何事和每件事物的任何人和每个人说话，继续和在。
    之上
而且不停地和在！之上
而且不停地和在！之上
并且，当他没有其他任何人说话时，他过去一直和他自己说话。
他过去一直在心里想着，"早安，喋喋不休者先生"。
"早安对你，"他过去一直答复他自己。
"好的日子，它不是吗？"
"是的它年时候"。
而且如此在，之上等等，和不停地！

5 LogoMedia Translate v.2:

喋喋不休者先生
喋喋不休者先生是的其中一个人们只是 couldn't 停止讲话。
他过去一直对任何人和每个人说大约任何事和每件事物，继续和在之上。
而且不停地和在！之上
而且不停地和在！之上
而且，当他 didn't 有其他任何人说话到，他过去一直对他自己说话。
他过去一直在心理想着的"早安，喋喋不休者先生，"。
他过去一直答复他自己的"早安到你，"。
"美好的日子，isn't 它？"
"是的它是为年的时候"。
而且如此在，之上和如此在，之上和不停地！

6 Systran:

chatterbox 先生
chatterbox 先生是不可能停止谈那些人民的之一。
他曾经与任何人和大家谈话关于任何东西和一切，继续不停和。
并且不停和！
并且不停和！
并且，当他没有任何人谈话对，他曾经与他自己谈话。
"早晨好，Chatterbox 先生，"他曾经对他自己说。
"对您的早晨好，"他曾经回复他自己。
"好天儿，不是它？"

"是它是在时期"。
等等，等等和不停!

7 *Transwhiz*

喋喋不休者先生是只是无法停止讲话的那些人们之一。
他过去一直与任何人和每个人谈论任何事和每件事物, 继续和之上。
而且不停地和之上!
而且不停地和之上!
并且, 当他没有有其他任何人要说话，他过去一直和他自己说话。
他过去一直在心里想着," 早安，喋喋不休者先生 " 。
"早安对你," 他过去一直答复他自己。
"好的日子, 它不是吗"?
"它年的时候的赞成票".
而且如此在,之上等等, 和不停地!

Appendix III

Table 11.6 Comparison of translation segments generated by machine translation systems for Extract 1

segments	Human Translation	Systran	Worldlingo	Google (SMT)	Kingsoft	LogoMedia	Transwhiz	Dr. Eye X
Mr Chatterbox	多嘴先生	chatterbox 先生	Chatterbox 先生	话匣子先生	喋喋不休者先生	喋喋不休者先生	喋喋不休者先生	唠唠叨叨的人先生
One of those who simply couldn't stop talking	名副其实的大嘴巴，说话是他最大的嗜好。	不可能停止该那些民的之一	不可能简单地停止该那些人的之一	这些人谁根本无法停止说话之一	只是无法停止讲话的那些人们之一	其中一个人们只是couldn't停止讲话	只是无法停止讲话的那些人们之一	完全不能停止交谈的那些人之一
(who simply couldn't stop talking)	他只要话匣子一打开，就很难停下来。							
He used to	不管遇到任何人	他曾经	他曾经	他曾经	他过去一直	他过去一直	他过去一直	他过去常常
Talk to anybody and everybody about anything and everything	他都可以和对方天南地北地聊个没完没了	与任何人和大家谈话关于任何东西和一切	与任何人和大家谈话关于任何东西和一切	跟任何人说话，每个人对任何事情，一切	和关于任何事物和事物的任何人和每个人说话	对任何人和每个人大约任何事和每件事物	与任何人和每个人谈论任何事情和每件事物	与任何人和每个人谈话任何事情和一切
Going on and on and on	(没完没了)	继续不停和	继续不停和	马上就要和	继续和在之上。	继续和在之上。	继续和之上	继续，和不停

(Continued)

segments	Human Translation	Systran	Worldlingo	Google (SMT)	Kingsoft	LogoMedia	Transwhiz	Dr. Eye X
And on and on and on	他就这样不停地讲呀讲！vs持续没完了的继续讲	并且不停和	并且不停和！	和和和	而且不停地和在：之上	而且不停地和在：之上	而且不停地他和在之上	并且任在上和不停
He used to talk to himself	多嘴先生也不会闲下来，	他曾经与他自己谈话	他曾与他自己谈话	他用自言自语	他过去一直和他自己说话	他过去一直对他自己说话	他过去一直和他自己说话	他过去常常自言自语
He used to say to himself	他还可以自己对自己说话：	他曾经对他自己说	他曾经对他自己说	他常对自己说	他过去一直在心里想着	他过去一直在心里想着的	他过去一直在心里想着	他过去常常对他自己说
He used to reply to himself	然后再回答自己：	他曾经回复他自己	他曾经回复他自己	他用回复自己	他过去一直答复他自己	他过去一直答复他自己的	他过去一直答复他自己	他过去常常对他自己说
For the time of year	Ellipse	它是在时期	它是在季度	它是一年的时间	它是一年时候	它是为一年的时候	它年的时候的赞成票	是年的时间
And so on and so on	然后就这样自言自语个不停。	等等	等等	等等	而且如此在，之上，等等	而且如此在，之上，和如此在	而且如此在之上等等	等等
And on and on	(然后就这样自言自语个不停。)	和不不停	和不不停	并在与上	和不停地	之上和不停地	和不停地	并且不停

Table 11.7 Glossary of Extract 1

Terms/Phrases in source language	Target language
Mr Chatterbox	多嘴先生
who simply couldn't stop talking	说话是他最大的嗜好
used to talk to anybody and everybody about anything and everything	不管遇到任何人，他都可以和对方天南地北地聊
going on and on and on.	没完没了
And on and on and on	就这样不停地讲呀讲
And on and on and on	持续没完没了的继续讲
used to talk to himself	也不会闲下来
reply to himself	回答自己
Nice day, isn't it?	今天天气真好啊。
Yes it is for the time of year.	是啊，是啊......
so on, and so on, and on and on	就这样自言自语个不停

Table 11.8 Comparison of translation segments generated by machine translation systems for Extracts 1 and 2 with Glossary

Segments	Human Translation	Dr Eye x w/o Glossary	Dr Eye x w Glossary
Mr Chatterbox was one of those people who simply couldn't stop talking.	多嘴先生是个名副其实的大嘴巴，说话是他最大的嗜好。	唠唠叨叨的人先生是完全不能停止交谈的那些人之一。	多嘴先生是完全不能停止交谈的那些人之一。
He used to talk to anybody and everybody about anything and everything, going on and on and on.	他只要话匣子一打开，就很难停下来。 不管遇到任何人，他都可以和对方天南地北地聊个没完没了。	他过去常常与任何人和每个人谈任何事情和一切，继续，和不停。	他过去常常与任何人和每个人谈任何事情和一切，没完没了
And on and on and on!	他就这样不停地讲呀讲！	并且在上和不停！	就这样不停地讲呀讲
And on and on and on!	持续没完没了的继续讲！	并且在上和不停！	就这样不停地讲呀讲
And, when he didn't have anybody else to talk to, he used to talk to himself.	即使没有谈话的对象，多嘴先生也不会闲下来，	并且，当他没有其他人要交谈时，他过去常常自言自语。	并且，当他没有其他人要交谈时，他也不会闲下来。
"Good morning, Mr Chatterbox," he used to say to himself.	他还是可以自己对自己说话:「早安！」	"早上好，唠唠叨叨的人先生，"他过去常常对他自己说。	"早上好，多嘴先生，"他过去常常对他自己说。
"Good morning to you," he used to reply to himself.	然后再回答自己:「早啊！」	"对你早上好，"他过去常常对他自己说。	"对你早上好，"他回答自己过去常常。

(*Continued*)

Segments	Human Translation	Dr Eye x w/o Glossary	Dr Eye x w Glossary
"Nice day, isn't it?"	「今天天气真好啊。」	"天气很好，不是吗？"	"天气很好，不是吗？"
"Yes it is for the time of year."	「是啊，是啊……」	"是是年的时间。"	"是啊，是啊……"
And so on, and so on, and on and on!	然后就这样自言自语个不停。	等等，等等，并且不停。	等等，等等，并且不停！
One morning the postman arrived with a letter for him.	一天早上，邮差来到叽哩呱啦小屋门前，轻轻敲了几下。叩！叩！叩！	一个早上邮差为他带着信到达。	一个早上邮差为他带着信到达。
"Morning Mr Chatterbox," said the postman.	多嘴先生打开大门，邮差递了一封信给他：「早安！多嘴先生，你的信！」	"早上唠唠叨叨的人先生，"邮差说。	"早上多嘴先生，"邮差说。
"Ah, good morning to you, Postman," replied Mr Chatterbox.	多嘴先生接过信，打开话匣子劈哩啪啦就说：「早安！	"啊，对你早上好，邮差，"唠唠叨叨的人先生回答。	"啊，对你早上好，邮差，"多嘴先生回答。
"Although, as I was saying to myself only yesterday, or was it the day before, I forget, however, it's not quite so good a morning, in my opinion, but I might be wrong, although I'm not very often, as it was the other day, Monday I think it was, or perhaps it was Tuesday, but never mind, because it is quite a good morning, don't you agree, yes of course you do, because that's what you said to me in the first place, and . . ."	我昨天才自己和自己道过早安。噢，不对不对，其实是前几天。我记得前些天，可能是星期一吧？哦！不对，可能是星期二，哎呀！都无所谓啦！你刚才……」	"虽然，我只是昨天正对我自己说，或者前天是它，但是，我忘记，在我看来，不确实如此好一个早上，但是我可能错误，虽然我经常不是，象它前些日子的那样，星期一我认为它是，或许那天是星期二，但是不要紧，因为是相当不错的早上好，你不同意，是当然你做，因为那是你首先对我说的，并且。.."	"虽然，我只是昨天正对我自己说，或者前天是它，但是，我忘记，不确实如此好一个早上，但是我可能错误，虽然我经常不是，象它前些日子的那样，星期一我认为它是，或许那天是星期二，但是不要紧，因为是相当不错的早上好，你不同意，是当然你做，因为那是你首先对我说的，并且。.."
And he went on and on all morning and the poor postman was late delivering all his letters.	他就这样不停地说了一个早上的话，可怜的邮差先生要派送的信都因此耽误了。	并且他整个上午不停走，不幸邮差晚递送他的全部信。	并且他整个上午不停走，不幸邮差晚递送他的全部信。

12 Crowdsourcing translation in contemporary China
Theories and practices

Cao Yixin

Crowdsourcing translation in contemporary China: theories and practices

Nowadays, we cannot ignore the huge contribution made by the grass-root users of the internet to the circulation of cultural products and the translation industry. Web page news is updating to the last second with their translation in diversified languages appearing on user-generated pages in different countries. Fansubbing groups and *manga* scanlation fanatics are uploading the newest version of their favorite films and *manga* with their own translations 24-hours within the works having been officially launched, and are, at the same time, circumventing censorships adroitly. Comparing with the long-established translation industry, where each formally published translation work has to undergo certain strict procedures to be on the market, the translations generated by the internet users reach their audiences in almost no time. In addition, the role of the translator is no longer limited to a small group of certificated professionals, but can be played by every internet user who is able to translate.

The all-pervasive penetration of the Web 2.0[1] concept and practice has made such translation activities possible and popular. In a typical Web 2.0 environment, the top-down flow of information of the past faces a challenge, the traditional media gatekeepers gradually lose their functions, and netizens are affecting how information is produced, transmitted, and consumed. Buzzwords have been springing up in recent years: "user innovation", "user-generation of content", and "user participation in localization" etc., among which "crowdsourcing" places itself, forming a new system of discourse confronting with the once central and dominant one.

The protesting discourse, as it appears, emerged after the development of communication technology and the internet. However, it is rather that the internet and the various new tunnels for on-line communication provide a platform for the protesting discourses to articulate themselves. Discourse and power are two sides of the same coin, and as Foucault (1980) holds: "power must be analyzed as something which circulates, or rather as something which only functions in the form of a chain. It is never localized here or there. . . . Power is employed and exercised through a net-like organization" (98). It is not that the internet that endows power to the user-translators, but that it delivers and disperses the once concentrated power into the users' hands.

Comparing with other terms, "crowdsourcing" contains both a centralized tendency and a decentralized tendency. The former shows that the mass online user creations are more or less organized by certain individuals, institutes, or even the government, which are all centers with different degrees of power. And the latter indicates that such production and consumption procedures, as well as the original material and the final product, are decided largely by the unknown crowd. The overlapped parts of "crowdsourcing" with those of the similar concepts such as "user innovation" and "user-generated content" might probably demonstrate that they are virtually attempts made to describe different facets of the same phenomena.

Under such a light, this article explores the development of crowdsourcing subtitle translation activities in China during the last decade, where the internet has been popularized in cities throughout the country, the grass-root users have been able to produce and consume texts much more conveniently than before, and the official internet media regulations have developed gradually from loose to tight. By probing into the characters and cultural implications of Chinese crowdsourcing translation communities, their development pattern, and their clash and converse with the official discourse, a better understanding of how the crowdsourcing pattern can be used in the future production of translation in China can be achieved.

Crowdsourcing: definitions

Before discussing crowdsourcing translation activities, it is necessary to look into the definition of crowdsourcing, how crowdsourcing has developed and been contextualized in different activities, and how it is related to translation.

Though the coinage of the term "crowdsourcing" has always been attributed to Jeff Howe, it first emerged on the internet by an anonymous user, which is in itself "typical of the Web 2.0 phenomenon" (Schenk and Guittard 2009: 4). Howe's article in the 2006 June issue of *Wired* magazine announces the public debut of "crowdsourcing". As defined by Howe in his blog article published in the same month:

> crowdsourcing represents the act of a company or institution taking a function once performed by employees and outsourcing it to an undefined (and generally large) network of people in the form of an open call. This can take the form of peer-production (when the job is performed collaboratively), but is also often undertaken by sole individuals. The crucial prerequisite is the use of the open call format and the large network of potential laborers.
> ("Crowdsourcing: A Definition" 2006)

Clearly, the first definition of crowdsourcing relates closely to the business circle. The term is a compound word of "crowd" and "outsourcing", with the latter being made use of in the established business institutions as a way of production or problem solving. The two vital prerequisites of crowdsourcing emphasized by Howe, "the open call" and "the large network of potential laborers", become yardsticks for measuring whether an activity is crowdsourcing. Many later theoretical attempts at defining the term evolve their discussions based on these two prerequisites. In his homonymous book two years later, Howe (2008) discusses in detail the origin, concept, examples, and cultural-political significance of crowdsourcing, and expanded its definition: "It's an umbrella term for a highly varied group of approaches that share one obvious attribute in common: they all depend on some contribution from the crowd" (280). Howe traces the origin of internet crowdsourcing to the co-design of the Linux system, a computer operating system openly inviting coders for its improvement since the 1990s. Open-source in nature, Linux is like a "bazaar", a place where the wisdom of the crowds converges and converses with each other. In contrast to the "cathedral", the symbol of a centralized pattern of production, "bazaar" embraces all the merits coming from the democratic "prosumers" who know exactly what they want (54–55). Some more recent examples, such as the Threadless.com T-shirt design competition and the business success of iStockphoto, etc., illustrate the web-community character of crowdsourcing production, a direction investigated by later researchers.

In retrospect, Howe's definition and discussion of crowdsourcing are eye-opening and inspiring, but too general, abstract, and capricious for serious academic discussion. Nevertheless, they successfully draw a panoramic blueprint for future studies on the internet crowdsourcing kingdom, especially for those taking the internet community as the primary playground for crowdsourcing activities. One area that the forthcoming scholars often investigated into is the business value of crowdsourcing, which has been taken as an effective tool for problem-solving.

Brabham (2008) launches the first acknowledged academic definition of crowdsourcing. Based on the case study of the Next Stop Design project, a project in 2009 encouraging members of an online community to design bus-stop shelters and using peer voting for selecting the top designs, Brabham explores the merits of crowdsourcing over the traditional public participation methods. Brabham's special concern goes to whether the participants regard such a kind of online participation as effective or not, as well as participants' motivations. He elaborates why crowdsourcing, a deliberative democratic process, has proven to be effective, with the term defined as: "not merely a web 2.0 buzzword, but is instead a strategic model to attract an interested, motivated crowd of individuals capable of providing solutions superior in quality and quantity to those that even traditional forms of business can" (79).

A series of discussions on how to define "crowdsourcing" emerged around 2010, and the definitions vary with different contexts. Vukovic (2009) undertakes a comprehensive study on enterprise crowdsourcing. Using a practice-based approach, Vukovic lists a few crowdsourcing sites, and proposes a classification of enterprise crowdsourcing according to their incentives, intellectual property rights, and information security. Vukovic and Bartonlini (2010) conduct a literature-based study on the same topic, looking into such aspects as the models of crowdsourcing, crowd types, incentives, quality assurance, legal factors, and social factors. Crowdsourcing is "a successful mechanism to harvest information and expertise from the masses" (425) in various domains. Other definitions of crowdsourcing include collective intelligence (Buecheler et al. 2010; La Vecchia and Cisternino 2010), a sheer business practice and an extension of outsourcing (Schenk and Guitarred 2009; Whitla 2009; Oliveira, Ramos, and Santos 2010; Sloane 2011), or a production process by voluntary users in the Web 2.0 environment (Mazzola and Di Stefano 2010; Wexler 2011).

Since 2010, articles have endeavored to review the existing discussions and definitions of crowdsourcing. For instance, considering that no existing literature by then has systematically portrayed the processes through which crowd intelligence is used to generate its power, Geiger et al. (2011) make the first attempt to reach a comprehensive taxonomy of crowdsourcing. They investigate altogether 49 crowdsourcing examples, looking for their organization pattern, crowdsourcing goals, as well as running mechanism; and classify them into 19 types, and finally into five clusters: integrative sourcing without remuneration, selective sourcing without crowd assessment, selective sourcing with crowd assessment, integrative sourcing with success-based remuneration, and integrative sourcing with fixed remuneration.

Estellés and González (2012), to reduce semantic confusion, make a more elaborate classification and redefinition of crowdsourcing after a scrutinized study of the existing literature up to 2011. By applying Tatarkiewicz's approach of reconstructing a concept, the authors investigate altogether 209 documents in terms of document type, definitions of crowdsourcing, nature of the crowd, initiators of crowdsourcing, and crowdsourcing processes. The rigid statistics they provide make it a milestone among the theoretical researches on crowdsourcing. Equally important, Estellés and González hold that the dispute between whether certain online activities can be regarded as crowdsourcing can be solved by studying the different initiations of individual crowdsourcing organizations. In addition, the specific area that a research investigates would affect its definition of crowdsourcing (198).

> Crowdsourcing is a type of participative online activity in which an individual, an institution, a non-profit organization, or company proposes to a group of individuals of varying knowledge, heterogeneity, and number, via a flexible open call, the voluntary undertaking of a task. The undertaking of the task, of variable complexity and modularity, and in which the crowd should participate bringing their work, money, knowledge and/or experience, always entails mutual benefit. The user will receive the satisfaction of a given type of need, be it economic, social recognition, self-esteem, or the development of individual skills, while the crowdsourcer will obtain and utilize to their advantage that what the user has brought to the venture, whose form will depend on the type of activity undertaken.
>
> (197)

This definition contains eight decisive factors for defining an activity as crowdsourcing: clear goals, recompenses and identifications of crowdsourcers, clearly defined compensation for crowdsourcers and clearly assigned process of participation type, as well as an open call and the use of the internet (10).

To conclude, from Howe's initial idea of "crowdsourcing" to Estellés and González's integrated redefinition, the concept has gradually been expanded to cover increasingly comprehensive online activities. Contextualized studies of crowdsourcing activities continue to draw a larger blueprint demonstrating the democratic nature, efficiency, and cost-effectiveness of this mode of production in a wide spectrum of businesses. Estellés and González's definition of crowdsourcing, though not directly, to a large extent incorporates the perplexing concepts of "crowdsourcing", "user-innovation", and "user generation content" rather than clarifying the boundaries between them. The latter is detrimental in terms of reaching the core of crowdsourcing, which is in nature, an information production and consumption revolution on the internet. Being both confined and resilient, Estellés and González's definition provides a feasible theoretical common ground for discussing the crowdsourcing cases of different fields and countries in or even before the Web 2.0 Age.

Crowdsourcing translation: theories and practices

Recent years have seen an augmentation of the research on crowdsourcing translation, but few systematic reviews have been made, especially when it comes to the theorization of the concept. Pérez-González (2014) introduces crowdsourcing as a newly immerging branch of audiovisual translation studies, and claims that "this term (crowdsourcing) designates the outsourcing of an audiovisual translation job, traditionally performed by professionals, to an undefined, often large group of individuals in the form of an open call" in the context of his discussions (307). This definition is noticeably similar to the first definition of "crowdsourcing" made by Howe in 2006, only adding "audiovisual translation" as a modifier to specify the field and industry which are applying "crowdsourcing". Although it is safe to re-write the succinct definition of crowdsourcing that can powerfully demonstrate the general running pattern of a crowdsourcing activity, we miss the entire backdrop of that which generates such a definition. While getting to know a "typical" crowdsourcing translation activity involves a task, a commissioner, and an undefined large group, we have no idea about the nature of the tasks, the identity of the commissioners, the relationship between the commissioners and the crowdsourcing translators, as well as the constitution of the crowd, etc. This definition only draws people's attention to the new trend in translation practices but does not tell why it deserves attention in the first place. Thus, a review of the literature on the theories and practices of crowdsourcing translation is necessary.

Literature included here are not only those directly under the term "crowdsourcing translation", which are few, but also those under the broader discussions of community translation, collaborative translation, user-generated translation, and even fansubbing, etc. All these similar terms, as long as they serve for crowd participation in the creation of certain products, can be regarded as crowdsourcing translation.

In general, the research altogether falls into two categories: theories and applications, with the former at its exploratory stage lacking a structured frame, and the latter concentrating on the technical level of crowdsourcing translation and specific cases.

Theoretical research on crowdsourcing translations can be classified into three parts. First, introductory researches such as a classification of the functions and goals of different on-line translation communities (Lu 2013), or a report of the management pattern, running mode, and the internal environment of crowdsourcing translation sites (Ray and Kelly 2011). Second, research on the information dissemination of crowdsourcing translations, for instance, how the internet has broken the linear translation production-consumption chain and dispersed it into a network (Gong 2012), or its impact on public perceptions of translation (McDonough Dolmaya 2012). Third, research on the ethics of crowdsourcing translation. Such issues as whether the translators are trained and paid, whether translation activities are becoming more visible, whether crowdsourcing could enhance the status of minor languages, and whether non-professional translators are able to generate new codes of practice when confronting with ethical choices in translation are examined carefully (McDonough Dolmaya 2011; Drugan 2011). Moreover, in the AMTA 2010 one-day workshop held in Denver, Colorado, myriad questions related to crowdsourcing translation were discussed, such as its impact on the translation profession and translation technology, its quality assurance and technological appropriateness, and its co-development with stakeholders (Désilets 2010). Valuable notes were taken around the issues of crowd motivation, monolingual contributors, professionalization in the crowd, business case, output quality, massive data sharing, and platform sharing, covering quite a large range of issues about crowdsourcing translation still waiting to be strictly studied.

On the other hand, applied research on crowdsourcing translations mainly address the following cases. First, there is human-machine translation: e.g., studies on the crowdsourcing post-editing framework and its application in the machine translation community (Aikawa, Yamamoto, and Isahara 2012); on the construction of cross-lingual or monolingual corpora via crowdsourcing (Negri et al. 2011; Hu 2012; Post, Callison-Burch, and Osborne 2012); or on the methods to help crowdsourcing translation in achieving professional quality (Zaidan and Callison-Burch 2011). In general, research from the human-machine perspective are fruitful, yet have mostly been conducted by computer scientists rather than researchers of translation studies. Second, there are comparisons between crowdsourcing translation and professional translation or machine translation for their quality, speed, and cost-effectiveness (Anastasiou and Gupta 2011; Sobol 2012). Third, evaluations have been made on other applications of crowdsourcing translations, such as fansubbing, social network and news translation, language learning, and humanitarian activities – for instance, crowdsourcing translation for the emergency response in Haiti after the 2010 earthquake (Munro 2013).

As can be drawn, researchers have made a variety of efforts on the topic of crowdsourcing translation. However, study cases are usually limited to a specific technique, a specific community, or a specific activity of crowdsourcing translation. Little research has been done on the features of crowdsourcing translation in a given area (for instance, a country), which indicates that regional differences in crowdsourcing and its functions in the target language cultures have been overlooked. Besides, synchronic studies far outweigh diachronic studies, which mean the inter-relationship (inheritable or developmental) between crowdsourcing translation, its internet predecessors, and pre-internet translation activities have been understated. Thus, present research results are far from being able to explain the changes and developments crowdsourcing translation has brought to a specific target culture, as well as its exclusive features in that culture. To conclude, studies on crowdsourcing translation suggest a need for further development from a historical and contextualized perspective.

Crowdsourcing translation activities in China: free and freedom

On the huge map of internet crowdsourcing translation, China is an underexplored area. Similar to their western counterparts, crowdsourcing translation activities in China have started with the fandom culture and Japanese *manga*, popularized with the fansubbing of English movies, and now extended to other genres of texts. This section gives a brief account of the social-cultural background for the rise of crowdsourcing translation in China, as well as how the major crowdsourcing translation communities have developed and evolved.

When tracing the development of the crowdsourcing translation activities in China, the social and technological contexts deserve attention. China is a country with neither a mature economic system nor a strictly regulated translation industry. The translation industry in China started in the 1980s after the Opening-up Policy, developed since the 1990s, and built up in the twenty-first century. Even today, the industry is still disproportioned, short of intellectual labors, lacking both a national standard of performable rules and an advanced evaluation system.

Crowdsourcing translation reveals the power imbalance between different countries. As Cronin (2013) states in *Translation in the Digital Age*, a book depicting, theorizing, and envisaging how the internet has and will bring about revolutions to the translation industry, under the internet environment "the circulation of cultural goods such as music, cinema, literature in English does not automatically have to bear the translation costs that are almost axiomatic for non-Anglophone cultures which seek global circulation of their own goods" (44). When contextualizing this statement in China, it is particularly true because almost all the present internet crowdsourcing translations have been done to import, rather than export the cultural products no matter in what forms. Those products in English, the *lingua franca* of today's world and an obligatory language course to be taken by Chinese students since primary school, make up the largest portion of such cultural import. Such cultural products can be in the form of movies, TV series, entertainment shows, news, documentaries, popular information and popular science articles, etc. Crowdsourcing translated Japanese *manga* and animations, Korean movies and entertainment programmes, and those media products from non-Anglophone cultures are also popular among particular fan groups, yet not as widely accepted, consumed, and acknowledged as those from the Anglophone cultures.

Cronin uses the terms "transferred or devolved cost" (44) to describe the phenomenon, indicating the translation cost that used to be borne by the information producers has been shifted to the consumers. The disintermediation of the information production and transmission process enables internet users to generate free texts and deliver them directly to the consumers, who are, largely, at the same time producers and consumers. Under such a mechanism, crowdsourcing translation is virtually a practice that disperses the innumerable digital texts to innumerable grass-root users who have the interest and ability to translate, because the production and translation of such texts are too costly considering the all-pervasive information explosion. Exploitations exist on two levels, one within a culture or a nation, largely taking the form of abusing the free labors of the users; the other crossing the borders of cultures and nations, demonstrating an imbalanced cultural flow. Despite the possible cultural hegemony existing in the crowdsourcing translation activities in China, which is against the democratic spirit of the internet, we can still discern in crowdsourcing the free flow and free choice of information inborn with the Web 2.0 Age. Viewing from the opposite perspective, the mass imports of foreign cultural products by grass-root internet users, as well as the prospering of numerous crowdsourcing translation communities, create a freer public domain where people are able to express their ideas, utilize their skills, and choose which texts bearing which ideology to transmit and consume. Thus, the crowdsourcing translation activities in China reveal a high degree of translator's manipulation of the original text. In addition, the practices of translators are more "visible" than before when considering their creative use of popular terms of the target language and culture in translation.

Nevertheless, though the World Wide Web has largely boosted cross-cultural interactions, the information flow always faces obstructions, no matter within a country or between different nations. The dominant discourse, usually that of the government of a country, would exert regulations on any cultural product imported through a legal channel, as well as endeavor to make the rules reach those circumventive cases. Crowdsourcing translation in China has always been touching on copyright issues and official censorship:

> Censorship is a coercive and forceful act that blocks, manipulates and controls cross-cultural interaction in various ways. It must be understood as one of the discourses, and often the dominant one, articulated by a given society at a given time and expressed through repressive cultural, aesthetic, linguistic ad economic practices.
>
> (Baker and Saldanha 2010: 28)

In China, a country exercising severe media censorship rules, a new book, movie, or TV series might need months or even years to enter, or may never enter the market legally, let alone the time spent on completing the translation and further editing. Take movie censorship, for example: before 2012, as regulated, no more than 20 new foreign movies can be broadcast in the registered cinemas per year. Although later the quota was stretched to 34, the increased proportion only includes the movies using 3D or IMAX techniques, with China's share in box-office of the introduced movies increased from the previous 13% to 25% (Gu 2014). Intentions to protect the local movie industry can be easily discerned from the rules, which both reassure the capital flow is in the positive direction for the benefit of the country, and the ideology of the introduced movies is not in conflict with the dominant ideology of China.

The crowdsourcing translation activities have challenged the official censorship through various channels. The most important one is uploading huge quantities of uncensored videos and web contents, which both violates the media law and infringes the copyright of the ST producers. In nature, crowdsourcing is a revolution brought by the rise of peer-to-peer technology, for the latter allows the inter-transmission of data directly between two computers, resulting in a faster, cheaper, and decentralized pattern of information sharing. The increasingly affordable and broader-banded internet in China since the year 2001 have been enabling more and more internet users to transmit larger or even super large documents with high efficiency. Seeing that the production and transmission of information are no longer pricey and beyond grasp, netizens started to upload self-made audios and videos, publish self-edited pictures and articles, and generate other forms of content, gradually replacing or canceling the "gatekeeper" role in the pre-internet era or the Web 1.0 Age.

According to the semiannual reports issued by the China Internet Network Information Center (CINNC) (2002, 2006, 2011a, 2015), an official institute responsible for internet affairs, the number of Chinese netizens has increased from 33.7 million in 2001, to 111 million in 2005, 457 million in 2010, and 649 million in 2014, now covering 47.9% of the entire population. The drastically ascending number calls for more comprehensive and penetrating regulations from the government's side for preventing internet crimes or infringements. However, in contrast to the rapid growth of the net kingdom, internet laws and regulations in China have been progressing slightly forward each year. As stated by Yu Zhigang (2013), professor of China University of Political Science and Law, in an investigation of the internet-related laws in China up to 2012, the current internet law system in China has many flaws in structure, legislation, and performance. "Chinese internet law system is lagging behind the development of time, because it is based on the Web 1.0 requirements" (90). The internet now is no longer a platform providing information, but rather a public domain for free communication. Social networks of the Web 2.0 Age are boosting the interaction between different users. Thus, Yu holds that new legislation should notice "the function of the internet and the formation of different internet communities" (90). In such communities, people communicate with each other rather than communicating merely with the machine. As demonstrated in another report issued by the CINNC (2011b), up to December 2010, 235 million netizens are using social network sites, 63.9% of which are active. Also, through the end of 2010, the youth netizens (netizens below the age of 25), which make up 46.3% of the entire internet population in China, contribute tremendously to the information production and consumption in internet entertainment and social network sites. About 66.6% of the youth netizens are involved with internet videos, 48.1% with internet literature, 74.8% with internet computer games, and 62% with social network sites (CINNC 2011c).

The preceding data are important for understanding the rise and development of crowdsourcing translation in China. On the one hand, crowdsourcing translation activities are mainly carried out on the social network sites. The internet communities provide the crowdsourcing translators a common platform to discuss and decide what and how to translate, as well as to accumulate feedbacks from the immediate audience. In terms of demography, the crowdsourcing translators in China are mostly educated youth that constitutes a considerable portion of the internet population. They are making their voices heard through the transmission and translation of foreign cultural products. On the other hand, official legislation and regulation on the internet nowadays, though endeavoring to catch up, still need a long way to go with the Web 2.0 era, where the surging user-produced web contents are no longer easy to control. Even if new policies and laws are tailored to the needs of the new environment, whether they can be effectively enforced in the massive information sea is still in question. During this transitional period of the lapse of a forceful and effective sanctioning power, the crowdsourcing translation activities in China constitute a counter-discourse of the youth netizens promoting an information democracy. By exploring the development pattern of the crowdsourcing translation communities, as well as the conflict and conversation between the dominant discourse and the crowdsourcing translators, we can achieve a better understanding of the nature and practicality of crowdsourcing translation in China.

From fan translation to crowdsourcing translation: utopias, resistance, and incorporation

In China, the crowdsourcing translation activities can be roughly classified into subtitle translation (developed from the fansubbing groups), *manga* scanlation (a compound word for translation plus the scanning of comic books), computer game "translation hacking" (a process involving both translation and the techniques of hacking into the game source codes), news and popular information translation, and literature translation. Each sub-genre of crowdsourcing translation, owning their own mechanism of production and targeted audience, clashes with the dominant ideology to different degrees. Among them, the crowdsourcing subtitle translation communities embrace the vastest audience groups, while conflicting most violently with official censorship and copyright laws. The following discussions would show how the fansubbing groups have been gradually growing into the crowdsourcing subtitle translation communities, under the influence and impact of different discourses.

As mentioned, since 2001, the internet in China has applied broadband technology and become increasingly affordable to private users. Peer-to-peer file sharing enables the netizens to upload and download videos beyond official regulations, pushing on the course of information globalization. Chinese youths of the internet age, growing up in a more tolerant cultural environment than their parents, better educated and media literate, started to seek the cultural products from other countries encoded with varying ideologies via the internet. Some of them, other than consuming the products for their own sake, have taken on the role of "cultural importer" by introducing the foreign, mostly western cultural goods to Chinese audiences. Motivated by the spirit of "sharing", Chinese fan-translation communities were born. At the very beginning, a typical Chinese fan-translation group constituted only a dozen members, and the source texts were mainly Japanese *manga*. Later on, television series in English gradually stepped into the spotlight and became a fad. Chinese fan-translators began to collaborate with overseas internet grass-root translation communities to acquire the latest videos. The warez[2] revolution all over the world has supported the rise of Chinese fansubbing communities; in particular, the 0-day warez has allowed fan-translators to get a copyrighted work within 24 hours after its release.

Backed up by the peer-to-peer technical foundation and stable sources of constantly updating videos, the fansubbing activities in China had already gained huge momentum around 2005. At that time, the most influential fansubbing communities in China such as 1000fr,[3] YDY Translate Extreme Team,[4] YYeTs,[5] and Ragbear[6] had already been formed, with their initiators and organizers being grass-root internet users. Non-profit in essence, these communities share similarities in their running patterns, while at the same time competing with each other. The competitions have been focusing on the speed, quality, language style of translation, as well as the quantity and variety of the source videos. For instance, YYeTs has been known for its translation quality, ydy for its translation speed and the broad spectrum of videos, and 1000fr once for its precision in wording and diction in translating the medical language in the American television series *Doctor House* (YYeTs 2009). All the source videos and translated subtitles would be uploaded to a server for free download, either open to all or to a circle of selected and registered users.

When it comes to the maintenance of the fansubbing communities, the initiator or the core members of a community shared the costs at the early stage. Later on, when a community gradually amassed its audience, it would start searching for exterior sponsors, mainly advertisers. The income was largely based on the click-through rate of the video download pages with advertisement banners, and has been used to sustain the everyday operation of the community. As reported in an article in *Nanfang Weekend* (Liu 2011), a newspaper advocating the opening-up and reform of China, Chinese volunteer subtitle translators regard their communities as self-sustained and self-sufficient utopias that are fighting both for their own development and the overall ideal of interment democracy, against the official power and ideology. Money has never been the motivation, not even self-developments such as language learning. The pivotal impetus for the fan translators is personal interest in foreign cultural products, and in sharing such products. Equally important is the zero tolerance of the pirate VCDs that are of poor translation quality. Although the statement against pirate videos sounds paradoxical since the fansubbers themselves have been transmitting warez files against internet laws, it reveals the sense of elite or even the heroic complex from the fan translators' side. The translators believe they are highly responsible for the social and cultural environment of the internet, and they insist that the non-profit sharing of information is not wrong. Judging from the biographies and comments of these youths, they gain great satisfaction from translating, uploading videos, and seeing their subtitles be appreciated by the audience.

However, any cultural activity cannot be devoid of interactions with other aspects of society, such as the economy, law, and power. As Even-Zohar's (1979) polysystem theory asserts, "sign-governed human patterns of communication (e.g., culture, language, literature, society) should be regarded as systems rather than conglomerates of disparate elements" (289). Such a conglomerated system is termed a "polysystem", and the translation system is no exception. The fansubbing communities in China, besides competing with each other to survive in the market, confront a more severe opponent, the dominant power exerted by the central government through censorship and law enforcement. While almost all the subtitle communities would automatically attach a statement: "the shared video and subtitle are only for study and share, please delete within 24 hours after download," it cannot exempt the fansubbers from their infringement of laws. The massive introduction of uncensored films and television programmes directly challenges the dominant ideology, and causes economic losses in the authorized film and television industry. Fansubbing subtitle translation communities, ever since they were born, have been colliding and conversing with the official discourse.

In 2009, the State Administration of Radio, Film and Television (incorporated with the General Administration of Press and Publication into the State Administration of Press Publication, Radio, Film and Television in 2003) ordered the regulation of the Bit Torrent websites, the hugest nest of downloadable videos. About 400 Bit Torrent websites were blocked in that year ("In the days without BT" 2009), including the famous Emule and BTChina, both owning millions of users. Bit Torrent, a typical protocol for peer-to-peer transmission, is the foundation for file sharing among the fan-translation communities and their audience. Thus, the blockage and sanctioning of the Bit Torrent sites posed a severe blow to the fansubbing communities. In fact, similar to the origin of the fansubbing translation activities, the governmental control over them also started from the west. The "Pirate Bay trial" in 2009 in Sweden prosecuted four initiators of the world's most used torrent tracking site by then, The Pirate Bay, and the final sentence was 1-year imprisonment and a fine of 30 million SEK (Ricknäs 2010). In 2014, the existing largest torrent site in China, the Shooter, was closed due to the "complaint from the 'The Motion Picture Association of America', who holds that the Shooter seriously violates the copyright laws" ("National Copyright Administration" 2014). The share of unauthorized videos all across the globe and its by-product, the fan-translated subtitles, has aroused economic disputes that lead to the amendment and enforcement of new laws.

For better development, many fansubbing subtitle translation communities in China have sought to "negotiate" with the official power by cooperating with authorized organizations, and it was from then that the crowdsourcing translation communities started to come into being. On the one hand, the crowdsourcing communities have inherited the translation experience and running patterns from the fansubbing predecessors. On the other, the increased sense of copyright protection and official cooperation reduced the risk of being "illegal". The fansubbers, accordingly, gradually turned into crowdsourcing translators with the legalization process of the user-generated translation activities. For instance, the rise of global open online courses brought about a new opportunity for the user translators. We can find the case of YYeTs, the largest subtitle translation group in 2010, who managed to collaborate with Netease, one of the most influential internet technology companies in China, in a programme called "Open Classes from World's Top Universities". By translating the subtitles for the open classes, the crowdsourcers received funding of 1 million RMB "not only for maintaining the server and other hardware, but also for paying the translation fee for the translators" (Wu 2011: 55). Since 2012, MOOC (Massive Open Online Courses) has become the mainstream of online open education, with Coursera, Udacity, edX as the most famous platforms for learning. These international MOOC platforms has cooperated with Guokr.com, a Chinese web community themed in popular science and technology, to recruit volunteer crowdsourcing translators with an open call. Standard certificates demonstrating the crowdsourcing translators' contribution to a specific open course would be issued to those who participate. Up to March 27, 2015, 64 Coursera MOOCs from different disciplines have been translated into Chinese.[7] From these cases, we can discern that the crowdsourcing translators, the used-to-be protesters of the official ideology and power, have gradually been incorporated with the latter. Although the protesting discourse from the crowdsourcers' side is still strong, that many subtitle translation communities are still dodging censorship and infringing copyright laws by uploading unauthorized videos and subtitles, the authorized or even paid practices is now making up an increasingly larger proportion of the entire map of crowdsourcing translation. The crowdsourcers and the official discourse have reached a common ground.

In other types of crowdsourcing translation communities, similar patterns of development can be traced: a tendency from "underground" practices to official activities, though the situations vary according to different platforms. Take literature and internet article translation communities as examples; their initial motivation for translation was also personal interests of studying and sharing foreign literature, news, entertainment information, and popular science articles, etc. During their development, these communities had either been weeded out by the market or went on the trail of profiting and legitimization. YeeYan, an open platform aimed at introducing the quintessence of foreign web contents, has started since 2006 to recruit qualified volunteer crowdsourcers to translate and publish literature works in foreign languages. As for the crowdsourcing translations of comics and computer games, such activities also confronted severe challenges. For game translation, the increasingly sophisticated anti-crack technologies of game companies have started to block the channel for the acquirement of the texts in the games, which makes the translation process more difficult, or even impossible. For comic and animation translation, the State Administration of Press Publication, Radio, Film and Television has been issuing documents such as "Notice of Further Regulation and Standardization of Website Animation Broadcast" every year to ban the upload of Japanese animations which are "violent, pornographic, and terrifying". Crowdsourcing translation communities for these genres are still struggling with the dominant discourse and are either working towards a legalization procedure, or have not yet found a way out.

Crowdsourcing translation: possible future directions

The development of and difficulties faced by the crowdsourcing translation communities in China might shed light on the future application of this pattern of translation production, which is vital in the modern world where information has become cheap and springs up in overwhelming amounts.

Many factors make crowdsourcing translation a prosperous field for contemporary China and the world. First, crowdsourcing translation is effective in translating multi-modal texts, which are parts of the global information explosion that is too costly and almost impossible if translated in a traditional mode. Second, the success of the crowdsourcing translation of mass open online courses proves that crowdsourcing translation communities can cooperate with official organizations. Third, the overwhelmingly single-direction transmission of cultural products through crowdsourcing translation hints that the non-Anglophone speaking countries can possibly "fight back" with the same strategy of translation. Thus, open calls for translation can be made by the official media, formal translation agencies, as well as the authorized internet platforms to recruit crowdsourcers to conduct translation. The division of an original text into different pieces largely reduces the time of translation; while the selection of the source text by the crowdsourcers is more market sensitive and effective than the traditional media gatekeepers, for the crowdsourcers come from the market and are alert about what the audience is crazy for. Thus, less waste in information production and transmission can be expected. In addition, crowdsourcing translation patterns can be tested on the translation of Chinese cultural products in multi-modal forms into English, such as open class and popular videos, etc., which would be a great channel for China to voice itself in the world.

Conclusion

The concept of crowdsourcing is still in development, as well as the practices and research on crowdsourcing translation. This chapter investigates the definition of crowdsourcing and crowdsourcing translation, their cultural implication in the context of nowadays China, and traces the development of crowdsourcing translation communities in the past few years. In this final conclusion, it has to be restated that in the Web 2.0 Age where the power of information production distributes directly into the hands of internet users, both the production and consumption of information shall be viewed with a new perspective. Trash information is updating every second in huge quantities, and trivial texts are distracting people from what really matters to their personal interest, leisure entertainment, and self-development. Crowdsourcing translation, a selection and re-editing process of the texts in foreign languages, has proven to be an effective filter of the supra-abundant information for its market sensitivity.

However, there are two long-term problems for the development of crowdsourcing translation activities in China. First, the overwhelmingly single direction of cultural products input, mainly from the Anglophone-spoken countries, reveals the problem of possible cultural hegemony. Second, the long-lasting clashes between the crowdsourcing translation communities and the official discourses, though now muted a little by the increasingly comprehensive internet laws and law enforcement, as well as the incorporation of the crowdsourcers into some more legally accepted translation activities, remains an obstacle for the future development of crowdsourcing translation. Thus, the power relations evolving around crowdsourcing translation need to be further explored.

Notes

1 Introduced by O'Reilly at the Web 2.0 Conference in the late 2004, the term spots the structural changes taking place along the development of the internet. The key of Web 2.0 lies in the user-generated contents, easy accessibility for individual users, and a participative culture that encourages interaction. Google, Amazon, EBay, Wikipedia are the typical Web 2.0-inspired sites harnessing the intelligence of the crowd (O'Reilly 2007), which inspired the later-on definition of "crowdsourcing" by Howe. To date, though the terms "Web 3.0 (semantic web)", "Web 4.0 (mobile web)", "Web 5.0 (emotional)", and even "Web 6.0" have emerged, they do not necessarily constitute the updated version of Web 2.0, but rather as complements based on predictions of technology. It is safe to conclude, among these versions, the Web 2.0 model is the only one started from large-scale real-life practices and from which came the concept of "crowdsourcing".
2 With the development of peer-to-peer technology, internet users start to distribute or trade copyrighted works without authorization. Such a work is called a "warez".
3 1000fr, with the full name in Chinese as "磬灵风软" (qing ling feng ruan), is among the earliest fansubbing communities in China. Its focus is English to Chinese translation of the subtitles of American television series. It was established around 2004 and became the most popular at once. However, due to disputes between the senior members, some of whom left the community and initiated a new one, 1000fr almost disintegrated in 2007. After that the reputation and the translation quality of 1000fr have degraded. Now 1000fr is still running as a non-profit translation community.
4 YDY Translate Extreme Team, with the full name in Chinese as "伊甸园字幕组" (yi dian yuan zi mu zu), is one of the earliest fansubbing communities in China. Its focus is English to Chinese translation of the subtitles of American or British television series. It was established around 2003 and experienced its golden period from 2005 to 2006. After the central government's ban of unauthorized publication of translated videos, YDY only opens to registered members. The registration procedure is strict, and members can have access to the download links of the videos.

5 YYeTs, with the full name in Chinese as "人人影视" (ren ren ying shi), is one of the earliest and the largest fansubbing community in China. Established in 2003, it went through difficulties from 2003 to 2005, YYeTs gradually became the largest and most popular fansubbing community. Other than translating English television series and films into Chinese, YYeTs also provides Chinese subtitles translated from French, Portuguese, and Hungarian, etc. YYeTs was closed due to the pressure from Motion Picture Association of America in 2014, and was re-opened in 2015.
6 Ragbear, with the full name in Chinese as "破烂熊乐园" (po lan xiong le yuan), was once one of the most popular fansubbing community in China. Its translation focus and development trace are similar to 1000fr and YDY Translation Extreme Team.
7 The statistics are made by Guokr, retrieved from http://mooc.guokr.com/post/609351/ on 27 March 2015.

References

Aikawa, Takako, Kentaro Yamamoto, and Hitoshi Isahara (2012) "The impact of crowdsourcing post-editing with the collaborative translation framework", *Advances in Natural Language Processing Lecture Notes in Computer Science* 7614: 1–10.

Anastasiou, Dimitra and Rajat Gupta (2011) "Comparison of crowdsourcing translation with machine translation", *Journal of Information Science* 37: 637–659.

Baker, Mona and Gabriela Saldanha (eds.) (2010) *Routledge Encyclopedia of Translation Studies*, Shanghai: Shanghai Foreign Language Education Press.

Brabham, Daren C. (2008) "Crowdsourcing as a model for problem solving: An introduction and cases", *Convergence: The International Journal of Research into New Media Technologies* 14: 75–90.

Buecheler, Thierry, Jan Henrik Sieg, Rudolf M. Füchslin, and Rolf Pfeifer (2010) "Crowdsourcing, open innovation and collective intelligence in the scientific method-a research Agenda and operational framework", in *Proceedings of the Alife XII Conference*, Odense, Denmark, 679–686.

China Internet Network Information Center 中国互联网络信息中心 (2002) 〈第9次中国互联网络发展状况统计报告〉 ("The 9th statistical report on Internet development in China"), available from www.cnnic.cn/hlwfzyj/hlwxzbg/200906/P020120709345368128648.pdf.

China Internet Network Information Center 中国互联网络信息中心 (2006) 〈第17次中国互联网络发展状况统计报告〉 ("The 17th statistical report on Internet development in China"), available from www.cnnic.cn/hlwfzyj/hlwxzbg/200906/P020120709345358064145.pdf.

China Internet Network Information Center 中国互联网络信息中心 (2011a) 〈第27次中国互联网络发展状况统计报告〉 ("The 27th statistical report on Internet development in China"), available from www.cnnic.cn/hlwfzyj/hlwxzbg/201101/P020120709345289031187.pdf.

China Internet Network Information Center 中国互联网络信息中心 (2011b) 2010年〈中国网民社交网站应用研究报告〉 ("Statistical report on the users' application of social Network sites in 2010, China"), available from www.cnnic.cn/hlwfzyj/hlwxzbg/201108/P020120709345277353319.pdf.

China Internet Network Information Center 中国互联网络信息中心(2011c) 2011年〈中国青少年上网行为调查报告〉 ("Statistical report on the youth's behavior on the Internet"), available from www.cnnic.cn/hlwfzyj/hlwxzbg/201108/P020120709345278379037.pdf.

China Internet Network Information Center 中国互联网络信息中心 (2015) 〈第35次中国互联网络发展状况统计报告〉 ("The 35th statistical report on Internet development in China"), available from www.cnnic.cn/hlwfzyj/hlwxzbg/201502/P020150203551802054676.pdf.

Cronin, Michael (2013) *Translation in the Digital Age*, London and New York: Routledge.

Désilets, Alain (2010) "AMTA 2010 workshop – collaborative translation: Technology, crowdsourcing, and the translator perspective", available from http://mt-archive.info/AMTA-2010-Desilets.pdf.

Drugan, Joanna (2011) "Translation ethics wikified: How far do professional codes of ethics and practice apply to non-professionally produced translation?" *Linguistica Antverpiensia, New Series – Themes in Translation Studies* 10, available from https://lans-tts.uantwerpen.be/index.php/LANS-TTS/article/view/280/178.

Estellés-Arolas, Enrique and Fernando González-Ladrón-de-Guevara (2012) "Towards an integrated crowdsourcing definition", *Journal of Information Science* 38(2): 189–200.

Even-Zohar, Ivan (1979) "Polysystem theory", *Poetics Today* 1: 287–310.

Foucault, Michel (1980) *Power/Knowledge: Selected Interviews and Other Writings 1972–1977*, translated by C. Gordon, London: Harvester Press.

Geiger, David, Stefan Seedorf, Thimo Schulze, Robert C. Nickerson, and Martin Schader (2011) "Managing the crowd: Towards a taxonomy of crowdsourcing processes", available from http://aisel.aisnet.org/cgi/viewcontent.cgi?article=1396&context=amcis2011_submissions.

Gong, Wen 公文 (2012) 〈论网络翻译传播模式〉 ("The communication model of net translation"), 《中国科技翻译》 (*Chinese Science and Technology Journal*) 25: 22–25.

Gu, Junzhu 古珺姝 (2014) 〈电影局否认进口片配额增加说法，称每年34部不变〉 ("China's film bureau denies the hearsay and claims the yearly quota of film importation is still 34"), 《新京报》 *Beijing News*, available from www.chinanews.com/gn/2014/02-11/5820379.shtml.

〈国家版权局：射手网因美方投诉被查〉 ("National copyright administration: The shooter is under investigation due to an American suit") (2014) 《南方周末》 (官方网站) (*Nanfang Weekend*), available from www.infzm.com/content/106364.

Howe, Jeff (2006) "Crowdsourcing: A definition", *Crowdsourcing Blog*, available from http://crowdsourcing.typepad.com/cs/2006/06/crowdsourcing_a.html.

Howe, Jeff (2008) *Crowdsourcing: How the Power of the Crowd Is Driving the Future of Business*, New York: Random House.

Hu, C. (2012) "Crowdsourced monolingual translation digital repository", unpublished doctoral dissertation, The University of Maryland, Maryland.

"In the days without BT: Successive ban of the BT download Sites" (2009), *Nanfang Weekend*, available from www.infzm.com/content/38462.

La Vecchia, Gioacchino and Antonio Cisternino (2010) "Collaborative workforce, business process crowdsourcing as an alternative of BPO", in Florian Daniel and Federico Mechele Facca (eds.) *Current Trends in Web Engineering, ICWE 2010 Workshops*, Berlin and Heidelberg: Springer, 425–430.

Liu, Zhibing 刘治兵 (2011) 〈乌托邦里也有快乐〉 ("There is also happiness in the Utopia"), 《南方周末》 (*Nanfang Weekend*), available from www.infzm.com/content/64924.

Lu, Yan 陆艳 (2013) 〈众包翻译应用案例的分析与比较〉 ("Researches on crowdsourcing translation"), 《中国翻译》 (*Chinese Translators Journal*) 3(34): 56–61.

Mazzola, Denia and Alexandra Di Stefano (2010) "Crowdsourcing and the participation process for problem solving: The case of BP", in *Proceedings of ItAIS 2010 VII Conference of the Italian Chapter of AIS*, Napoles: ItAIS, 42–49.

McDonough Dolmaya, Julie (2011) "The ethics of crowdsourcing", *Linguistica Antverpiensia, New Series – Themes in Translation Studies* 10, available from https://lans-tts.uantwerpen.be/index.php/LANS-TTS/article/view/279/177.

McDonough Dolmaya, Julie (2012) "Analyzing the crowdsourcing model and its impact on public perceptions of translation", *The Translator: Studies in Intercultural Communication* 18: 167–191.

Munro, Robert (2013) "Crowdsourcing and the crisis-affected community", *Information Retrieval* 16(2): 210–266.

Negri, Matteo, Luisa Bentivogli, Yashar Mehdad, Danilo Giampiccolo, and Alexxandro Marchetti (2011) "Divide and conquer: Crowdsourcing the creation of cross-lingual textual entailment corpora", in *Proceedings of the 2011 Conference on Empirical Methods in Natural Language Processing*, Edinburgh, UK, July 27–31 (670–679). Stroudsburg, PA: Association for Computational Linguistics.

Oliveira, Fabio, Isabel Ramos, and Leonel Santos (2010) "Definition of a crowdsourcing innovation service for the European SMEs", in Florian Daniel and Federico Mechele Facca (eds.) *Current Trends in Web Engineering, ICWE 2010 Workshops*, Berlin and Heidelberg: Springer, 412–416.

O'Reilly, Tim (2007) "What is web 2.0: Design patterns and business models for the next generation of software", *Communications and Strategies* 65(1): 17–37.

Pérez-González, Luis (2014) *Audiovisual Translation: Theories, Methods and Issues*, London and New York: Routledge.

Post, Matt, Chris Callison-Burch, and Miles Osborne (2012) "Constructing parallel corpora for six Indian languages via crowdsourcing", in Chris Callison-Burch, Philipp Koehn, Christof Monz, Matt Post, Radu Soricut, and Lucia Specia (eds.) *WMT '12 Proceedings of the Seventh Workshop on Statistical Machine Translation*, Montrèal, Canada, 7–8 June (401–409). Stroudsburg, PA: Association for Computational Linguistics.

Ray, Rebecca and Nataly Kelly (2011) "Crowdsourced translation", available from www.commonsenseadvisory.com/Portals/_default/Knowledgebase/Article Images/110201_R_GL _Crowdsourcing_Preview.pdf.

Ricknäs, Mikael (2010) "Pirate bay appeals looks set to start in September", *PC World*, available from www.pcworld.com/article/191304/article.html.

Schenk, Eric and Claude Guittard (2009) "Crowdsourcing: What can be outsourced to the crowd, and why", in *Workshop on Open Source Innovation*, Strasbourg, France, available from http://raptor1.bizlab.mtsu.edu/s-drive/DMORRELL/Mgmt%204990/Crowdsourcing/Schenk%20and%20Guittard.pdf.

Sloane, Paul (2011) "The brave new world of open innovation", *Strategic Direction* 27(5): 3–4.

Sobol, Forest Julia (2012) "Translation in transition: The feasibility and effectiveness of crowdsourced translation versus professional translation", PhD dissertation, Arizona: The University of Arizona.

Vukovic, Maja (2009) "Crowdsourcing for enterprises", in *Services-I, 2009 World Conference on IEEE*, Los Angeles, CA, 6–10 July (686–692). Washington, DC: IEEE Computer Society.

Vukovic, Maja and Claudio Bartolini (2010) "Towards a research agenda for enterprise crowdsourcing", in Tiziana Margaria and Bernhard Steffen (eds.) *Leveraging*

Applications of Formal Methods, Verification, and Validation, Berlin and Heidelberg: Springer, 425–434.

Wexler, Mark N. (2011) "Reconfiguring the sociology of the crowd: exploring crowdsourcing", *International Journal of Sociology and Social Policy* 31(1/2): 6–20.

Whitla, Paul (2009) "Crowdsourcing and its application in marketing activities", *Contemporary Management Research* 5(1): 15–28.

Wu, X.F. (2011) "Subtitle groups: Behind the localization of American television series", *World Affairs* 1: 52–55.

Yu, Z.G. 于志刚 and Xing Feilong 刑飞龙 (2013) 〈中国网络法律体系的现状分析和未来建构 – 以2012年12月31日为截止时间点的分析〉 ("Analysis on the internet legal system in China and its future construction"), 《辽宁大学学报 (哲学社会科学版) 》 (*Journal of Liaoning University (Philosophy and Social Sciences Edition)*) 7: 82–94.

YYeTs (2009) 〈中国字幕组以及YYeTs字幕组的历史简介〉 ("A brief introduction to the subtitle groups in China and YYeTs"), available from http://blog.sina.com.cn/s/blog_57036da80100d9gr.html.

Zaidan, Omar F. and Chris Callison-Burch (2011) "Crowdsourcing translation: Professional quality from non-professionals", in *Proceedings of the 49th Annual Meeting of the Association for Computational Linguistics*, Portland, Oregon, June 19–24 (1220–1229). Stroudsburg, PA: Association for Computational Linguistics.

Index

accuracy 22, 80
alignment 102, 141; alignment tool 139, 141–142; bilingual 100
authoring 120

clarity 21
computational linguistics 155, 184
computer-aided translation 4, 64, 120, 138–140, 142, 144–145, 224; computer-aided translation software 3, 100; computer-aided translation system 102, 138, 224; computer-aided translation technology 145, 150; computer-aided translation tool 100–101, 120, 122, 125, 141, 144–146
computer-assisted translation 120, 122–123
computer translation 5–6, 209, 215; computer translation system 6, 209, 224; corpus-based 215; rule-based 215, 217
concordance 145–146
conference translation 52
controlled authoring 4, 120, 122–123, 125, 132; controlled authoring tool 123
controlled language 1–2, 30, 36, 38–39
corpus 85, 100, 161, 179, 186
corpus rhetoric 83
cost 23
crowdsourcing 6, 236–240, 248–249; crowdsourcing translation 6, 236, 236–245, 248–250
customer satisfaction 12, 178

data 1, 80, 100, 161, 167, 173, 177, 213; data mining 42, 64
dynamic equivalence 84

faithfulness 209–210
fidelity 19, 209–210, 221–222
fluency 210, 221–222
free translation 5–6, 209, 214, 220
frequency 70, 80

human factor 1–2, 6, 9, 26, 51
Human-targeted Translation Edit Rate 187, 189
human translation 23, 167, 173, 180, 189, 220–221, 223

information 181, 236; information extraction 64; information processing 64; information retrieval 64
intelligibility 19, 39
interpreting 2, 51–52, 61

knowledge presentation 64

literal translation 5, 176, 209
localization 8, 26, 224; web 1; website 1, 8, 10, 12, 16, 25; localization project 80–81

machine translation 1–2, 4–7, 9, 12, 19, 23–24, 26, 30, 36, 38, 51, 57, 64, 153–155, 167, 173–176, 178–181, 183–185, 209–211, 212, 214, 220, 222, 224; controlled language 48–49; example-based 215, 218, 220; interactive 189; knowledge-base 217, 219; machine translation evaluation 23, 184; machine translation output 8, 12, 22, 24; machine translation system 8, 13, 16, 36, 39, 41–42, 183–184, 187, 209–211, 214–215, 220–222, 224; machine translation tool 225;

post-edited 12–13, 24–25; raw 13, 19, 22–25; rule-based 219; statistical 215; statistics-base 219–220
meaning 1, 30, 173, 180, 189

natural language processing 3, 64, 100, 118
noise 111; noise ratio 114
norm 30, 44, 102

output quality 3

parts of speech 31
post-editing 2, 5, 8, 12–13, 22–23, 145, 151, 154, 185, 189; maximal 24–25; maximum 22; rapid 22, 24–25
practical translation 2, 51, 61
pre-editing 12
productivity 6, 139, 150, 209, 214, 220, 224
project management 144, 150

quality assessment 2–3
quality estimation 183, 185

readability 21–22, 189, 214
recall 110
recipient evaluation 23–24
reusability 124

segment 92, 95, 141, 222
segmentation 66, 72; segmentation tool 66; text 66
semantics 32–33
sense mining 1, 30, 36, 38–39, 43
software design 3
source language 1
source text 8

tagging POS 66–68
target text 8
term 64–65, 74, 78, 100, 105, 122, 127, 142; candidate 65, 67–73, 75, 80, 142; extracted 64; term autonomy 124; term candidate 103
termbase 64, 100, 118, 123–124, 126, 129, 140, 142, 145, 150

term extraction 2–3, 64–65, 68, 79–81, 100–101, 142; automatic 3, 65, 100, 102; bilingual 101–102, 104; term extraction algorithm 65, 73, 80; term extraction method 2, 64–65, 68; term extraction system 100, 102, 104; term extraction tool 2–3, 64–65, 80–81, 100–102, 106, 115, 132
terminology 3, 100, 118, 128, 142; terminology database 118, 140; terminology management 3, 127; terminology management software 100; terminology management system 3, 64, 118, 125–126, 129, 132; terminology mining 4; terminology technology 138; terminology tool 125
term recognition 2, 65, 74, 76, 80
translatability 1, 5, 8, 12–14, 16, 25
translation 3, 12, 51–52, 64, 84, 126, 139, 185, 214; human-quality 24; professional 12; reference 188–189
translation cost 8
translation encyclopedia 2, 51
translation equivalent 101, 104
Translation Error Rate 186
translation memory 100, 120, 139–142, 145, 150, 213, 224; author-specific 215; translation memory database 140; translation memory exchange 144
translation process 8
translation project 64–65
translation quality 22, 64, 183, 189, 214, 222, 224; translation quality assessment 83–84
translation software 80
translation technology 1–2, 6, 51, 56–57, 100–101, 115, 138
translation workflow 183

usability 11, 221; website 12
user expectation 3, 108
user experience (UX) 1, 7, 9–15, 18, 20, 22, 25
user-friendliness 11
user preference 24–25
user satisfaction 22

website translation 12–13